BENTHAM'S THEORY OF FICTIONS

The International Library of Philosophy

PHILOSOPHY OF MIND AND LANGUAGE
In 8 Volumes

BENTHAM'S THEORY OF FICTIONS

C K OGDEN

First published in 1932 by
Kegan Paul, Trench, Trubner & Co Ltd

Reprinted in 2000, 2001 (twice) by
Routledge
2 Park Square, Milton Park, Abingdon, Oxon OX14 4RN

Transferred to Digital Printing 2002

Routledge is an imprint of the Taylor & Francis Group

Printed and bound by Antony Rowe Ltd, Eastbourne

© 1932 C. K. Ogden

All rights reserved. No part of this book may be reprinted or reproduced
or utilized in any form or by any electronic, mechanical, or other means,
now known or hereafter invented, including photocopying
and recording, or in any information storage or retrieval system, without
permission in writing from the publishers.

The publishers have made every effort to contact authors/copyright holders
of the works reprinted in the *International Library of Philosophy*.
This has not been possible in every case, however, and we would
welcome correspondence from those individuals/companies
we have been unable to trace.

These reprints are taken from original copies of each book. In many cases
the condition of these originals is not perfect. The publisher has gone to
great lengths to ensure the quality of these reprints, but wishes to point
out that certain characteristics of the original copies will, of necessity, be
apparent in reprints thereof.

British Library Cataloguing in Publication Data
A CIP catalogue record for this book
is available from the British Library

Bentham's Theory of Fictions
ISBN 9780415434522
Philosophy of Mind and Language: 8 Volumes
ISBN 0-415-22576-0
The International Library of Philosophy: 56 Volumes
ISBN 0-415-21803-9

BENTHAM IN OLD AGE

(By permission of the National Portrait Gallery)

CONTENTS

v

ILLUSTRATIONS

THE THEORY OF FICTIONS

PART I
GENERAL OUTLINE

I. Linguistic Fictions 7
II. Fictions in Psychology 59
III. Elliptical Fictions 66
IV. Fiction and Metaphor 70
V. Exposition 75
VI. Language as a Sign-System 105

PART II
SPECIAL PROBLEMS

I. Motion, Rest, and Relativity . . . 109
II. Substantive and Adjective 114
III. The Fiction of Right 118
IV. The Fiction of an Original Contract . . 122
V. Analysis, Physical and Linguistic . . . 126
VI. Summary 137
Appendix A. Legal Fictions 141
Appendix B. The Classification of Fictions,
             by George Bentham . . . 151
Index 157

Bentham's Theory of Fictions

INTRODUCTION

By C. K. OGDEN

I.—ORIGINS AND INFLUENCES

IF the History of Philosophy ever comes to be rewritten so that philosophers are assessed rather for their ability to recognize the linguistic basis of ' philosophy ' than for their attempts at an imaginative reformulation or a static analysis of the legacies of various types of Word-magic, many surprising revaluations will be necessary.

Bacon, Hobbes, Locke, Berkeley, Hume . . . Mill, Bradley, Russell—such is the tradition, with appropriate variants for the three final links, which is generally supposed to constitute the English contribution to the highest or the deepest Thought of humanity. To his five great predecessors Bentham acknowledges his debt. It is the purpose of the present volume to give some indication of the debt which future generations may acknowledge to Jeremy Bentham, when he has taken his place as sixth in the line of the great tradition—and in some respects its most original representative.

From D'Alembert as well as from Horne Tooke Bentham also derived suggestions for his remarkable anticipations of the modern approach to the symbolic tangle by which physics and psychology are alike confronted ; but quite apart from all such influences, there are certain features of his treatment of Fictions which suggest that he would have arrived quite independently at the analysis which posterity has hitherto so completely neglected.

Ghosts, no less than his horror of Legal Fictions, can be

shown to have played their part in determining the intensity and pertinacity of his researches. For over sixty years he struggled with the primary technique of linguistic psychology ; for nearly eighty years he was acutely conscious of the problem of fictional entities.[1]

As an infant, instead of the travel or history which fascinated him hardly less than ordinary tales of imagination, he was set to read the Fables of Phaedrus, but their arbitrarily fictional character annoyed him. " Fables, inasmuch as they are stories in which inferior animals are represented as talking together like men and women, never had any charm for me." This was at the age when English children of the last two centuries were afflicted by the collects, and Bentham *père*, though sane enough in some respects, did not refrain from subjecting his offspring to such linguistic tribulations.

Equally potent in impressing on a sensitive mind the power of Word-magic was the influence of his grandmother, who would nightly insist on giving her blessing before he climbed the stairs to her bed in the old Barking house. Seventy years later, the memory was still fresh :

" Previous to the ceremony, I underwent a catechetical course of examination, of which one of the questions was— ' Who were the children that were saved in the fiery furnace ?' Answer—' Shadrach, Meshach and Abednego ' ; but as the examination frequently got no farther, the word *Abednego* got associated in my mind with very agreeable ideas, and it ran through my ears, like Shadrach, Meshach, and *To-bed-we-go*, in a sort of pleasant confusion which is not yet removed." [2]

This same old lady also assisted him to consolidate his experience of the mystery of Fictions ; for on her walls hung a ' sampler ' depicting Adam, Eve, and the forbidden fruit.

[1] Cf. *The Theory of Legislation*, uniform with the present volume, where this aspect of Bentham's work is related to his achievement in the general field of Jurisprudence (Introduction, pp. xi ff.).

[2] *Works*, Vol. X, p. 18. Later, when too old to be his grandmother's bedfellow, he " became the sole occupant of a large unfurnished room —a fit place for the visitation of nocturnal visitors ; and then and there it was that the devil and his imp appeared to me " (*Ibid.*, p. 20).

" One thing alone puzzled me ; it was the forbidden fruit. The size was enormous. It was larger than that species of the genus *Orangeum* which goes by the name of the forbidden fruit in some of our West India settlements. Its size was not less than that of the outer shell of a cocoa nut. All the rest of the objects were, as usual, in *plano* ; this was in *alto*, indeed in *altissimo relievo*. What to make of it, at a time when my mind was unable to distinguish fictions from realities, I knew not."

SPECTRES AND BOGEYS

His grandmother's mother was a " matron of high respectability and corresponding piety ; well-informed and strong-minded. She was distinguished, however ; for, while other matrons of her age and quality had seen many a ghost, she had seen but *one* ". And, added Bentham in his old age, " this subject of ghosts has been among the torments of my life. Even now, when sixty or seventy years have passed over my head since my boyhood received the impression which my grandmother gave it, though my judgment is wholly free, my imagination is not wholly so ". His infirmity was not unknown to the servants.

" It was a permanent source of amusement to ply me with horrible phantoms in all imaginable shapes. Under the Pagan dispensation, every object a man could set his eyes on had been the seat of some pleasant adventure. At Barking, in the almost solitude of which so large a portion of my life was passed, every spot that could be made by any means to answer the purpose was the abode of some spectre or group of spectres. The establishment contained two houses of office : one about ten yards from the kitchen, for the use of ' the lower orders ', another at the farther end of the little garden, for the use of ' the higher ', who thus had three or four times the space to travel, on these indispensable occasions, more than that which sufficed for the servile grade : but these shrines of necessary pilgrimage were, by the cruel genius of my tormentors, richly stocked with phantasms. One had for its autocrat no less a personage than ' Tom Dark ' ; the other was the dwelling-place of ' Rawhead and Bloody Bones '. I suffered dreadfully in consequence of my fears.

I kept away for weeks from the spots I have mentioned ;
and, when suffering was intolerable, I fled to the fields."

So dexterous was the invention of those who worked
upon his apprehensions " that they managed to trans-
form a real into a fictitious being.   His name was *Palethorp* ; and Palethorp, in my vocabulary, was synonymous
with hobgoblin ".   The origin of these horrors was this :—

" My father's house was a short half-mile distant from the
principal part of the town, from that part where was situated
the mansion of the lord of the manor, Sir Crisp Gascoigne.
One morning, the coachman and the footman took a conjunct walk to a public house kept by a man of the name
(Palethorp) : they took me with them ; it was before I
was breeched.   They called for a pot of beer ; took each of
them a sip, and handed the pot to me.   On their requisition,
I took another ; and when about to depart, the amount
was called for.   The two servants paid their quota, and I
was called on for mine.   *Nemo dat quod non habet*—this
maxim, to my no small vexation, I was compelled to
exemplify.   Mr. Palethorp, the landlord, had a visage harsh
and ill-favoured, and he insisted on my discharging my
debt.   At this very early age, without having put in for my
share of the gifts of fortune, I found myself in the state
of an insolvent debtor.   The demand harassed me so
mercilessly that I could hold out no longer : the door
being open, I took to my heels ; and, as the way was too
plain to be missed, I ran home as fast as they could carry
me.   The scene of the terrors of Mr. Palethorp's name and
visitation, in pursuit of me, was the country-house at
Barking : but neither was the town-house free from them ;
for, in those terrors, the servants possessed an instrument
by which it was in their power, at any time, to get rid of
my presence.   Level with the kitchen—level with the
landing-place in which the staircase took its commencement—were the usual offices.   When my company became
troublesome, a sure and continually repeated means of
exonerating themselves from it, was for the footman to
repair to the adjoining subterraneous apartments, invest
his shoulders with some strange covering, and, concealing
his countenance, stalk in, with a hollow, menacing, and
inarticulate tone.   Lest that should not be sufficient, the
servants had, stuck by the fireplace, the portraiture of a
hobgoblin, to which they had given the name of Palethorp.
For some years I was in the condition of poor Dr. Priestley,

on whose bodily frame another name, too awful to be mentioned, used to produce a sensation more than mental."

THE DEVIL AND HIS IMP

Another instance of the influence of fictional horror occurred when the child was about nine :

" I went to see a puppet-show : there were Punch and Joan—the devil, whom I had seen before ; but I saw, for the first time, the devil's imp. The devil was black, as he should be ; but the devil's imp was white, and I was much more alarmed at his presence than at that of his principal. I was haunted by him. I went to bed ; I wanted to sleep. The devil appeared to me in a dream ; the imp in his company. I had—which is not uncommon in dreams, at least with me—a sort of consciousness that it was a dream ; with a hope that, with a little exertion, I might spring out of it : I fancied that I did so. Imagine my horror, when I still perceived devil and imp standing before me. It was out of the rain into the river. I made another desperate effort. I tried to be doubly awake ; I succeeded. I was in a transport of delight when the illusion altogether vanished : but it was only a temporary relief ; for the devil and the imp dwelt in my waking thoughts for many a year afterwards."

A little later Literature played its part. His French tutor, La Combe, induced his father to give him the *Lettres Juivres*, which filled his mind with vague terrors : " I could not understand the book, but I was frightened by the accounts of the vampires in it." [1] The story of the Goat of the Cave in *Robinson Crusoe* also disturbed him : " It was a moot point with me whether it was a goat or the devil. I was indeed comforted to find it was a goat." *The Pilgrim's Progress* frightened him still more : " I could not read it entirely through. At Westminster School, we used to go to a particular room to wash our feet : there I first saw an imperfect copy of *The Pilgrim's Progress* ; the devil was everywhere in it, and in me too. I was always afraid of the devil : I had seen him sowing tares, in a picture at Boghurst ; how should

[1] *Works*, Vol. X, pp. 11 and 21.

I know it was not a copy from the life ? " And he had actually seen the devil, in the puppet-show ; " I dreamt about him frequently : he had pinched me several times, and waked me. . . . How much less unhappy I should have been, could I have acknowledged my superstitious fears ! but I was so ashamed. Now that I know the distinction between the imagination and the judgment I can own how these things plagued me, without any impeachment of my intellect."

OXFORD

On the opposite page appears a portrait[1] of Bentham at Oxford, shortly after his arrival there at the age of twelve and a half, in 1760. " Paternal authority ", he wrote at the age of eighty, " compelled me to hammer out and send in, as a candidate for admission into the customary academical collection of half lamentational, half congratulational, rhythmical commonplaces, the subject of which was the loss of one thing and the acquisition of another, a copy in Sapphics (*sic*) the first stanza of which

[1] First in the possession of the Earl of Shelburne, then of Sir John Bowring, and now in the National Portrait Gallery. The artist was a certain Mr. Fry, and the stanza in question reads :—

> " Eheu Georgi ! jamne Britannica
> Gestare taedet sceptra pia manu
> Linguisque perculsum Senatum
> Et populum Patre destitutum ? "

Dr. Johnson made some criticisms of these verses but pronounced them " a very pretty performance of a young man ". Bentham was not impressed by Johnson's emendations and gave them to a lady who wanted Johnson's signature. He later (1776) " belonged to a dinner club, of which Johnson was the despot " ; and in a note written in 1785 he refers to him as " the pompous vamper of commonplace morality—of phrases often trite without being true ".

A further sidelight on the picture is a note in the diary of Bentham *père*, dated June 27-8, 1760 : " Paid for a commoner's gown for my son, £1, 12s. 6d. Paid for a cap and tassel, 7s." We are also told that a grievous annoyance to Bentham, at Oxford, was the formal dressing of the hair. " Mine ", he said, " was turned up in the shape of a kidney ; a quince or a club was against the statutes ; a kidney was in accordance with the statutes. I had a fellow-student whose passion it was to dress hair, and he used to employ a portion of his mornings in shaping my kidney properly." (*Works*, Vol. VIII, pp. 36, 39, 41, 51, 142 ; Vol. I, pp. 241–2.)

BENTHAM AT OXFORD, *aetat* 12½

(*By permission of the National Portrait Gallery*)

INTRODUCTION

INTRODUCTION

figures in a whole length portrait of me, in my academical dress."

At Oxford he found a physical and intellectual environment that distressed him considerably ; but in due course he succeeded in moving his rooms in Queen's College from " the two-pair-of stairs' floor, on the farther corner of the inner quadrangle, on the right hand as you enter into it from the outer door ", to the ground-floor, " on the right hand of the staircase, next on the left hand, as you go from the outer quadrangle to the staircase that leads to the former ones "—partly as a result of these childhood experiences.[1]

The first chamber " was a very gloomy one. It looked into the churchyard, and was covered with lugubrious hangings. Bentham's fear of ghosts, and the visitations of spiritual beings was strong upon him ; and the darkness of the chamber and its neighbourhood added to his alarms".[2]

On this grim foundation was to be built a theory of symbols applicable not only to the sins of the law and the confusions of philosophy but even to the respect and awe with which otherwise worthless individuals can be invested, *qua* dignitaries. In the *Constitutional Code* this attribute is described as " altogether curious—deplorable, considering how mischievous it is ". First, of course, there is the obvious fact of association, the potency of the symbol. " The dignitary has in every instance for its immediate efficient cause, or rather instrument, some symbol perceptible to sense—to the sense of hearing at the least ; an appellation—most commonly in addition to it some symbol perceptible to the sense of sight, an embroidered imitation of a star, a ribbon of a particular

---

[1] *Works*, Vol. X, p. 39.

[2] Throughout his life Bentham retained a vivid impression of his own early experiences at the hands of uneducated domestics, and in his educational writings he constantly urges that children should as far as possible be rescued from their ministrations. On this occasion he comments (*Ibid.*, p. 64) : " My fear of ghosts had been implanted in my mind from earliest infancy by the too customary cultivation of that most noxious weed, domestic servants." And, as is well known, J. S. Mill was among the first to profit by his enlightened policies.

shape and colour, a medal. Of this power of symbols or signs over opinions the cause lies in the association of ideas—in the principle of association between idea and idea." But there is more to it than mere association—and here came the ghosts :

" The curious circumstance is the irresistible force with which, in this instance, the cause operates in the production of the effect. Here are a set of men whom, taken in the aggregate, I cannot, upon reflection, look upon as fit objects of a greater portion of esteem and respect, nor even of so great a portion as an equal number of men taken at random. At the same time, spite of myself, by the idea of any one possessed of any of these symbols, a greater degree of those social affections is excited than is excited by the idea of any one not possessed of any one of those symbols. Whence this inconsistency ? By a continually renewed train of association, commencing at the earliest dawn of reason, this opinion of the constant connexion between the possession of the external symbol in question and the mental quality in question, has been created and confirmed : for the revival of the erroneous opinion, a single instant suffices at all times : for the expulsion of it, nothing less than a train of reflection can suffice.

To this case I feel a very conformable parallel may be seen in the case of ghosts and other fabulous maleficent beings, which the absence of light presents to my mind's eye. In no man's judgment can a stronger persuasion of the non-existence of these sources of terror have place than in mine ; yet no sooner do I lay myself down to sleep in a dark room than, if no other person is in the room, and my eyes keep open, these instruments of terror obtrude themselves ; and, to free myself of the annoyance, I feel myself under the necessity of substituting to those more or less pleasing ideas with which my mind would otherwise have been occupied, those reflections which are necessary to keep in my view the judgment by which the non-existence of these creatures of the imagination has so often been pronounced. The cause of these illusions were the stories told by servants in my childhood.

The tale of the apparition of ghosts and vampires is not more fabulous than is in general the tale of worth, moral or intellectual, as applied to these creatures of a monarch who form the class of state dignitaries." [1]

[1] *Works*, Vol. IX, pp. 83–4.

LEGAL FICTIONS

At the age of sixteen, while Bentham was still at Oxford and attending Blackstone's lectures, a new and even more sinister symbolic product was forced on his attention ; for in Blackstone's approach to jurisprudence he found at all points a direct antithesis to the orthological clarity which his early horror of darkness made imperative. In the *Fragment on Government* he noted the tone of regret in which Blackstone refers to the historical development of the English language as a legal medium :—

> " The case is this. A large portion of the body of the Law was, by the bigotry or artifice of Lawyers, locked up in an illegible character, and in a foreign tongue. The statute he mentions obliged them to give up their hieroglyphics, and to restore the native language to its rights.
> This was doing much ; but it was not doing everything. Fiction, tautology, technicality, circuity, irregularity, inconsistency remain. But above all, the pestilential breath of Fiction poisons the sense of every instrument it comes near." [1]

Says Bentham's Editor, John Hill Burton, writing in 1828 to point the moral : " The ' Fictions of Law ', of which the English practice is so full, were repeatedly and earnestly attacked by Bentham, both collectively and in detail. The example shown to the world, of falsehoods deliberately, and on a fixed system, told in the very workshops of justice, and by those who are employed to support truth and honesty, he looked upon as holding out a pernicious example to the public. Without any sarcastic or reprehensory qualification, a Fiction of Law may be defined in general as the saying something exists which does not exist. and acting as if it existed ; or *vice versa.*"

Where the purpose of the Fiction is desirable, it should have been achieved directly, without falsehood or ambiguity, by the Legislature. But whether used to a good or a bad purpose, it is an assumption of arbitrary power.

[1] *Works*, Vol. I, p. 235.

b

" A fiction of law ", says Bentham, " may be defined a wilful falsehood, having for its object the stealing legislative power, by and for hands which durst not, or could not, openly claim it ; and, but for the delusion thus produced, could not exercise it." [1]

It is true, continues Burton, that new Fictions are not now invented—at least on any considerable scale ; and those formerly created have become a fixed part of the law, uniform in their operation.   " It is still the case, however, that from the nominal repetition of the fraud under which they were originally perpetrated, they are a cumbrous and costly method of transacting judicial business.   But they have a much worse influence than this.   By the obscurity and complexity with which they surround operations which might be simple and open, they afford concealment to fraud and professional chicanery ;   they exclude the unprofessional man from the means of knowing what the lawyer is doing among the windings of the professional labyrinth, and they show him that the law countenances palpable falsehoods." And he quotes Bentham as follows :—

" When an action, for example, is brought against a man, how do you think they contrive to give him notice to defend himself ?   Sometimes he is told that he is in jail ; sometimes that he is lurking up and down the country, in company with a vagabond of the name of Doe ; though all the while he is sitting quietly by his own fireside : and this my Lord Chief Justice sets his hand to.   At other

[1] " Thus ", he continues by way of example, " by the system of pleading anterior to the late Uniformity Act, the defendant over whom the Court of King's Bench extended its jurisdiction, was said in the writ to have been in the custody of the Marshall of the King's Bench Prison for an offence, though no such circumstance had taken place. The court had originally no jurisdiction over any one who was not so in custody ; the lie was told that the court might have an excuse for interfering ; the court would not allow the lie to be contradicted, and it assumed jurisdiction accordingly. The origin of this class of fictions was of the most sordid character—the judges and other officers of court being paid by fees, a trade competition for jurisdiction took place ; each court trying to offer better terms to litigants than the others, and adopting the fictions as a means of accomplishing this object. Of another class are the Fictions as to Common Bail, Fines and Recoveries, Docking, Entails, etc."

times, they write to a man who lives in Cumberland or
Cornwall, and tell him that if he does not appear in Westminster Hall on a certain day he forfeits an hundred pounds.
When he comes, so far from having anything to say to
him, they won't hear him : for all they want him for, is to
grease their fingers."

THE WAY OUT

It was to an analysis of Language that Bentham turned
in the first instance for weapons against an evil that had
its origin primarily in Word-magic. But he had great
faith in the progress of Science as such, and above all of
Physics. " In knowledge in general, and in knowledge
belonging to the physical department in particular, will
the vast mass of mischief, of which perverted religion is
the source, find its preventive remedy. It is from physical
science alone that a man is capable of deriving that mental
strength and that well-grounded confidence which renders
him proof against so many groundless terrors flowing from
that prolific source, which, by enabling him to see how
prone to error the mind is on this ground, and thence
how free such error is from all moral blame, disposes him
to that forbearance towards supposed error, which men
are so ready to preach and so reluctant to practise." [1]

Hence his dissatisfaction with D'Alembert whose treatment, in his Encyclopedical Map, of the Irregularities of
Nature he regarded as presenting itself " in the character
of a blotch, to which a sponge might apply a not incongruous cure ". For Bacon there was some excuse :

" In the time of the English Philosopher, the mind was
annoyed and oppressed by terrors which in the time of his
French disciple had lost, though not the whole, the greater
part of their force. In Bacon's time—in the early part of
the seventeenth century—everything in nature that was, or
was supposed to be, *extraordinary*, was *alarming* ; alarming,
and in some shape or other, if not *productive, predictive* at
least of human misery. In this place, as in other places—
at this time, as at other times—*Ghosts* and *Witches* composed a constant part of the population, *Devils* an occasional

[1] *Works*, Vol. VIII, p. 13.

one. Patronized by Queen Elizabeth, Dee had not long ceased to hold converse with his disembodied intimates : Lilly was preparing for the connexion he succeeded in forming with *his*. To burn heretics, to hang witches, and to combat devils, were operations, for all which Bacon's Royal Patron held himself in equal and constant readiness." [1]

THE DEVELOPMENT OF THE THEORY

In 1775 Jeremy Bentham at the age of twenty-seven wrote :—

" What we are continually talking of, merely from our having been continually talking of it, we imagine we understand ; so close a union has habit connected between words and things, that we take one for the other ; when we have words in our ears we imagine we have ideas in our minds. When an unusual word presents itself, we challenge it; we examine it ourselves to see whether we have a clear idea to annex to it ; but when a word that we are familiar with comes across us, we let it pass under favour of old acquaintance.

The long acquaintance we have had with it makes us take for granted we have searched it already ; we deal by it, in consequence, as the custom-house officers in certain countries, who, having once set their seal upon a packet, so long as they see, or think they see that seal upon it, reasonably enough suppose themselves dispensed with from visiting it anew."

Fictions of Law, he added, " are mightly pretty things. Locke admires them ; the author of the *Commentaries* adores them ; most lawyers are, even yet, well pleased with them : with what reason let us see ".[2]

In 1780, the year before Kant published his *Critique of Pure Reason*, Bentham printed his preliminary treatise on Jurisprudence, but "found himself unexpectedly entangled in an unsuspected corner of the metaphysical maze ", and decided to hold up publication till he had set his mind at rest.

What was this unsuspected corner ? Nine years later, in 1789, he had sufficiently satisfied himself of the

[1] *Ibid.*, p. 78.
[2] *Works*, Vol. X, pp. 74–5.

general validity of his Critical Elements to allow them to be formally published, with "a patch at the end and another at the beginning", as *An Introduction to the Principles of Morals and Legislation*, "a great quarto volume of metaphysics". The edition was very small, "and half of that devoured by rats":—the definitive reprint only appearing in 1823, with corrections by the Author.

That his earlier troubles were partly due to the mere magnitude of his undertaking is clear from a further admission. "I had got into a mizmaze", he says. "I could not see my way clearly; it was a dark forest—for the vast field of the law was around me with all its labyrinths." But it is significant that many of the most illuminating footnotes are concerned with linguistic difficulties, and particularly with the ramifications of fictional analysis

In the Preface itself we are warned that the truths at the basis of political and moral science "are not to be discovered but by investigations as severe as mathematical ones, and beyond all comparison more intricate and extensive. The familiarity of the terms is a presumption, but it is a most fallacious one, of the facility of the matter. Truths in general have been called stubborn things; the truths just mentioned are so in their own way. They are not to be forced into detached and general propositions, unincumbered with explanations and exceptions. They will not compress themselves into epigrams. They recoil from the tongue and the pen of the declaimer. They flourish not in the same soil with sentiment. They grow among thorns; and are not to be plucked, like daisies, by infants as they run. Labour, the inevitable lot of humanity, is in no track more inevitable than here."

In Chapter X, where the intricacies of the psychology of Motivation come up for discussion, reference is made to the apparent contradictions into which any one who confines himself to ordinary language will be led. "His propositions will appear, on the one hand, repugnant to truth ; and on the other hand, adverse to utility. As paradoxes, they will excite contempt ; as mischievous paradoxes, indignation. For the truths he labours to convey, however important, and however salutary, his reader is never the better ; and he himself is much the worse. To obviate this inconvenience, completely, he has but this one unpleasant remedy ; to lay aside the old phraseology and invent a new one. Happy the man whose language is ductile enough to permit him this resource. To palliate the inconvenience, where that method of obviating it is impracticable, he has nothing left for it but to enter into a long discussion, to state the whole matter at large, to confess that for the sake of promoting the purposes, he has violated the established laws, of language, and to throw himself upon the mercy of his readers."

To which Bentham adds as a note : " Happily language is not always so intractable but that, by making use of two words instead of one, a man may avoid the inconvenience of fabricating words that are absolutely new. Thus instead of the word *lust*, by putting together two words in common use, he may frame the neutral expression, *sexual desire* ; instead of the word *avarice*, by putting together two other words also in common use, he may frame the neutral expression, *pecuniary interest*. This, accordingly, is the course which I have taken. In these instances indeed, even the combination is not novel ; the only novelty there is consists in the steady adherence to the one neutral expression, rejecting altogether the terms of which the import is infected by adventitious and unsuitable ideas." And furthermore : " In the catalogue of motives, corresponding to the several sorts of pains and pleasures, I have inserted such as have occurred to me. I cannot pretend to warrant it complete. To make sure of rendering it so, the only way would be to turn over the dictionary from beginning to end ; an operation which, in a view to perfection, would be necessary for more purposes than this."

In connexion with the classification of Offences (Chapter
XVI) we find an elaborate note on the genera generalissima
of Fictions in the field of law.   Powers, it is here laid
down, " though not a species of rights (for the two sorts
of fictitious entities termed a *power* and a *right* are altogether disparate) are yet so far included under rights
that wherever the word *power* may be employed the
word *right* may also be employed.   The reason is, that
wherever you may speak of a person as having a power,
you may also speak of him as having a right to such
power : but the converse of this proposition does not
hold good ; there are cases in which, though you may
speak of a man as having a right, you cannot speak of
him as having a power, or in any other way make any
mention of that word.   On various occasions you have a
right, for instance, to the services of the magistrate : but
if you are a private person, you have no power over him ;
all the power is on his side.   This being the case, as the
word *right* was employed, the word *power* might perhaps,
without any deficiency in the sense, have been omitted.
On the present occasion however, as in speaking of trusts
this word is commonly made more use of than the word
right, it seemed most eligible, for the sake of perspicuity
to insert them both."

And here comes a personal digression.   It might have
been expected, says Bentham, that since the word *trust*
had already been expounded, the words *power* and *right*,
upon the meaning of which the exposition of the word
trust is made to depend, would be expounded also, since
no two words can stand more in need of it than these do.

" Such exposition I accordingly set about to give, and
indeed have actually drawn up ; but the details into which
I found it necessary to enter for this purpose, were of such
length as to take up more room than could consistently be
allotted to them in this place. With respect to these words,
therefore, and a number of others, such as *possession, title,*
and the like, which in point of import are inseparably
connected with them, instead of exhibiting the exposition
itself, I must content myself with giving a general idea of

the plan which I have pursued in framing it : and as to everything else, I must leave the import of them to rest upon whatever footing it may happen to stand upon in the apprehension of each reader. Power and right, and the whole tribe of fictitious entities of this stamp, are all of them, in the sense which belongs to them in a book of jurisprudence, the results of some manifestation or other of the legislator's will with respect to such or such an act. Now every such manifestation is either a prohibition, a command, or their respective negations ; viz. a permission, and the declaration which the legislator makes of his will when on any occasion he leaves an act uncommanded. Now, to render the expression of the rule more concise, the commanding of a positive act may be represented by the prohibition of the negative act which is opposed to it. To know then how to expound a right, carry your eye to the act which, in the circumstances in question, would be a violation of that right ; the law creates the right by prohibiting that act. Power, whether over a man's own person, or over other persons, or over things, is constituted in the first instance by permission : but in as far as the law takes an active part in corroborating it, it is created by prohibition, and by command ; by prohibition of such acts (on the part of other persons) as are judged incompatible with the exercise of it ; and upon occasion, by command of such acts as are judged to be necessary for the removal of such or such obstacles of the number of those which may occur to impede the exercise of it. For every right which the law confers on one party, whether that party be an individual, a subordinate class of individuals, or the public, it thereby imposes on some other party a *duty* or *obligation*. But there may be laws which command or prohibit acts, that is, impose duties, without any other view than the benefit of the agent ; these generate no rights : duties, therefore, may be either *extra-regarding* or *self-regarding* ; extra-regarding have rights to correspond to them : self-regarding, none."

That a correct exposition of the words *power* and *right* must enter into a great variety of details will be obvious. " One branch of the system of rights and powers, and but one, are those of which property is composed : to be correct, then, it must, among other things, be applicable to the whole tribe of modifications of which property is susceptible. But the commands and prohibitions, by which the *powers* and *rights* that compose those several modifications are created, are of many different forms : to comprise the exposition in question within the compass of a single paragraph would therefore be impossible ; to take as many paragraphs for it as would be necessary in order to exhibit these different forms, would be to engage in a detail so ample that the analysis of the several possible species of property would compose only a part of it. This labour, uninviting as it was, I have accordingly undergone : but the result of it, as may well be imagined, seemed too voluminous and minute to be exhibited in an outline like the present."

He explains that he might have cut the matter very short, by proceeding in the usual strain, and saying that a power was a faculty, and that a right was a privilege, and so on, following the beaten track of definition." But the insanity of such a method, in cases like the present, has been already pointed out ; [1] a power is not a—any thing ; neither is a right a—any thing : the case is, they have neither of them any superior genus ; these, together with *duty, obligation,* and a multitude of others of the same stamp, being of the number of those fictitious entities of which the import can by no other means be illustrated than by showing the relation which they bear to real ones."

Finally, there is the sort of linguistic difficulty which presents itself when we speak of any one in whose hands a trust exists, as the person who possesses, or is in possession of it, and thence of the possession of the trust abstracted from the consideration of the possessor. " However different the expression, the import is in both cases the same. So irregular and imperfect is the structure of language on this head, that no one phrase can be made to suit the idea on all the occasions on which it is requisite it should be brought to view ; the phrase must be continually shifted, or new modified : so likewise in regard to conditions, and in regard to property. The being invested with, or possessing, a condition ; the being

---

[1] See *Fragment on Government*, Chapter V (*Works*, Vol. I, p. 293).

in possession of an article of property, that is, if the object of the property be corporeal; the having a legal title (defeasible or indefeasible) to the physical possession of it, answers to the being in possession of a trust, or the being the person in whose hands a trust exists. In like manner, to the *exercise* of the *functions* belonging to a trust, or to a condition, corresponds the *enjoyment* of an article of property; that is, if the object of it be corporeal, the *occupation*."

The mists of language are not easily dispelled. "These verbal discussions are equally tedious and indispensable. Striving to cut a new road through the wilds of jurisprudence, I find myself continually distressed for want of tools that are fit to work with. To frame a complete set of new ones is impossible. All that can be done is, to make here and there a new one in cases of absolute necessity, and for the rest, to patch up from time to time the imperfections of the old." This, at least, is the verdict of one who feels sure of his ground—who has reached definitive conclusions. But there can be little doubt that the temporary *impasse* of 1780 was due to Bentham's lack of an adequate foundation for his Theory of Fictions; and that the years between were largely devoted to the further reflection necessitated by the intricacies of the subject—culminating in the intensive effort of 1813–1815 with which the present volume is chiefly concerned.

In a letter to Dumont written on 11th May 1802, and preserved in the Bentham-Dumont MSS. in the Library of Geneva University, Bentham himself stresses the continuity of his work on Fictions. Various examples, from Hobbes to Rousseau, are cited as evidence of the tendency to word-magic. "In the invention or choice of a fundamental principle for morals or politics, what writers of all parties and descriptions have aimed at hitherto has been the hitting upon some cant word or short form of words, such as should serve as a sort of hook on which to hang the opinions of which their prejudices and passions have been productive." Finally:

" All this from the first to the last J. B. has constantly protested against as so many . . . delusive falsehoods, so many sheet anchors to error, corroboratives to obstinacy, provocatives to violence, bars to true instruction, masks to ignorance. At the age of 16 at his first entrance upon the study of law, he resisted (as he mentions in his anonymous work . . . *A Fragment on Government*) the fiction of the Original Contract. At the age of 28, in and by that work, he entered his public protest against it.

None of those other works, notwithstanding all their celebrity, presented themselves to his mind as anything better than a mere useless heap of words. Fascinated by Rousseau [1] on other accounts to the highest pitch of fascination, he never could bring himself to fancy so much as for a moment that from the Contract Social or any one passage in it he had ever received the smallest ray of intelligence.

The same principle of delusion which was so convenient to writers was equally convenient to readers : as in the one class each had his favourite set of tenets to establish, so in the other each had his set of favourite tenets to adhere to and occasionally to propagate."

AS AN INSTRUMENT OF DISCOVERY

The Theory of Fictions was elaborated in order to cope with the symbolic factor in all its ramifications, legal, scientific, and metaphysical ; and in the list of ' Instruments ' by which his various discoveries were made possible, it appears as No. 1, epitomized as follows :—

" Division of entities into real and fictitious ; or say, division of noun-substantive into names of real entities, and names of fictitious entities :

By the division and distinction thus brought to view, great is the light thrown upon the whole field of logic, and thereby over the whole field of art and science, more especially the psychical and thence the ethical or moral branch of science.

[1] " Rousseau having in view the recommending of a Democracy (recommending for 25 millions or any greater number of millions a democracy more democratical than the democracy of 25 thousand which he was born under and best acquainted with) invented his fiction of a Social Contract—a Contract according to which any number of millions, without ever having communicated with each other, agree to govern one another in conformity to certain ends without anything said about either means or ends."

It is for the want of a clear conception of this distinction
that many an empty name is considered as the representative
of a correspondent reality ; in a word, that mere *fictions*
are in abundance regarded as *realities*.

D'Alembert is the author in whose works [1] the notion
of this distinction was first observed by me :—*être fictif* is
the expression employed by him for the designation of the
sort of object for the designation of which the appellation
fictitious entity has ever since been employed.

In speaking of the faculties of the mind, the same
distinction will also be found occasionally brought to view
in the philosophical works of Voltaire.

By attention to this distinction it is that I was enabled
to discover and bring to view, in the case of a numerous
class of words, their incapacity of being expounded by a
definition in the ordinary form, viz. the form *per genus et
differentiam*, which form of definition it has, with how little
success and benefit soever hitherto, perhaps universally
been the practice to bestow upon them ; and at the same
time to bring to view the only instructive and useful exposition of which the words of this class are susceptible,
viz. the exposition by *paraphrasis*—the only form of exposition by which the import attached to them is capable
of being fixed, and at the same time placed in a clear and
determined point of view.

See, in particular, the class of political, including legal,
fictitious entities, in respect of which, by indication of the
relation which the import of the word in question bears in
common to the fundamental ideas of pain and pleasure, a
distinct and fixed meaning is thus given to a numerous
tribe of words, of which, till that time, the meaning has
been floating in the clouds and blown about by every blast
of doctrine—words to the which, in the mind of many a
writer, no assignable ideas, no fixed, no real import, had
been annexed." [2]

Instrument No. 2 is the division of entities, real and
fictitious together, into physical and psychical ; by means
of which, as we shall see, he maintained that considerable
light could be thrown both upon the origin and the
formation of language, and on the connexion between
the nomenclature of psychology on the one hand and
that of physics and physiology on the other. " There is

[1] *Mélanges de Litterature et de Philosophie.*
[2] *Works*, Vol. III, p. 286.

7. Vol. 1. p. 154. l. 7. After "autres" put homme

8. V. 1. p. 230 l. 19. After "fiction" omit ridicule [the distinction between real & fictitious entities is a point of great importance in ideology on account of the multitude of words which are names of fictitious entities].—

9. V. 1. p. 255 l. 3 from the bottom After "bien qu'il" omit "ne"

10. V. 1. p. 263 l. 5 for "proportions" put proposition

11. V. 1. p. 336. l. After "portent" Add (if you will) si un corps de droit n'est pas complet ce que lui manque pour l'être sera dans la forme de Droit non écrit. Mais de Droit non écrit le caractère ... et d'être incertain & inconnu a ... une quantité connue une quan ... connu qui la modifie, le ... i.—

Note After "défendu" peut ... rendent la liberté de ... que d'autres lois avaient ordonné.

2. V. l. 2. p. 33 l. 5 from the bottom

no name of a psychical entity which is not also the name of a physical entity, in which capacity alone it must have continued to have been employed, long before it was transferred to the field of psychical entities and made to serve in the character of a name of a psychical, and that most commonly a fictitious, entity."

A CENTURY OF NEGLECT

Since Bentham himself so clearly indicates the importance which he attached to the Theory of Fictions as an Instrument, it is all the more surprising that his biographers, interpreters, and critics have almost all [1] been content to dismiss it with a contemptuous reference.

From his immediate disciples Bentham could hardly expect much understanding. James Mill had his own ideas of the way in which the linguistic borderlands should be handled, but the old terminology of 'abstraction' and 'generalization' failed to meet the case. J. S. Mill further confused the issue by his inconclusive reversion to the nominalist-realist controversy. Bowring was not to be taken seriously as an interlocutor on such subjects,[2] and Dumont was hardly less obtuse when any of the subtler problems of analysis had to be glossed over in the interests of the wider public for whom he so successfully catered.

Having elsewhere [3] endeavoured to give Dumont full credit for his devoted labours, we may here without injustice draw attention to his very obvious shortcomings as an interpreter of the more fundamental aspects of Bentham's thought. On the opposite page is reproduced in facsimile a page from the Miscellaneous Corrections which Bentham put together immediately after he received the first volume of the *Traités* [4] :—

[1] Sir Leslie Stephen, however, in his account of Bentham in *The English Utilitarians*, provides a detached and intelligible summary.

[2] *Works*, Vol. X, p. 562 ; cf. *The Theory of Legislation*, Introduction, p. xiii (International Library of Psychology).

[3] *Op. cit.*, *The Theory of Legislation*, Introduction, pp. xi ff.

[4] By kind permission of the Librarian of the University of Geneva. The date of the letter is May 21, 1802, and the reference, *Inv.* mss. 532 (MS. DUM 33) f. 98.

" After ' *fiction* ' omit ridicule (the distinction between real and fictitious entities is a point of great importance in ideology on account of the multitude of words which are names of fictitious entities)."

Dumont, finding the word *fiction* in Bentham's descriptive material, and with the full text of the *Introduction* before him, had assumed that a fiction must be something absurd, and embellished it accordingly. No better evidence of the distance at which he followed his master could be required ; and it is not altogether surprising that in a moment of pique Bentham declared in his old age : " He does not understand a word of my meaning."

Even the *Dictionary of National Biography* allows itself to conclude that Bentham " made no very valuable contributions to logic " though " it was the subject of his inquiry for many years " ; indeed, " his ideas on that subject, which relate chiefly to exposition and method, will be found in his nephew's work." Professor Halévy, otherwise Bentham's most learned and sympathetic expositor, has referred to the said contributions as " les longs et inutiles manuscrits " ; [1] and Mr. Everett would have us believe that " the MSS. from which Bentham's disciples were to edit the voluminous publications of his later years contain, almost without exception, papers written by Bentham between 1770 and 1790. His later writings were either completions of plans sketched in his early years, or works published then which it would have been dangerous to avow earlier, or applications to contemporary political or legal situations of views arrived at in youth or early manhood." [2] Nevertheless, almost all the MSS. with which the present volume is concerned bear a date subsequent to 1812, *i.e.* more than twenty years after the period in question.

---

[1] *L'Evolution de la Doctrine Utilitaire*, 1789–1815, p. 357.

In the latest orthodox History of Philosophy, therefore, Professor Bréhier, relying on Halévy's estimate, gives two pages of his two thousand (*Histoire de la Philosophie*, Vol. II, Part III, 1932, pp. 764–7) to Bentham ; while twenty are allotted to Schelling, thirty to Maine de Biran, and forty-six to Auguste Comte.

[2] *The Education of Jeremy Bentham*, 1931, p. 197.

It is clear that Bentham's interest in these matters was due in part to the dislike of ' legal fictions ' which inspired his attack on Blackstone ; but as a writer on jurisprudence, he was dealing with linguistic problems at a level very different from that to which he found himself impelled to proceed when investigating the terminological ultimates of psychology, utilitarianism, and a universal language. Jurists have regarded his philosophic subtleties as irrelevant ; philosophers have felt safe in neglecting the subtleties of a jurist. But now that the linguistic foundations of jurisprudence are urgently in need of orthological scrutiny, while the profundities of philosophy are resolving themselves into grammatical and psychological misunderstandings, the time is ripe for a readjustment of historical values.

THE PHILOSOPHY OF ' AS-IF '

One result of this neglect has been that during the last twenty years a flourishing new movement in philosophy has taken credit for the discovery of what should have been a commonplace in every history of English thought, had the orthological approach been given due attention.

The *Philosophy of As If*, which was hailed by pragmatists as a masterpiece when it appeared in Germany, remained untranslated for thirteen years ; the present writer made himself responsible for an English version.[1]

---

[1] Vaihinger's work first appeared in 1911, though the nucleus had been written in 1876. The English translation (1924) was based on the sixth German edition of 1913, and the relevant passages are pp. 187–8 of the former and 354–7 of the latter. From both it is clear that Vaihinger had not read Bentham in the original, but took his account of Bentham's views from Mill, who never realized the significance of his master's linguistic researches.

In the preparation of the historical sections of *The Meaning of Meaning*, prior to the translation of Vaihinger, it became obvious that Bentham's work on language required many months of undivided attention ; and the task of pointing out his claim to priority in the matter of fictions was left to others. Yet not one of the scores of able reviews, essays, and monographs to which *The Philosophy of As If* gave rise so much as hinted at the Englishman's researches over a century ago.

There is no doubt that Hans Vaihinger reached his conclusions independently of Bentham, but it is time that the achievement of the earlier thinker should be recognized.

The account of fictions given by Bentham in the following pages, supplemented by the version of his nephew (the reaction of a youth of twenty-seven to the life-work of an octogenarian), provides a complete answer to Vaihinger's query " whether Bentham applied his methods consciously " ; and makes it impossible to conclude with him that " it was his successors who first recognized in assumptions, false as hypotheses, important and useful fictions ".

The chief defect of Vaihinger's monumental work was its failure to lay stress on the linguistic factor in the creation of fictions.   The next step would have been to make good this omission, had not that step already been taken by Bentham a century ago.   " To language, then— to language alone—it is that fictitious entities owe their existence ; their impossible, yet indispensable existence."

THE MATERIAL

For the study and interpretation of the Theory of Fictions thus gradually and consistently developed we are fortunately provided with abundance of material. Owing to Bentham's peculiar methods of composition, to which reference is made on a subsequent page,[1] the main principles to which he attached importance are set forth on no less than seven distinct occasions.

First comes the section dealing with Fictions in relation to Methodization by Denomination (*Logic*, Chapter IX, § IV) [2] the MS. of which is dated 7th, 8th, and 9th of August 1814.   Bentham had then just acquired Ford Abbey in Devonshire,[3] where, perhaps for the first time in his life, he found ideal conditions for his reflective

---

[1] See p. cl.   [2] *Works*, Vol. VIII, pp. 262–4.
[3] Now Forde Abbey, in Dorset.

labours. It was to the analysis of Fictions that he first turned his attention ; and during September and October he was able to amplify the classification (which in August was only a " commenced catalogue " [1]) in the elaborate essay which occupies the first place in the present volume.

The *Chrestomathia* itself was published in its entirety in the summer of 1815,[2] which serves to date the summary in Appendix IV, Section 18, in connexion with the planting of a Ramean Tree.[3] In the later classification in Section 1 of the Appendix on Universal Grammar,[4] relational Fictions are stressed. There is a parallel section in Chapter VI of the Essay on Language,[5] where the subject is dealt with in relation to Conjugates ; and a briefer re-statement for the application of the theory to Scales of Logical Subalternation.[6] Finally, there is a useful summary in the fragmentary Appendix to the *Nomography*,[7] where the various " Instruments of Invention and Discovery employed by Jeremy Bentham " are detailed under fifteen separate heads.

In April and July 1928,[8] attention was drawn to the essentials, and further instalments of the present work continued to appear from 1929 to 1932.[9] It has seemed best to separate the exposition of points of detail from the main body of the text ; which can thus be judged, to some extent, apart from its many variants and applications.

[1] See p. xxxvi below.
[2] *Works*, Vol. IV, p. 532 (letter to the Governor of Virginia).
[3] *Works*, Vol. VIII, pp. 119–120.
[4] *Ibid.*, p. 187.
[5] *Ibid.*, pp. 325–6.
[6] *Ibid.*, p. 267.
[7] *Works*, Vol. III, p. 286. See pp. xxvii ff. above.
[8] *Psyche*, Vol. VIII, No. 4 and Vol. IX, No. 1. In the following year The Orthological Institute invited Mr. John Wisdom, of St. Andrew's University, to examine Bentham's theories of Division, Definition, and Archetypation from the standpoint of the logico-analytic school. His conclusions (*Interpretation and Analysis*, 1931) are referred to below, pp. xlviii ff. and lx–lxi.
[9] *Psyche*, Vol. X, Nos. 2 and 4 (October 1929 and April 1930), Vol. XI, No. 3 (January 1931), Vol. XII, Nos. 3 and 4 (January and April 1932).

c

II.—THE THEORY

BENTHAM'S PROLEGOMENA[1]

[*As stated on page* xxxiii, *this is Bentham's earliest systematic survey* (*dated August* 1814) *of the field which he covered shortly afterwards in greater detail, though from a somewhat different angle*]

" OF methodization, in so far as performed by denomination, the subjects, the immediate subjects are *names* and nothing more. Things ? Yes ; but no otherwise than through the medium of their names.

It is only by means of *names*, viz. simple or *compound*, that things are susceptible of arrangement. Understand of arrangement in the *psychical* sense ; in which sense, strictly speaking, it is only the ideas of the things in question that are the subjects of the arrangement, not the things themselves. Of *physical* arrangement, the subjects are the things themselves—the animals, or the plants, or the minerals disposed in a museum ; of *psychical*, the *names*, and, through the names, the *ideas* of those several objects, viz. as disposed in a systematic work on the subject of the correspondent branch of Natural Philosophy—on the subject of Zoology, Botany, or Mineralogy.

If of this operation (viz. methodization by denomination) things were the only subjects, after names of *persons*, names there would be none other than names of *things* ; but of names that are *not* names of *things*, there are abundantly more than of names that are.

By *things*, bodies are here meant, portions of inanimate substance.

By this denomination we are led to the distinction, the

---

[1] *Works*, Vol. VIII, pp. 262-4.

comprehensive and instructive distinction, between *real* entities and *fictitious* entities; or rather, between their respective *names*. Names of real entities are masses of proper names—names of so many individual masses of matter; of *common* names—names respectively of all such individual masses of matter as are of such or such a particular description, which by these names is indicated or endeavoured to be indicated.

Words—viz. words employed to serve as names—being the only instruments by which, in the absence of the *things*, viz. the *substances* themselves, the ideas of them can be presented to the mind; hence, wheresoever a word is seen, which, to appearance, is employed in the character of a *name*, a natural and abundantly extensive consequence is a propensity and disposition to suppose the existence, the real existence, of a correspondent object—of a correspondent thing, of the thing of which it is the name, of a thing to which it ministers in the character of a name.

Yielded to without a sufficiently attentive caution, this disposition is a frequent source of confusion—of temporary confusion and perplexity; and not only so, but even of permanent error.

The class of objects here meant to be designated by the appellation of *names* of fictitious entities require to be distinguished from names of *fabulous* entities; for shortness, say—fictitious require to be distinguished from fabulous entities. To render whatsoever is said of them correctly and literally true, the idea of a *name* requires all along to be inserted, and the grammatical sentence composed and constructed in consequence.

Fabulous entities are either fabulous persons or fabulous things.

Fabulous entities, whether persons or things, are supposed material objects, of which the separate existence is capable of becoming a subject of belief, and of which, accordingly, the same sort of picture is capable of being drawn in and preserved in the mind, as of any really existent object.[1]

Of a *fabulous* object, whether person or thing, the idea (*i.e.* the *image* delineated in the mind by the name and accompanying description) may be just the same, whether a corresponding object had or had not been in existence, whether the object were a historical or a fabulous one.

Fictitious entities (viz. the objects for the description of which, throughout the whole course of the present work, this appellative is meant to be employed) are such, of which, in a very ample proportion, the mention, and consequent fiction, require to be introduced for the purpose of discourse ; their names being employed in the same manner as names of substances are employed ; hence the character in which they present themselves is that of so many names of substances. But these names of fictitious entities do not, as do the above-mentioned names of fabulous entities, raise up in the mind any correspondent images.

Follows a sort of commenced catalogue of these fictitious entities, of these names of fictitious entities ; from which the common nature, in which, as above, they all participate, will presently become perceptible. Like the names of real and those of fabulous entities, all these words, it will be seen, are, in the language of grammarians, *noun-substantives*. All these fictitious entities are, accordingly, so many fictitious substances. The properties which, for the purposes of discourse, are attributed to them, are so many properties of all substances.

That the properties belonging to substances, to bodies in general, are attributed to them—that they are spoken of as if possessed of such properties—appears from the *prepositions* by which the import of their respective names is put, in connexion with the import of the other

[1] Examples : Gods of different dynasties ; kings, such as Brute and Fergus ; animals, such as dragons and chimaeras ; countries, such as El Dorado ; seas, such as the Straits of Arrian ; fountains, such as the fountain of Jouvence.

words of which the sentence, the grammatical sentence, is composed.

Physical and *psychical.* Under one or other of these two denominations may all fictitious entities be comprised.

Let us commence with physical :

I. *Motion, motions.* In the physical world, in the order of approach to real existence, next to *matter* comes *motion.* But motion itself is spoken of as if it were *matter* ; and in truth, because, in no other way—such is the nature of language, and such is the nature of things—in no other way could it have been spoken of.

A *ball*—the ball called *the earth*—is said to be *in* motion. By this word *in*, what is it that is signified ? *Answer :* What is signified is that *motion* is a *receptacle, i.e.* a hollow substance ; and that in this hollow substance, the ball called the earth is lodged.

A motion, or the motion we say of a body. The body is one portion of matter, the motion is another, which proceeds of, that is *from*, that substance.

Of names of motions (*i.e.* of names of species, or modifications of motion) vast, not to say infinite, is the number and variety.

Genus generalissimum is a term employed by the logicians of old, to indicate the name of any one of those aggregates which is not contained in any other aggregate that hath as yet received a name.

The idea of *motion* necessarily supposes that of a moving body—a body which is in motion, or in which the motion is ; necessarily supposes—*i.e.* without the one idea, at any rate, without the one image, the other cannot be entertained.

The idea of motion does not necessarily suppose that of another body, or the idea of the motion of another body, or the idea of another body, from which, or from the motion of which, the motion in question proceeds or did proceed. The planets, that they are in motion, is matter of observation—whence the motion took its rise is matter of inference, or rather of vague conjecture. On the earth's surface, we see various bodies in the act of deriving motion from various *primum mobiles*. But the *primum mobile*, if any, from which the earth itself derived the motion *in* which it is at present, what can we so much as conjecture in relation to it ?

Where a motion of any kind is considered as having place, it is considered either with reference to some *person* who is regarded as the author of it, or without such reference. In the latter of these cases, motion, and nothing else, is the word employed : in the other case, *action* or *operation* ; and in respect of it, the author is termed *agent* or *operator*.

II. *Quantity*. Next to motion and motions, come quantity and quantities.

Quantity is applicable in the first place to *matter*, in the next place to *motion*.

Of and *in* are the prepositions in the company of which it is employed.

A *quantity* of ink is *in* the ink-glass which stands before me. Here *ink*, the real substance, is *one* substance ; *quantity*, the *fictitious* substance, is another which is proceeding, or has proceeded, from ink, the real one.

The ink which is in the ink-glass, exists there *in* a certain quantity. Here *quantity* is a fictitious substance— a fictitious receptacle—and in this receptacle the ink, the real substance, is spoken of as if it were lodged.

In this word *quantity*, may be seen the name of another *genus generalissimum* ; another aggregate than which there is no other more capacious in the same nest of aggregates.

When *quantity* is considered, it may be considered either with or without regard to the relation between part and whole ; and if considered, in one or other of these ways it cannot but be considered ; the division is, therefore, an exhaustive one.

When quantity is considered, or at least. attempted to be considered, without regard to the relation between part and whole, it is considered with reference to *figure*.

But if, without regard to the relation between part and whole, the idea of figure be indeed capable of being entertained, it is indeterminate and confused.

Quantity, according to the logicians of old, is either continuous or discrete. By continuous quantity, they mean quantity considered with regard to figure, and without regard to the relation between part and whole. By *discrete* quantity, they mean quantity considered with regard to the relation between part and whole, and without regard to figure.

If the three branches of mathematical discipline be separately considered, continuous quantity is the subject of *geometry* ; discrete quantity, the subject of *arithmetic* and *algebra*.

But it is only by *arithmetic* that either in relation to any proposition appertaining to geometry, or in relation to any proposition in algebra, any clear conception can be obtained. Divide a circle into any number of parts—for instance, those called degrees ; clear and distinct ideas are obtainable respecting the whole, and those or any other parts into which it is capable of being divided, or conceived to be divided. Refuse all such division ; the best idea you can obtain of a circle will have neither determinate form nor use.

III. *Quality.* Quality is *applicable to* matter, to motion, and to quantity.

Of and *in* are the prepositions in the company of which it is employed.

Qualities of bodies, or say ' portions of matter ', animate or inanimate, are good and bad, viz. with reference to man's use.

Qualities of motion, *i.e.* of motions, are quick and slow, high and low, viz. with reference to any object taken as a standard, uninterrupted and interrupted, etc.

Qualities of quantities are great and little, determinate and indeterminate, *i.e.* with reference to man's knowledge of them, or conception concerning them.

Qualities of quantities are qualities either of bodie

(*i.e.* portions of matter) or of portions of space, considered
with reference to quantity in the exclusion of every other
quality.

Property is, in one of the senses of the word, synonymous, or nearly so, to quality.

As we speak of the *quality* of a *quantity*, so do we of
the *quantity* of a *quality*.

When men speak of the quantity of a quality, instead
of saying quantity of a quality they commonly say a
degree—in a high degree, in a low degree ; instead of
' high ', we say sometimes, in a ' great ' degree ; instead
of low, in a ' small ' degree.

Degree, in French *degré*, is from the Latin *gradus*,
a step or stair ; that which is said to be a *high* degree
is considered as situated upon the upper steps of a staircase. *Scale*, in French *échelle*, is from the Latin *scala*,
a ladder ; whether the word be staircase or ladder, the
image is to the purpose here in question much the same.

IV. *Form* or *Figure*. No mass of matter is *without
form* ; no individual mass of matter but has its boundary
lines ; and by the magnitude of those lines, and their
position with reference to one another, the *form*, the
figure, of the mass is constituted and determined.

But neither is any portion of *space* without its form.
Form or figure, or say ' to possess form or figure ', is,
therefore, a property or quality of space as well as of
matter ; it is a property common to matter and space.

A mass of matter may have throughout for its bounds
or limits either another mass, or other masses, of matter,
or a portion of space, or in some parts *matter*, in others
space.

A portion of space cannot, in any part, have for its
bounds anything but matter.

A mass of matter is said to exist in a certain form ; to
be *of* a certain form or figure ; to be changed *from* one
form *into*, or to, another.

V. *Relation*. In so far as any two objects are regarded
by the mind at the same time—the mind, for a greater

or less length of time, passing from the one to the other—by this transition, a fictitious entity termed *Relation*, a relation, is considered as produced.

The one of these objects—*either* of these objects—is said to *bear* a relation to the other.

Between the two objects, a relation is said to exist or to have place.

The time during which the two objects are regarded, or kept under consideration is, as above, for shortness spoken of as the same time. It should seem, however, that with exactly the same degree of attention objects more than one cannot be regarded, considered, examined, surveyed, at exactly the same instant, or smallest measurable portion of time ; but that, on the occasion and for the purpose of comparison, the mind is continually passing and repassing from the one to the other, and back again, *i.e.* vibrating, viz. after the manner of the pendulum of a clock.

This motion, viz. *vibration* (the motion acquired by an elastic *cylinder* or *prism*, in which the length is the prevalent dimension, on its being suddenly dragged, impelled, or drawn, and let go in a direction other than that of its length), being the simplest of all recurrent motions, is the sort of motion best suited, or rather is the only sort of motion in any degree at all suited to the purpose of *comparison*.

Hence it seems to be that, in speaking of a *relation*, any number of objects greater than two are not brought to view ; for, on this occasion, the preposition employed is always *between*, never *among*. By the preposition *between*, the number of the objects in question is restricted to *two* ; restricted universally and uncontrovertibly.

Hence it is that, in methodical division, the *bifurcate* mode is the only one that is completely satisfactory."

THE VOCABULARY OF FICTION

Two brief passages indicating the point of view from which this preliminary outline was subsequently filled in, and supplementary to the material in the text of *The Theory of Fictions* below,[1] may conveniently be interpolated here.

The first is a note on the statement that " for the purpose of rendering, in the best manner in which we are able, an account of the motion of such bodies as are in motion, and of the rest of such as are at rest, certain fictitious entities are, by a sort of innocent falsehood, the utterance of which is necessary to the purpose of discourse, feigned to exist and operate in the character of causes, equally real with, and distinct from, the perceptible and perceived effects, in relation to which they are considered in the character of causes." It runs as follows :—

" The necessity to which we are subjected by the imperfection of the instrument for the purposes of discourse, the necessity of mixing falsehood with truth, on pain of being without ideas, as well as without conversation, on some of the most interesting of the subjects that lie within the pale of our cognizance, is productive but too abundantly of misconception and false reasoning ; and this not only in the physical department of the field of thought, discourse, and action, but also in every other.   On pain of having some of the most interesting subjects of thought, discourse, and action undiscoursed of, and even unthought of, we set to work the powers of our imaginations in the creation, as it were, of a multitude of imaginary beings, all spoken of as if they belonged to the class of bodies or substances ; and on the occasion, and for the purpose of the creation, we attach to them a name or sign, called a part of speech : viz. a species of word, termed a noun substantive ; the same species of word as that of which, in the character of a common name, we make use for the designation of real entities, appertaining strictly and properly to the class of substances.   Beholding at a distance, in the dress of a man, sitting and playing upon an organ, an automaton figure, constructed for that purpose by the ingenuity of the

[1] The body of the text, pp. 1–140, will be referred to as *The Theory of Fictions*.

mechanist, to take this creature of human art for a real man, is a sort of mistake which, at a certain distance, might happen for a time to be made by the most acute observer. In like manner, beholding a part of speech cast in the same mould with the name of a real entity, a really existing substance, no wonder if, on a variety of occasions, to the mental eye of a very acute observer, this fictitious entity thus accoutred should present itself in the character of, and be regarded and treated as if it were a real one. How should it be otherwise, when on every occasion on which, and by every person by whom it is spoken of at all, it is spoken of as if it were a real entity ? And thus in a manner an universal attestation is given to the truth of a set of propositions, the falsity of which, when once brought to view, cannot in any instance fail to be recognized." [1]

The second is one of Bentham's numerous asides on the implications of the theory for Psychology :—

" What is here meant is, not that no such fictions ought to be employed, but that to the purpose and on the occasion of instruction, whenever they are employed, the necessity or the use of them should be made known.

To say that, in discourse, fictitious language ought never, on any occasion, to be employed, would be as much as to say that no discourse on the subject of which the operations, or affections, or other phenomena of the mind are included, ought ever to be held : for no ideas being ever to be found in it which have not their origin in sense, matter is the only direct subject of any portion of verbal discourse ; on the occasion and for the purpose of the discourse, the mind is all along considered and spoken of as if it were a mass of matter : and it is only in the way of fiction that when applied to any operation, or affection of the mind, anything that is said is either true or false.

Yet in as far as any such fictions are employed, the necessity of them, if, as in the case just mentioned, necessary, or the use of them, if simply useful, should be made known. Why ? In the first place, to prevent that perplexity which has place in the mind, in as far as truth and falsehood being confounded, that which is not true is supposed to be true ; in the next place, by putting it as far as possible in the power of the learner to perceive and understand the use and value, as well as the nature of the instruction communicated to him, to lighten the burthen of the labour necessary to be employed in the acquisition of it." [2]

[1] *Works*, Vol. VIII, p. 129.   [2] *Ibid.*, p. 174.

What is remarkable about these amplifications of the theory is the modernity of their outlook in relation to scientific method. The vocabulary of As-If is of relatively recent origin, and Suppositions, Theories, Assumptions, Hypotheses, Fictions may be advanced, or approached, from many points of view. Each has been used in some connexion as a synonym for all the others.

When, as opposed to stating a fact, we lay down a proposition to form the basis of discussion or argument, we may do so in the belief that it will be verified, in the hope that its consistency may lead to knowledge, or, regardless of fact, simply in order to provide something to talk about. Similarly our attitude to the existence of our referents has three grades.

In relation to these six situations we are apt to use six terms somewhat as follows :—" I believe that the planetesimal *hypothesis* will be verified ". " The *theory* of evolution seems to be consistent and comprehensive." " On the *assumption* that $2 \times 2 = 5$." " My *idea* of Bentham is that of a sensitive and kindly man." " The *conception* of ectoplasm is still decidedly vague." " A centaur is as much a *fiction* as Hamlet or the golden age."

We have also a variety of alternative locutions symbolizing beliefs in the applicability of our references, taking the form " that this will be the case ", " that this formula will work ", " that this hypothesis (theory, assumption) is true ". And we have graded linguistic expressions for beliefs as to the place, or whereabouts, of certain particular referents. Including certainty, we get the full probability range symbolized as follows. It is a fact (certainly) that ; the (probable) hypothesis that ; the (possible) theory that ; let us assume that (the impossible). And as regards place : the perception of this (certainly) here ; the idea of that (probably) there ; the conception of that (possibly) somewhere ; that (impossible) fiction.

From the point of view of verification, then, we are concerned with various degrees of the hypothetical, from the generalizations or laws which we assume, the hypotheses, suppositions, and proposals which we believe or doubt pending further evidence, to fictions proper (which are excluded from the universe of fact though their tenancy of the higher reaches of methodology is sponsored by the imagination), and finally to the impossibilia, which conflict even with our symbol structures (nonsense) or with the nature of our sensations (as that one and the same logistic patch can be both red and green). In a sense, then, a shift from the language of fictions into that of probability is a form of translation from substantival into adjectival symbolism ; whose adequate notational exploration may eventually attract the more sophisticated geographers of Symbolic Distance.

' Impossible ', moreover, is the opposite both of ' possible '(= not contradicting the laws) and, in terms of belief, ' possible ' (= not-unbelievable). And since the believable (*can*) is either certain (*must*, *will*) or not certain (*may*), the impossible (*cannot*) may also function linguistically as the extreme of a psychological scale from certain belief to certain disbelief—with a middle range, probable, neither believed nor disbelieved, but doubted.[1]

The statistical grounds for the various degrees of belief constitute the formal theory of probability, which thus becomes an inquiry into the various forms of contextual complication whose analysis can be mathematically treated. These grounds involve two factors :—

(*a*) The relative frequency of realization of any event.

(*b*) The reliability with which this realization can be expected in further cases.

When, therefore, we are exercised about the reasons for our beliefs, the statistical probability of any statement, we endeavour to give a numerical value to our expectation in terms of uniform contexts. If this is the case, to say

[1] See the writer's *Opposition* (1932), p. 75. It is to this middle range that Bentham would presumably have relegated those " inferential entities " (*Theory of Fictions*, pp. 8–10) whose reification is desiderated by physics and circumspection alike.

with certain mathematicians that the probability attaches to the ' proposition ' is to talk in terms of fictions which will be misleading if we regard them as ultimates. Similarly, to suppose that there is a world of ' subsistent entities ' and ' assumptions ' independent of the world of fact is to allow ourselves to generate linguistic fictions ; and it was with the avoidance of these fictions that Bentham was primarily concerned.

THE TECHNOLOGICAL APPROACH

It seems that philosophical and logical discussion has always consisted in the translation of common discourse into some technical analytic language which, it has been hoped, would provide proper devices for the efficient detection and correction of errors. Such translations have generally been vitiated by the introduction of irrelevant material into the analytic language. The simplicity and directness of the Benthamic translation is a welcome shock to minds familiar with the traditional irrelevances, because it is concerned from the outset with practical and linguistic issues. His analytic method throws into relief certain crucial turning-points in thought that have usually been dismissed as merely verbal. Perhaps his most important insistence is that words, no matter what their other developments in use may be, must, in so far as they are names used to refer beyond themselves, be interpreted as referring ultimately to something real and observed.

Language, according to Bentham—here anticipating the most striking feature of Bergson's presentation—is essentially a technological apparatus for dealing with the world of things in space. What is ' there ' to be talked about is primarily a nexus of individual bodies, and when we seem to be talking about other sorts of entities our language is metaphorical—whatever the alleged status of its referents. All such fictional and metaphorical jargon is not only capable of translation but, for purposes of serious discussion or of technology, must be translated into something less deceptive.

The inevitable tendency is for logical translators to neglect this feature of language until it is too late to give it adequate attention. Makeshifts consequently mar the final results, or, as more often happens, entities are invented to correct distortions of reference and to populate the world with fictions. Bentham's powerful and original prophylactic device for such linguistic aberrations is the archetype [1] which at the start fixes the reference of words to observed entities, and at the same time provides the foundation and framework for a verbal expansion to any degree of explicitness and exhaustiveness that we may need for accurate translation. In fact, the two processes of archetypation and phraseoplerosis may carry translation beyond its primary function into what is usually called logical analysis ; Bentham with characteristic vigour calls it the analysis of fictions.[2] The expansion catches, analyses, and traces lines of reference for, those planetary adjectives and opaque metaphors that confuse the best minds even in the most familiar jargons. The archetypes, which are usually actual or pictured bodies in rest or in motion, act as symbolic and logical lenses and bring fictional terms to focus on a man's experience, or dissolve them into their original nothingness. This is more than even the most highly complicated logics have achieved, and Bentham's technique is as simple as it is original.

INCOMPLETE SYMBOLS

The nearest approach of modern philosophers and logicians to the subject of Bentham's inquiry is the attempt to define an ' incomplete symbol '. At certain points the logistic method of exposition is very like Bentham's " giving phrase for phrase " in the process of archetypation (p. lxxviii).

[1] See *Theory of Fictions*, pp. 86 ff.
[2] See Professor Buchanan's *Symbolic Distance*, 1932.

The primary endeavour of this new ' critical ' philosophy, according to those who favour the terminology which suggested the technique, is to analyse something that is called ' the meaning ' of a small [1] number of words and phrases, such as ' brother of ', ' *a* is a multiple of *b* ', ' this is red ', ' x is good '.

This process of analysis may start with such a question as " What do *I mean* when I say ' this is a chair '," or " What is the *correct analysis* of ' x ' is beautiful ", or " What are the *constituents of the thing, meaning,* or *relation* called ' brother of '."

The " correct analysis of ' meanings of words ', *i.e.,* ' concepts ', *i.e.* ' universals ' '", is called *definition.* [2]

The general theory of symbols from which this account of analysis appears to be derived moves between two ultimates :—

(1) immediate experience which is made up of sensa like patches of colour in temporal-spatial order, and

(2) universals which may come into immediate experience as qualities, but do not depend on any space or time relations for their order, which is logical and not primarily experiential.

Sentences, on this logico-analytic theory, are divided into at least four kinds :—

(*a*) Those that contain only proper names, such as " I see this patch now here " ;

(*b*) Those that assert the presence or existence of absolutely determinate qualities (or universals), such as " There is this absolutely determinate red (quality) here now " ;

---

[1] The complications which would arise if other examples were hazarded may be gathered from the care with which the range is restricted.

[2] Wisdom, *Interpretation and Analysis,* p. 17. It is, however, worth noting that other logico-analysts would not necessarily subscribe to such a statement. It is true that Russell has sometimes written as if his analysis of the number concept was also a definition of it, but that seems to have been due to a confusion of motive. When analysing ' number ' as it actually occurred in propositions used by mathematicians, he was not defining it ; and when he *was* defining, he was exhibiting a new entity (a class of classes of classes) with similar formal properties.

(c) Those that contain general terms or apparent variables which refer conjunctively, alternately, or disjunctively to sensa or universals, such as " All the colours in my field of vision are shades of red ", or " Some of the colours in my field of vision are shades of red ", or " Either x, or y, or z, etc., is a shade of red."

This last class of sentences express chiefly logical constructions and are, according to some logisticians, incomplete symbols ; according to others, however, all propositions are incomplete symbols. The notation of Russell's *Principia* provides the means for analysing them ; and when analysed they can be shown to be indirect references to propositions of the types (a) and (b) and the relevant sensa or universals.

Type (d) sentences contain combinations of symbols that make nonsense ; they really originate in type (c), but when the *Principia* analysis fails to carry their references back to types (a) and (b) they are placed in type (d). Examples would be " A is between B ", or, according to one authority, " Two is a number " ; but this field is very chaotic—a sort of epistemological dump. Indeed, it would seem to follow from any interpretation of the Theory of Types (another of Russell's ingenious legacies to his logistic epigoni [1]) that the ultimate nature of ' facts ', ' propositions ', and ' scientific objects ' is irremediably controversial ; there are so many analyses that have not been carried out, and each new case seems to bring up new difficulties. For the same reason the domain of nonsense is for the most part vague, and is apparently increasing its population with great rapidity.

Bentham would agree as to the ultimacy of immediate experience and sentences of type (a). He would put type (b) sentences into type (c), which is the class of fictions. He would agree that some analysis was necessary,

[1] For an examination of the Theory of Types as a valid symbolic device, and of possible alternatives, see Max Black, *The Nature of Mathematics*, 1932, Section I (International Library of Psychology).

d

but it would consist of archetypation and phraseoplerosis rather than in the operations of the *Principia*. The differences in the degrees of efficiency of these two analytical devices would then account for the major differences in classification. A better analytical machinery, designed on the same lines as that of Bentham, could probably reclaim a great deal of that sort of ' nonsense ' which consists in metaphorical distortion—if such reclamation were desirable.

In the account already referred to,[1] the analysis of ' definition ' employs certain other assumptions which seem to be common to this group of logicians. The ontological status of ' universals ' is no longer stressed in the latest formulations of the system. Definite statements are, however, made about qualities, which emerge from the consideration of patches and facts.

In the sentence ' This is red ', we are told that " both ' this ' and ' red ' name elements in the world. ' This ' names the sort of element which can be the subject in a patch and red the sort of element which can be a predicate in a patch." But though they are *elements* in the world, " still, if we make a list of the facts in the world, we shall find on it neither this nor a shade of red ". The shade is a *quality*. A *fact* is a configuration of objects, and " some objects can take either the position of subject or that of predicate. These are qualities." Qualities are not obvious, but are " detected by philosophical inspection ".

Bentham believed that language must contain fictions in order to remain a language, *i.e.* that a language which ' mirrored ' reality would be impossible. If the logico-analysts were to believe that ' logical constructions ' must *necessarily* occur in language they would profoundly modify their attitude to the problem ; for it would follow that there could be no atomic propositions and all analyses would be relative. Whether some hierarchical analysis is possible must remain doubtful. What is at any rate

[1] See p. xlviii, note.

clear is that we could not talk of *the* analysis of a given proposition. This is the real bone of contention between the logico-analytic temperament and the technological approach of Bentham. The latter realized that the problem is eminently a *practical* one—the classification of thought by simplifying and revealing the structure of language ; and therefore a task for whose performance no eternally valid rules can be promulgated. The logico-analysts postulate an ideal language—perfect even in its well-disposed irregularities—which requires methodical articulation in accordance with a preconceived metaphysical scheme. That is why they restrict their analysis to phrases like ' This is red ' which approximate to ideals of linguistic excellence, and neglect entities like ' right ', ' power ', etc., which so strongly attracted Bentham. Hence the sterility of their method.[1]

If Bentham's statements are approached from their standpoint he will necessarily appear to be muddled.

---

[1] For a critical discussion of logical analysis from this point of view, see Max Black, *loc. cit.*

It is, however, frequently possible to translate the language of fictions into that of incomplete symbols. Thus, taking the word Liberty, we can proceed as follows :—

I. *Liberty* is a fiction = ' Liberty ' is an incomplete symbol.

' Liberty ' is an incomplete symbol = ' Liberty ' is not a name for anything nor a descriptive phrase for anything, though it is used as if it were, but sentences in which it occurs can be translated into sentences using only genuine proper names and descriptive phrases.

II. *Liberty* is a fiction = (i) ' Liberty ' is an incomplete symbol and

(ii) Anyone using such a sentence as ' Liberty is desirable '

(a) Means what he would mean if he were using ' Liberty ' as an incomplete symbol only (*i.e.* as a fiction in sense I) ; and

(b) Believes that ' Liberty ' is a name for something or a descriptive phrase for something.

III. *Liberty* is a fiction = *Liberty* is a fiction in sense II ; and

(c) Anyone using the word ' Liberty ' believes with respect to certain properties that they apply to what ' Liberty ' is a name for (or a descriptive phrase for).

Memo : It does not follow that there is an x such that the person using ' Liberty ' believes that ' Liberty ' is the name for it ; nor that there is an x such that the person believes that these properties apply to it.

Thus when he insists that fictions have a sort of verbal reality—*i.e.* we seem to be predicating something about them, though strictly the predicates are being applied only to *names*—he is readily misunderstood to be supposed to be asserting that the names stand for *nothing* ; in which case he would appear to have been " very much misled ", and to be saying " what someone with an imperfect understanding of logical constructions would say ".[1]

Nevertheless, the fact that such a misunderstanding of his position is possible makes it important to examine in greater detail certain passages in which he speaks of fictions as blameless and inevitable, while yet regarding them as a source of misunderstanding, controversy, and even war.[2]

QUALITIES AS FIRST-ORDER FICTIONS

Fictions, Bentham has explained, " owe their existence entirely to language ", but we are under the necessity of talking about them in terms which pre-suppose their existence ; they may even be said to have a sort of *verbal* reality, so to speak.[3] We still have to talk about them *as if* they were ' there ' to be talked about ; and for all ordinary purposes those most directly related to our senses, or to a ' tangible ' archetype, in so far as they are nearer to physical reality, may on occasion be spoken of as ' real '.

This is best understood by reference to the status of what are called *qualities*—entities regarded as ultimate by nearly all systems in which an analysis of propositions has been attempted.

Bentham's starting-point is, as we have seen, the

---

[1] Wisdom, *op. cit.*, pp. 78 and 88.

[2] *Works*, Vol. VIII, p. 328. See *Theory of Fictions*, p. 14 ; and cf. p. 60.

[3] *Works*, Vol. VIII, pp. 126 and 198. See *Theory of Fictions*, pp. 16 and 37.

noun-substantive, which may be the name either of a
real or a fictitious entity :—

" Incorporeal as well as corporeal substances being included, real entities are those alone which belong to that
universal class designated by the logicians by the name of
substances.

Substances are divided by them into corporeal and
incorporeal. Under the name of corporeal are included all
masses of matter, howsoever circumstances in respect of
form, bulk, and place.

Of corporeal substances, the existence is made known
to us by sense. Of incorporeal, no otherwise than by
ratiocination ; they may on that account be termed
inferential." [1]

To the class of inferential entities belong, " 1. The soul
of man in a state of separation from the body. 2. God.
3. All other and inferior spiritual entities." With inferential entities we are advised elsewhere [2] not to trouble
ourselves unduly ; they being best " left in the places in
which they are found ". Real and fictitious entities are
our more immediate concern :—

" By a real entity, understand a substance—an object,
the existence of which is made known to us by one or
more of our five senses.[3] A real entity is either a person or
a thing, a substance rational, or a substance not rational.

By a fictitious entity, understand an object, the
existence of which is feigned by the imagination—feigned
for the purpose of discourse—and which, when so formed,
is spoken of as a real one."

These sorts of fictitious entities " may be classed in
different ranks or orders, distinguished by their respective

---

[1] Another of Bentham's many references to Berkeley is added at
this point : " According to those who agree with Bishop Berkeley,
matter belongs to the class of those entities of which the existence is
inferential ; impressions and ideas being, in that case, the only perceptible entities. But, in the case of matter, the justness of the
inference is determinable, at all times determinable, by experimental
proof : if of the wall opposite me, I infer the non-existence and run
that way as if there were no wall, the erroneousness of the inference
will be but too plainly perceptible on my forehead ; which is not the
case in any one of these other instances " (*Works*, Vol. VIII, p. 189).

[2] *Theory of Fictions*, p. 10.

[3] " Say, in a word, where the object is a tangible one," says Bentham
elsewhere (*Theory of Fictions*, p. 60).

degrees of vicinity to the real one ".[1]   And here comes one of the most important passages in which qualities, as fictions, are assigned to their different levels.

" To substance we ascribe qualities ; to motion also we ascribe qualities.   It is by this circumstance that of motion the import is placed, as it were, nearer to that of substance than that of qualities.   Substances have their qualities— they are large, small, long, short, thick, thin, and so forth ; motions have their qualities—they are quick, slow, rising, falling, continued, discontinued, regular, irregular, and so on.

If, then, *motion* be termed a fictitious entity of the *first* order, viz. that which is nearest to reality, mobility, and so any other quality, may with reference to it be termed a fictitious entity of the *second* order.

Here, then, we have an additional class of fictitious entities, of fictitious substances.   We have largeness, small-ness, length, shortness, thickness, thinness ; we have, moreover, quickness, slowness.   We might have as well as rising, risingness ; as well as falling, fallingness ; as well as continued, continuedness, as well as discontinued, dis-continuedness ; we have as well as regular, regularity ; as well as irregular, irregularity ; attributes as well of sub-stances as of motions.

Already has been brought to view, though as yet without special notice, a different sort of conjugate, the noun-adjective—large, small, long, short, thick, thin and so forth.

This sort of conjugate, in what consists its difference from that which is the name of a quality ?   In this :—when we speak of *largeness*, there is largeness ; we speak of the fictitious substance so denominated, without reference made to any other object.   On the contrary, when we say *large*, we present the idea of that same quality, but accompanied with the intimation of some other substance which is endued with that quality—some other object in which that quality has existence, and is to be found.   We put the mind upon the look-out for that other object, without which it is satisfied that the expression is incomplete ; that the idea presented by it is but, as it were, the fragment of an idea—a fragment, to the completion of which the idea of some object in which the quality is to be found is necessary.

In a word, the *substantial name* of a quality presents the idea, in the character of a complete idea, conceivable

[1] *Works*, Vol. VIII, p. 325 (=*Theory of Fictions*, p. 114).

of itself ; the *adjectival denomination* of that same quality presents the idea in the character of an incomplete idea, requiring for the completion of it the idea of some object in which it may be seen to *inhere*." [1]

That qualities are typical fictions is further emphasized in the account given of Abstraction,[2] which may be supplemented by a passage dealing with the principles of education, where it is laid down that " no portion of matter ever presents itself to *sense* without presenting at one and the same time a multitude of simple ideas, of all which taken together the *concrete* one, in a state more or less correct and complete, is composed ".

Though naturally all these ideas present themselves together, " the mind has it in its power to detach, as above, any one or more of them from the rest, and either keep it in view in this detached state or make it up into a compound with other simple ideas, detached in like manner from other sources. But for the making of this separation—this abstraction, as it is called—more *trouble*, a stronger force of *attention*, is necessary than for the taking them up in a promiscuous bundle, as it were ; in the bundle in which they have been tied together by the hand of Nature : that is, than for the consideration of the object in its *concrete* state." [3]

What is to be understood by *concrete* is made clear in the elaborate gloss on the term itself :—

" From a Latin word, which signifies *grown up along with* ; viz. along with the subject which is in question, whatever it be : it is used in contradistinction to the word *abstract*, derived from a Latin word which signifies *drawn*

[1] *Works*, Vol. VIII, p. 326 (=*Theory of Fictions*, pp. 116–7).
[2] *Ibid.*, pp. 121 ff.
[3] *Ibid.*, p. 26. In an entry in Bentham's Memorandum Book dated 1831, " February 16, the day after arrival at the age of 83 . . . J. B. the most ambitious of the ambitious ", we find the following—
" *Logic.*—Abstraction is one thing, association another ; relation comprehends both ; the one the converse of the other ; *relation* is the most abstract of all abstractions.
Each thing is—the whole of it, what it is ; but we may consider the whole of it together, or any one or more parts of it at a time, as we please ; thus we make—thus we have abstracted—abstract ideas." (*Works*, Vol. XI, p. 72).

off from ; viz. from the subject in question, as above. An *orange*, for example, has a certain *figure*, whereby, in connexion with a certain *colour*, it stands distinguished from all other fruits as well as from all objects of all sorts. Take into consideration this or that *individual* orange ; the ideas presented by the *figure* and *colour*, whereby it stands distinguished not only from other fruits but even from other *oranges*—from other fruits of the same kind—are *concrete* ideas ; for they *grew up*, as it were, together in the mind, out of the individual object, by which they are excited and produced : they are amongst the *elements*, out of which the aggregate conception, afforded and presentable to us by that individual object, is formed. The orange being no longer in sight—now, of the figure and colour observed in that individual orange, consider such parts or appearances as are to be found in all *other* oranges as well as in *that* one. The idea thus formed is *an abstract idea* : it being a portion *drawn off*, as it were, from the *aggregate idea* obtained, as above, from the *individual object*. Being abstracted and slipt off from the individual stock, and thereupon planted in the mind, it has there taken root, and acquired a separate and independent existence. Without thinking any more of that individual orange in particular, or of oranges in general, or of so much as of *fruits* in general, take now into consideration *figure* at large, and *colour* at large. Here, at one jump, the mind has arrived at an idea not only *abstract* but vastly *more* abstract than in the case last mentioned. Instead of *figure* and *colour*, let us now say *sensible qualities*. Under this appellation are included not only *figure* and *colour* but *smell, taste,* and many others ; it is therefore *abstract* in a still *higher* degree."

Thus, in talking about sensible or sensory qualities, we are already dealing with fictions of a high order ; and we must go back to the concrete situation if we are to understand the part played by such fictions in predication. " Everything which can happen to a corporeal subject is resolvable into this, viz. the having been, during the length of time in question, either in a state of motion or in a state of rest." Similarly, everything that can be said of that same corporeal subject " is resolvable either into this, viz. that during the length of time in question it has been, or has been capable of being, in a state of *motion* ; or into this, viz. that it has been, or has been capable of being in a state of rest ". Sight, hearing, and smell present no exceptions.[1]

"In either case, by what is said of the corporeal subject in question, a quality may be said to be ascribed to it, to be attributed to it, to be said to belong to it ; it may be said to be possessed of, endued, endowed with that same quality ; the quality is spoken of as being in that same subject, belonging to, appertaining to, inherent in that same subject.

If, in speaking of the quality as being in the subject, no more than a single point of time is brought to view, the quality thus attributed may be styled *actual*, or *momentary*, or *transient* ; if it be considered as either being, or capable of being, in the subject for an indeterminate length of time, the quality may be styled *potential, habitual,* or *permanent.*

When a quality is spoken of as appertaining to this or that subject, that which on this occasion is most frequently meant to be designated and is, therefore, most apt to be brought to view, is an habitual or permanent quality.

In consideration of its being attributed to a subject, a quality is also frequently styled an *attribute*—an attribute of that same subject ; and in consideration of its belonging to a subject, it is also frequently styled a *property*—a property of, or belonging, or appertaining to, or inherent in, that same subject."

Suppose, then, a portion of the matter of language so constructed "as to present to view a quality, whether actual or habitual, as appertaining to this or that given corporeal subject ; let it be considered what are the objects of which this portion of the matter of language must have contained the signs. These are : 1. the subject, 2. the quality. But to say that the quality in question is *in* the subject in question, is to affirm the existence of a certain relation between that subject and that quality, viz. the sort of relation of which the word *in* is the sign. Thus, then, to the sign of the subject and the sign of the quality must be added the sign of the relation."

[1] " In case of *sight*, the object said to be seen may be at rest, but the light, but for which it would not have been seen, has been in motion : and so in the instances of *hearing* and *smell* ; in hearing, the air ; in smell, the odoriferous particles " (*Works*, Vol. VIII, p. 337).

But what is here affirmed " is that in the subject in question the quality in question *is* ; in other words that *between* the subject and this quality there *exists* the relation in question. Thus, then, to complete the texture of the proposition, to the sign of the subject, the sign of the *quality* and the sign of the *relation* must be added the sign of existence—the sign by which existence is brought to view—the sign by which existence is asserted to have, or to have had place, viz. the existence of the relation between the subject and the attribute."

The number of words employed in the minimum proposition " Sugar is sweet " are no more than *three* ; " but in the form of expression, an abbreviation may be observed. Sweetness (the quality of sweetness) is in sugar. Sugar, the name of the subject—a corporeal subject ; sweetness, the name of the quality ; the quality consisting in the aptitude, in consequence of the necessary actions, to produce in the *sensorium* of men the perception termed by the same name." [1]

In the further treatment both of the subject of a proposition and of predication, the fictitious nature of qualities is also emphasized. In discussing the question of singular and plural subjects, he remarks that the individuals designated by a plural name are either all determinate, all indeterminate, or some determinate, others indeterminate.

" 1. All determinate—for instance the members of one official *board* actually in existence.

2. All indeterminate—for instance the intended members of an official board, not in existence but in contemplation to be established.

3. Some determinate, some indeterminate—of this sort, are the names of all *species* and *genera* of things ; of aggregate objects which have, have had, or will have, a real existence ; for in and by every such specific or generic name are designated, in the first place, all the individuals which are considered as being at the time in question endowed with the specific quality indicated by the name. In the next place, all that ever were. In the last place, all which ever

[1] *Ibid.*, p. 337.

will be, and by the supposition these last neither *have* nor ever have had existence."

A specific name, therefore, "partakes at once of the nature of the name of a real entity and of a name of a fictitious entity. It is the name of a real entity considered as applied to any one of the individuals now or before now in existence, which were endowed with the specific property, or to the whole number of them, or to any part of the whole number of them put together. It is as yet the name of a fictitious entity, considered as applied to all or any one or more of those individuals which, with that same specific character belonging to them, are considered as about to come into existence."

In this it differs from the name of a quality, "for a quality is an object altogether fictitious, an object which, considered as distinct from the subject in which it is spoken of as *inhering*, neither has, nor has had, nor ever will have existence ; for as often as it is spoken of as if it were *in* a body, *i.e.* a tangible substance, or in some other object which is spoken of as if it were a body, it is spoken of as if it were a substance, a tangible substance, which, by the supposition, it is not ".[1]

Predication is either real or verbal.[2] It is verbal "when the design is merely to give intimation of the import of the word which, on the occasion in question, is

---

[1] *Ibid.*, p. 335.

[2] " Different as they are in themselves, that is, in the design in pursuance of which they are employed, these two modes of predication are very liable to be confounded.

When the predication is *real*, the purpose of it—the purpose of the proposition in which it has place—is always, as above, to convey an intimation that in the entity in question which, or the name of which, is the *subject* of the proposition in question, a certain quality to which expression is given in and by the Predicate, has existence.

When the predication is *verbal*, purely verbal, the design is not to give intimation of any quality as having existence in any subject, but merely to convey an intimation of a certain relation between the import of one word and the import of another ; no such object as the nature of the quality designated by either being on that occasion meant to be brought into view.

The reason for holding up to view this distinction is, that sometimes, when the effect or design of the proposition is of one sort, it is liable to be misconceived, by being conceived to be of the other sort ". (*Works*, Vol. VIII, p. 336).

employed in the character of a sign, as " An oak is a plant " or " A dog is an animal ". It is real " when the design of the proposition is to convey information concerning the nature of the object signified ; when it declares the existence of some quality in the subject named ". Only a quality can be the object or matter of a real predication—but " a quality being but a fictitious entity, the predicate, if the predication be real, can never be anything but the name of a fictitious entity ".

How then can Bentham speak of ' real qualities ', which " belong to the objects " to which they are ascribed?[1] If we take the phrase ' real qualities ' in isolation there is an apparent contradiction, as in the case of the reality of the ' rights ' of the ordinary man—which Bentham is not concerned (at that level) to deny.[2] But here again it would be rash to assume that he is muddled.[3] " To be spoken of at all ", we are told, " *every* fictitious entity *must* be spoken of *as if* it were real ".[4] Since, therefore, no quality can be real, all talk about qualities in this context must be interpreted at the level for which it was intended. Having stated in more than a dozen carefully worded passages that all qualities, attributes, or predicates of whatever kind are inevitably and typically ontological fictions, Bentham could hardly expect to be misunderstood if for the sake of brevity he occasionally used language as the majority of his readers would also use it.

Thus when we find amongst the MSS. relating to qualities this isolated allusion to ' real ' qualities, and the equally unguarded remark that " the name of the attribute or predicate may be either the name of a real or the name of a fictitious entity ",[5] we can be fairly certain that by ' real ' Bentham here meant—first order

[1] *Works*, Vol. VIII, p. 211(=*Theory of Fictions*, p. 51).
[2] *Works*, Vol. VIII, p. 126 (=*Theory of Fictions* p. 138).
[3] *Contra* Wisdom, *Interpretation and Analysis*, p. 120. Cf. p. lxxix.
[4] *Works*, Vol. VIII, p. 19. The italics are ours. Cf. " *Fictitious* as they are, entities of this description could not be spoken of at all if they were not spoken of as *real* ones ". *Ibid.*, p. 126.
[5] *Ibid.*, p. 333.

fictions such as ordinary language is forced to introduce
by any form of predication.

This interpretation is supported by the instructive
passage in which figurative language is distinguished
from that which for all practical purposes may be treated
as non-figurative. " Fiction ", we have been told, " in
the simplest case in which language can be employed,
becomes a necessary resource ". But if all language be
thus figurative, how can it escape the condemnation to
which rhetoric in general is liable ? " To this it may be
answered : The discourse that, in this particular sense,
is *not* figurative is that in which no other figures are
employed than what are absolutely necessary to, and
which, consequently, are universally employed in, the
conveyance of the import intended to be conveyed."[1]

Thus only can we avoid undue pedantry in expression.
The penalty may be, as Bentham remarks in another
connexion, that by " confining himself to the language
most in use, a man can scarce avoid running, in appearance, into perpetual contradictions ; "[2] but the alternative, at any rate in the case of fictions such as quality,
would be to remodel the very structure of the grammar
of substantive and adjective on which Indo-European
languages are based. Some idea of the effects of such
a procedure on communication may be gathered from
the recent attempts of logicians who have not yet aban-
doned the search for " incomplete symbols " to discover
what sort of sentences may, in their terminology, be said
to " express facts ".[3]

For Bentham, as for anyone who accepts a Theory of
Fictions founded on linguistic psychology rather than on
logical assumptions, the term ' real ' can have no use
other than as a pointer indicating a high degree of symbolic
approximation to a technological ideal.

[1] *Theory of Fictions*, p. 74.
[2] *Introduction to the Principles of Morals and Legislation*, Chapter X, § 2.
[3] *Mind*, 1931, pp. 204 and 475.

III.—EXPANSIONS AND APPLICATIONS

WORDS, THOUGHTS, AND THINGS

THOUGH Bentham's views on Language and Linguistic Psychology are essentially part of his general Theory of Fictions, there are many passages scattered through his writings in which the symbolic factor is dealt with as a separate problem. A useful starting-point for an estimate of the importance which Bentham attached to linguistic analysis is provided by his notes on Nomenclature and Classification, where instructions are given for the planting of a Ramean tree.[1]

The distinction between names of real and names of fictitious entities " which in some of his Encyclopaedical remarks, D'Alembert was, it is believed, the first to bring to view ", will, he says, " be found to pervade the whole mass of every language upon earth, actual or possible ".[2] The names of the various branches of the *Porphyrian* or *Ramean* tree are names of *real* entities ; [3] those of the branches of the (Benthamic) Encyclopaedical tree [4] are names of *fictitious* entities, though to a con-

[1] *Works*, Vol. VIII, pp. 118 ff. (*Chrestomathia*, Appendix IV, § 18).

[2] " Even by Bishop Berkeley, by whom, as if to out-scepticize the sceptics, and foil them at their own weapons, the existence of the table he was writing upon was denied, the *name* of the table would have been allowed to be, in common intendment at least, the name of a *real entity* ; and, even in his own view of the matter, the table (an utensil which required wood to make it of and a saw, etc., to make it with) would have been allowed to approach somewhat nearer to the state of reality than a sort of entity such as *quality*, as a *relation*, in the making of which *thoughts* have been the only *materials* and words the only *instruments* ".

[3] " Say, strictly speaking, names of so many aggregates or classes, of objects *in* which *real entities* are included ; for, strictly speaking, *individual* objects are the only real entities : considered in themselves, the *aggregates* or *classes* in which those *real entities* are regarded as included, are no more than so many *fictitious bodies*, put together by the mind for its own use ".

[4] See *Works*, Vol. VIII, p. 8.

siderable extent references made to correspondent names of real entities are included in them.

This division of entities forms the basis of one exhaustive division of the whole stock of nouns substantive. "Strict, to the highest pitch of strictness, as is the propriety with which the *entities* here called *fictitious* are thus denominated, in no instance can the idea of *fiction* be freer from all tincture of blame : in no other instance can it ever be equally beneficial; since, but for such fiction, the language of *man* could not have risen above the language of *brutes*."

This being the minimum of explanation which will "prevent the whole field of fictitious entities from presenting itself to the eye of the mind in the repulsive character of an absolutely dark spot", more cannot be said "without wandering still further from the main subject, and trespassing beyond hope of endurance upon the reader's patience".

The endeavour to trace the principal relations between the fields of thought and language, including, of course, a survey of Universal Grammar, led Bentham to develop the Theory of Fictions in relation to "the discoveries, half-concealed or left unperfected", of Horne Tooke : the upshot being that "almost all names employed in speaking of the phenomena of the mind are names of fictitious entities. In speaking of any *pneumatic* (or say *immaterial* or *spiritual*) object, no name has ever been employed that had not first been employed as the name of some *material* (or say *corporeal*) one. Lamentable have been the confusion and darkness produced by taking the names of *fictitious* for the names of *real* entities".

In this misconception he traces "the main if not the only source of the clouds in which, notwithstanding all their rivalry, Plato and Aristotle concurred in wrapping up the whole field of *pneumatology*. In the phantoms generated in their own brains, it seemed to them and their followers that they beheld so many realities. Of these fictitious entities, many will be found of which, they being, each of them, a *genus generalissimum*, the names are consequently incapable of receiving what is commonly understood by a definition, viz. a definition *per genus et differentiam*. But, from their not being susceptible of *this* species of exposition, they do not the less stand in need of *that* species of exposition of which they are susceptible." [1]

The conclusion is significant : " Should there be any person to whom the ideas thus hazarded present themselves as having a substantial footing, in the nature of *things*, on the one hand, and the nature of *language* on the other— it will probably be admitted that a demand exists for an entirely new system of *Logic*, in which shall be comprehended a *theory of language, considered* in the most general point of view ".[2]

THE LINGUISTIC BASIS OF LOGIC

This " entirely new system of logic ", with its linguistic orientation arising out of the analysis and classification of Fictions, was Bentham's chief concern (apart from Codification as such) during the last twenty years of his life. In addition to the purely fictional material (dealt with primarily under the caption ' Ontology '), it comprises :—

(i) The application of Linguistic Psychology to differentiate Symbol, Thought, and Referent, in any system of Communication.

(ii) The principles of classification, whereby symbolic Order is established by hierarchical Division (Dichotomy).

---

[1] " Examples of these *undefinable* fictitious entities are :

   1. Physical fictitious entities—*motion, rest, quality, etc.*
   2. Ethical fictitious entities—*obligation, right, power, etc.*
   3. Ontological fictitious entities—*condition, certainty, impossibility, etc.*

Of the demand for a *species* or *mode* of *exposition* adapted to the nature of this class of appellatives, hints may be seen in an anonymous tract published by the author, A 1776, under the title of *A Fragment on Government*, etc., pp. 179–85 [= *Works*, Vol. I, p. 283 ff.] "

[2] *Works*, Vol. VIII, pp. 119–20.

(iii) The rationale of Definition, including the Exposition of Names of Fictional entities.

(iv) The linguistic analysis of Propositions, for the detection of Elliptical Fictions.

(v) The foundations of Universal Grammar.

The sense in which Bentham uses the term logic is made clear in the fragmentary treatise which actually bears that name. *Logic*, he says, may be defined as " the art which has for its object, or end in view, the giving, to the best advantage, direction to the human mind, and thence to the human frame, in its pursuit of any object or purpose to the attainment of which it is capable of being applied ". And by way of explanation :—

> " That of all definitions that have been or can be given of this art this is the most *extensive*, seems upon the face of it to be sufficiently manifest.
>
> That it is the most *useful*, will, it is believed, be no less so, for it is in this modern definition alone, and not in any preceding one, that its relation to practical *use* in any shape has been directly held up to view.
>
> That it is the most proper, will, at the same time, appear from the account given of logic, by those who were the first to hold it up to view in the character of an art, and that an attainable one ; in a word, by its inventors, viz. Aristotle and his followers, not to speak of his at present almost unknown predecessors." [1]

We are concerned, in fact, with " the entire field of human thought and action. In it is accordingly included the whole field of art and science ; in it is moreover included the field of ordinary, *i.e.* unscientific *thought*, and ordinary, *i.e.* unartificial action—or say *practice*, including, together with the whole contents of these respective fields (viz. all the subjects, not only of human action but of human thought), all entities, not only real but fictitious ; not only all real entities but all fictitious ones that have ever been feigned, or remain capable of being feigned : fictitious entities, those necessary *products of the imagination*, without which, unreal as they are, *dis-*

[1] *Ibid.*, p. 219.

e

course could not, scarcely even could *thought*, be carried on, and which, by being *embodied, as it were, in names*, and thus put upon a footing with real ones, have been so apt to be mistaken for real ones." [1]

Let us begin, therefore, with the thoughts. " Words are the signs of thoughts ; proportioned only to the degree of correctness and completeness with which thoughts themselves have been conceived and arranged can be the degree of correctness and completeness given to their respective signs. Of speech, though the correction, extension, and improvement of thought be, and that to a prodigious degree, a consequence, yet the more immediate and only universally regarded object is but the communication of thought." To communication, in general, we shall return. Bentham himself proceeds :—

" But by anything less than an entire proposition, *i.e.* the import of an entire proposition, no communication can have place. In language, therefore, the *integer* to be looked for is an entire proposition—that which logicians mean by the term logical proposition. Of this integer, no one part of speech, not even that which is most significant, is anything more than a fragment ; and, in this respect, in the many-worded appellative, *part of speech*, the word *part* is instructive. By it, an intimation to look out for the integer of which it is a part may be considered as conveyed. A word is to a *proposition* what a *letter* is to a word.

A sentence—in that which by Grammarians is meant by the word sentence—the matter either of no more than a single proposition, or that of any number of propositions, may be contained." [2]

Hence the supreme importance of the linguistic factor ; for what is thus ' embodied ' (as it were) must be, as it were, disembodied and separately re-interred. " The words employed, and the compounds formed of them in the shape of propositions—in one or other of these classes of objects may be seen the source of every instance of error or perplexity, every cause of deception to which discourse can give rise ; if it be in the structure of the propositions, or in the sort of connexion given to them

[1] *Ibid.*, p. 219.   [2] *Ibid.*, p. 188.

that the *imperfection* has, or is supposed to have, its source, logic (in which grammar may be considered as included) is the name of the art or science, by which alone the remedy, if obtainable, can be obtained ; if it be *in the import* attached to the words taken singly, sometimes it is to logic, sometimes it is to metaphysics, that any endeavours to remedy it are referred." For Bentham, however, ' metaphysics ' resolved itself into a misunderstanding of the Theory of Fictions ; and logic, as commonly understood, was for him little more than a similar misunderstanding of the grammatical principles here " considered as included ".[1]

Amongst the last entries in Bentham's Memorandum Book (1831, he being then in his eighty-fourth year) is the following :—

> " Wherever there is a word, there is a thing ;. so says the common notion—the result of the association of ideas.
>
> Wherever there is a word, there is a thing ; hence the almost universal practice of confounding *fictitious* entities with *real* ones—corresponding names of fictitious entities with *real* ones. Hence, common law, mind, soul, virtue, vice.
>
> Identity of nomenclature is certificate of identity of nature ; diversity of diversity :—how absurd, how inconsistent, to make the certificate a false one " ![2]

ARISTOTELIAN VERBALISM

The ' common notion ' of the correspondence of words and things lay, for Bentham, at the very root of the system of traditional logic. It vitiated the entire Aristotelian doctrine, with its claim to provide an instrument for the attainment of knowledge, correct and complete. " So much for profession ; now for the result. For about two thousand years, little more or less, the precepts of this art have been before us ; and the result is that of the whole amount of things knowable there is not a single one concerning which the smallest particle of knowledge has been found obtainable by means of it. On the con-

[1] *Ibid.*, p. 221.   [2] *Works*, Vol. XI, p. 73.

trary the nature of it is now—or may now—be seen to
be such that, by means of it, of no one thing can any sort
of degree of knowledge—at any time, by any possibility—
be obtained." And the indictment proceeds as follows :—

" Experience, Observation, Experiment, Reflection, or
the results of each and of all together ; these are the means,
these are the instruments by which knowledge—such as is
within the power of man—is picked up, put together, and
treasured up ; and of no one of these, in the whole mass of
the Aristotelian logic, is so much as a syllable to be found.

The *import of words*—in this short expression will, in
truth, be found the subject, the only subject of it ; in such
or such a manner the import of this or that word agrees or
disagrees with the import of this or that other.

On this occasion, a notion, and that an erroneous one—
a proposition, and that a false one—was all along involved ;
this is, that to each word was an import naturally inherent,
that the connexion between the sign and the thing signified
was altogether the work of nature.

What is now pretty generally, and at the same time,
pretty clearly understood, is that the connexion between a
word and its import is altogether arbitrary, the result of tacit
convention and long-continued usage; and, of the truth of this
proposition, the short proof is the infinite diversity of languages
—the infinite multitude of signs by which, in the different
languages, the same object has been found represented.

The case is, that so firmly connected by habit are the
connexions between these signs, and the things which they
have respectively been employed to signify and present to
the mind, that, in Aristotle's time, men had not learned
sufficiently to distinguish them from one another : and of
this inability one consequence, and thereby one proof, was
their aptitude, as often as they observed a word which, in
its grammatical form, purported to be the name of a thing
(that form being the form that had been given to such
words as were really, and in truth respectively, the names
of things) to infer the existence of a particular sort of real
thing corresponding to that word ; the observation not
having been as yet made that the purposes of human
converse could not in any instance have been attained,
unless to such words as are names of real entities, a mixture,
and that a large one, had been added of words which are
but so many names of so many purely fictitious entities." [1]

[1] *Works*, Vol. VIII, pp. 238–9.

In short, " it was by fancying that everything could be done by putting together a parcel of phrases, expressive of the respective imports of certain *words*, mostly of certain *general* words, without any such trouble as that of applying *experiment* or *observation* to *individual things*, that, for little less than two thousand years, the followers of Aristotle kept *art* and *science* nearly at a stand ".[1]

As such, the method of the Aristotelians " was not simply worthless, it was positively pernicious. It was pernicious by drawing aside and keeping mankind for so many ages out of the only instructive track of study . . . into and in this uninstructive one. But out of an ill-directed pursuit, it will sometimes happen that useful results may collaterally, and, as it were by a side-wind, be brought to light." And here follows a remarkable anticipation of the modern approach to the philosophy of the Middle Ages—as an exercise in operational technique:—

> " Though of all the propositions thus demonstrated or demonstrable, the value was, is, and ever will be equal to O ; though logical demonstration, the fruit of all this labour, was and is delusion ; yet of the operations which had no other object than the formation and maturation of this fruit, many there are which have been, and will ever continue to be found, applicable to and continually applied to real and most important uses.

[1] *Ibid.*, p. 110. Bentham is quite prepared (p. 218) to substitute "the followers of Aristotle " for Aristotle himself, in any passage where injustice may have been done to the original by Sanderson. Sanderson's *Compendium* was the standard treatise of the eighteenth century, and Bentham fully acknowledges his own debt to Aristotle's logical work : " In that storehouse of instruction the author found at any rate a considerable number of the tools or instruments which he has had to work with ". Of his detailed criticism, the following, on the Fifth Post-Predicament and the Tenth Predicament, may serve as a specimen : " A word is now introduced in the character of the name of a Post-Predicament, and to the word no determinate idea is attached. In the way of specification, what is given is not the modification of an idea, but a multitude or number of significations or senses in which it has happened to this same word to have been employed. Eight in number are these specifications ; eight, according to a statement in a succeeding chapter, is the number of these its different significations. Two, and no more, were the different significations included in the Predicament termed *habitus*, habit. These two form two out of the eight significations ascribed to *habere*, to have, this last of the Post-Predicaments " (p. 236).

The demonstration of the Aristotelian may in this respect be compared to the philosopher's stone. The *stone* was a *nonentity* ; but in seeking for this nonentity, real entities, pregnant with real and important uses, were discovered in no inconsiderable numbers ; for though the stone was never discovered, multitudes of substances applicable to the purposes of medicine and the arts were brought to light." [1]

THE FUNCTIONS OF LANGUAGE

Bentham's own approach to the linguistic factors involved in all interpretation, in all symbolic analysis, is, as we have already indicated, essentially technological. There is the operator, the machine, the operation, the raw materials, the product, and so forth ; there is the thinker or speaker with his ideas and emotions, there are the words and their ways, there are the entities real and fictional which the words through the thought which they symbolize may stand for.

Language, according to Bentham, must be regarded primarily as a system of *communication*. It has, of course, both solitary and social uses ; it is used for designation as well as for discourse, for intransitive as well as transitive purposes ; indeed " it is to its intransitive use that discourse ", or transitive language, " is indebted for its existence ".[2] But whatever the importance of the intransitive use, for purposes of interpretation and analysis it is clearly secondary.

Though the operational or technological approach to language adopted in all Bentham's writings makes it necessary for him to stress its communicative (transitive)

[1] *Works*, Vol. VIII, pp. 233–4. Cf. the similar verdict a few pages later : " In respect of miscarriage and success, the character and lot of the art of logic, as taught by Aristotle, may be considered as a sort of prototype of the art of alchemy, as taught by the searchers after the universal medicine, the universal solvent, and the philosopher's stone. In both instances, in respect of the ultimate object, a complete failure was the result : but, in both instances, in the course and in consequence, of the inquiry, particular discoveries of no small use and importance were brought to light ".
[2] *Ibid.*, pp. 228, 301.

side, he was equally aware of the importance of the notational (intransitive) development :—

" By its transitive use, the collection of these signs is only the vehicle of thought ; by its intransitive use, it is an instrument employed in the creation and fixation of thought itself. Unclothed as yet in words, or stripped of them, thoughts are but dreams : like the shifting clouds of the sky, they float in the mind one moment, and vanish out of it the next. But for these fixed and fixative signs, nothing that ever bore the name of *art* or *science* could ever have come into existence. Whatsoever may have been the more remote and recondite causes, it is to the superior amplitude to which, in respect of the use made of it in his own mind, man has been able to extend the mass of his language, that, as much as to anything else, man, it should seem, stands more immediately indebted for whatsoever superiority in the scale of perfection and intelligence he possesses, as compared with those animals who come nearest to him in this scale.

Without language, not only would men have been incapable of communicating each man his thoughts to other men, but, compared with what he actually possesses, the stock of his own ideas would in point of number have been as nothing ; while each of them, taken by itself, would have been as flitting and indeterminate as those of the animals which he deals with at his pleasure." [1]

Of more interest, in view of its bearing on the technique of interpretation, is the distinction between the emotive and referential use of symbols. Words may be used either to refer ourselves and others to the things about which we are thinking, or to arouse emotions ; [2] to convey information, says Bentham, or for the purpose of excitation. The passage is one of considerable historical interest :—

" In respect of its transitive function, it is the medium of communication between one mind and another, or others.

This communication may convey information purely, or information for the purpose of excitation, say—more simply, and, when as above explained, not less precisely— information or excitation ; to one or other of these ends and purposes, or both, will language in every case be directed."

[1] *Ibid.*, pp. 228–9.
[2] *The Meaning of Meaning*, third edition, 1930, pp. 223 ff.

In so far as *information* is the end, the understanding is the faculty to which the appeal is made ; in so far as *excitation* is the end, the will.

" [For] the purpose of simple communication, neither in act nor in wish need the philanthropist wish to apply any restriction to the powers of language. Of such communication, evil, it is true, may be the subject as well as good ; but, in the mixed mass, good, upon the whole, predominates ; and it cannot be rendered apt for the one purpose without being rendered proportionably apt for the other.

Considered as applied to the purpose of excitation, the case may at first sight present itself as being, in some respects, different. In regard to passion, and thence in regard to affection, which is but passion in an inferior degree and always liable to be raised to higher degree, repression, not excitation, may appear to be the object to be wished for ; passion being, in every part of the field, the everlasting enemy of reason, in other words, of sound judgment, *alias* correct and all-comprehensive judgment.

But even to the lover of mankind, an acquaintance with the powers of language, even when applied to this dangerous purpose, is not without its use : for by the same insight by which the mode of increasing its powers in this line is learned, the mode of repressing them, when and in so far as applied to pernicious purposes, is learned along with it. In the case of moral, as in that of physical poison, an acquaintance with the nature and powers of the disease is commonly a necessary preliminary to an acquaintance with the proper nature and mode of applying the most efficient, and, upon the whole, the most benignant remedy." [1]

For Rhetoric in general, and particularly political rhetoric, Bentham had little use. The logic of it is of a piece with its morality : " a perpetual vein of nonsense, flowing from a perpetual abuse of words—words having a variety of meanings, where words with single meanings were equally at hand ; the same words used in a variety of meanings in the same page ; words used in meanings not their own, where proper words were equally at hand ; words and propositions of the most unbounded signification, turned loose without any of those exceptions or modifications which are so necessary on every occasion

[1] *Works*, Vol. VIII, pp. 301–2.

to reduce their import within the compass, not only of right reason, but even of the design in hand, of whatever nature it may be : the same inaccuracy, the same inattention in the penning of this cluster of truths on which the fate of nations was to hang, as if it had been an oriental tale, or an allegory for a magazine ; stale epigrams, instead of necessary distinctions ; figurative expressions preferred to simple ones ; sentimental conceits as trite as they are unmeaning, preferred to apt and precise expressions ; frippery ornament preferred to the majestic simplicity of good sound sense ; and the acts of the senate loaded and disfigured by the tinsel of the playhouse."

The criticism is verbal ? " True, but what else can it be ? Words—words without a meaning or with a meaning too flatly false to be maintained by anybody, are the stuff it is made of. Look to the letter, you find nonsense —look beyond the letter, you find nothing." [1]

THE TECHNIQUE OF DEFINITION

To analysis we must oppose both generalization and synthesis. Generalization is the converse of analysis, which presupposes its performance. " By the combination made of the ideas of a multitude of individuals or sorts of individuals, in virtue of some ·property which is supposed to belong to them in common, and which is thus made to serve as a bond of ideal union by which they are bound together into one *aggregate*, and that aggregate recorded and fixed by one common name—*generalization* is formed. By the *division* and *sub-division* of an aggregate thus found, correspondent names, whether single-worded or many-worded, being either formed or made for the several parts which are the results of the several acts of division and sub-division, *analysis*, *i.e.* the *resolutive* division and decomposition of the antecedently formed artificial aggregate, is performed."

Thus, on the *Porphyrian tree*, if we work in the direction

of *generalization*, and set out either from *Homo* or *Brutum*, or from a sub-species, or an individual of either species, we may arrive, immediately or through *sensitivum, vivens* and *corpus*, at least at *substantia*. But working in the direction of *synthesis*, the course taken is exactly the reverse. " By imagination, the idea and practice of *logical, noological, metaphysical* analysis, was deduced from that of *physical*. Physical is either *mechanical* or *chemical*. *Physical* analysis is an instance of a *real* and *material* operation ; *logical*, of an *immaterial*, and thus in some sort, a fictitious one, of the same name."

Synthesis is apt to be considered not only as the opposite but the exactly co-extensive correlate of analysis. " If the coincidence were thus complete, *synthesis* and *generalization* would be exactly synonymous, and ought to be interconvertibly employed. This, however, is not the case. Of any number of ideas, how heterogeneous soever, the putting together may be termed *synthesis*. But in so far as the term *analysis* is applied, the ideas comprehended in the subject in which the operation is to be performed are by the supposition *homogeneous*. The subject analysed is an aggregate or *genus*, which is divided into *species*, those into *sub-species*, and so on. The only case in which *synthesis* is exactly opposite and correspondent to, and no more than co-extensive with analysis, is when between the ideas put together there is that sort of conformity from which the act of putting them together receives the name of *generalization*."

Analysis and *synthesis*—*analytic method* and *synthetic method*—are locutions which are often very loosely used. " The same operation which by one person is called by one of these names shall by another person be called by the other. By giving to every supposed explanation the name of *an analysis*, Condillac, in his Logic, thinks he has explained everything ; and thus it is that he explains nothing. *Analysis* (he says) *is nothing but a language well made*. He sees not, that it is of an act of synthesis (the declared object of his antipathy) that every name, which is not, in the grammatical sense, a *proper* name, is the sign and the result : and that, were it not for that despised and much vituperated agent, his favourite and exclusively lauded instrument would not have a subject on which to operate." [1]

The further the operation of analysis by dichotomy is continued, the longer and more complex the names that would tend to be given to the continually diminishing aggregates. " In a synoptic table, an instrument designed for the eye rather than the ear, this inconvenience may, under favour of a well-adapted language, remain for some time almost imperceptible ; but in a running discourse, a discourse designed for the ear as well as the eye, it would probably become intolerable. In ordinary discourse, therefore, at the second if not at the very first operation, the necessity will be felt of substituting, in the instance of each aggregate, in the place of the two-worded appellative exhibited by the table, a single-worded one. Thus, in English, to the two-worded appellative *material substance,* on the occasion of the first division made of the import of the universal appellative body— *a fortiori* to the three-worded appellative *living material substance*—a single-worded appellative, so it were that the English language . . . afforded one [will require to be substituted] ; *a fortiori* again, on the occasion of a second division to the three-worded appellative, *insensitive living body*, or the four-worded appellative, *insensitive living corporeal substance*, will require to be substituted another single-worded appellative, such as a plant or vegetable and so in the case of the opposite result of this same division, viz. animal."

The logician here finds himself driven to the same sort of expedient as " is wont to be employed by the algebraist, who to a heap of *a*'s, *b*'s, and *c*'s, mixed up with a heap

---

[1] *Ibid.*, Vol. VIII, p. 75. It is therefore hardly sufficient to say with Halévy (*Philosophic Radicalism*, p. 457) that for James Mill " to analyse is to decompose into elements and to reduce to principles, so as subsequently to make possible the synthesis of the phenomenon considered ", whereas for Bentham to analyse is only " to enumerate and to distinguish ".

of x's, y's, and z's, forms to himself, in the shape of a single s, a concise and most commodious substitute ". Moreover, at every step in the track of exhaustive division, " the condivident aggregates, or two prongs which are the result when added to the divided aggregate which forms the stem, exhibit a definition, and that of the *regular* kind, a definition *per genus et differentiam* of the two aggregates thus brought to view ".[1]

For Bentham, then, definition *per genus et differentiam* is definition proper, and in this respect he accepts the convention of traditional logic. " By logicians, when speaking of a *definition*, is commonly meant, as of course, the mode termed in Latin *definitio per genus et differentiam* ; definition, afforded by the indication of a more extensive collection of objects, to which the object in question belongs—some *genus* (as the phrase is) of which it is the *species*—together with the indication of some peculiar character or quality by which it stands distinguished from all other objects included in that same collection— from all other *species* of that same *genus* : and this form is that which, when what is considered as a *definition* is given, is the form constantly intended and supposed to be given to it." [2]

Traditional logic, however, has neglected the problem of Fictions. " By him who undertakes to give a definition in this form, what is necessarily, howsoever tacitly, assumed, is that there exists in the language a word, serving as the name of a *genus* of things, within which the *species* of things indicated by the word he thus undertakes to define is comprehended. But words there are, and in no small abundance, of which definitions of this sort are frequently undertaken to be given—or which are supposed to be as clearly and generally understood as if definitions in this form could be and had been given of them—but for which, all this while, no such more extensive denomination is afforded by this or any other language ; and among them, words which in law and

---

[1] *Ibid.*, p. 292.   [2] *Works*, Vol. III, p. 593.

politics are in continual use, and upon the signification of which questions of prime and practical importance are continually turning."

Take, for instance, says Bentham, the words *right, power, obligation.* " Now, in the way in question—namely, by indication of so many superior genuses of things, of which these words respectively designate so many species, it is not possible to define these words. No one of these three words can you thus define. The word *man* (for example) you *can* thus define : you may do so, by saying that he is *an animal* ; and then stating a quality by which he is distinguishable from other animals. Here, then, is a word you can and do thus define. Why ? Because, comprehending in its import that of this same word *man*, stands that same word *animal*, by which is accordingly designated a *genus* of which *man* is a *species.* So likewise in regard to *operations* : for example, that of *contracting*, in the *civil* branch of the field of law ; and that of *stealing*, in the *penal* branch of that same thorny field. *Contracting* is one *species of operation* ; *stealing* is another. But this you cannot say in the instance of *right*, or *power*, or *obligation* : for a right is not a *species* of anything ; a power is not a *species* of anything ; an obligation is not a *species* of anything."

In short, " the objects of which the words *man, animal, substance* are names are extensive sorts or kinds of *real* entities ; the objects of which the words *right, power, obligation* are names are *not* sorts or kinds of any *real* entities ", but so many *fictitious* entities.

To cope with fiction, therefore, a different technique is required, and for this purpose Definition proper must be treated as a part of the wider problem of Exposition. It is then seen that for expounding or explaining the import of the name of any fictitious entity, " the nature of the case affords but one resource ; and that is, the finding some class of real entities, which is more or less clearly in view as often as, to the name of a class of

fictitious entities, any clear idea stands annexed—and
thereupon framing two propositions ; one, in which the
name of the fictitious entity is the leading term ; the
other, in which the name of a corresponding class, either
of real entities, or of *operations* or other *motions* of real
entities, is the leading term :—this last so ordered, that,
by being seen to express the same import, it shall explain
and make clear the import of the first. This mode of
exposition has been termed *paraphrasis—paraphrase* :
giving *phrase* for *phrase* ".[1]

For lack of this distinction, all attempts to define
words of the description in question, such as *right, power,*
and *obligation,* have proved abortive. " In a work
entitled *A Fragment on Government,* published by the
Author in 1776 without a name, and long since out of
print, indication was, for the first time, given of the
utter impossibility of doing that which, in such numbers,
men have been continually supposing themselves to have
done. Instead of a *superior genus*, what on this occasion
has been brought forward has been some term or other
bearing in its import such a resemblance to the term in
question as to be capable of being, on some occasions,
with little or no impropriety, employed instead of it.
A right is a power—or a power is a right—and so forth ;
shifting off the task of definition, backward and forward,
from one word to another ; shifting it off thus at each
attempt and never performing it." [2]

A *right* is not itself a species of anything, " but *right*
has divers species, perfectly and clearly distinguishable ;
namely, by means of the *benefits* which they respectively
confer, and the *sanctions* by which they are respectively
created : and for each of these species a separate exposition
would be found requisite. *Give us our rights*, say the
thousands and the millions. *Give us our rights*, they say,
and they do well to say so. Yet, of all who say so, not
one perhaps can say, not one perhaps ever conceived

[1] For Paraphrasis, cf. *Theory of Fictions*, pp. 86 ff.
[2] *Works,* Vol. III, p. 594.

clearly, what it is he thus calls for—what sort of a thing *a right* is." [1]

They do well to say so, because although rights, as entities, are fictitious, any sentence in which rights are spoken of can be translated, by means of archetypation and paraphrasis, into a statement at another level in which all the referents are real entities. " From the observations by which the words ' duties ' and ' rights ' are here spoken of as names of fictitious entities, let it not for a moment so much as be supposed that in either instance the reality of the object is meant to be denied, in any sense in which in ordinary language the reality of it is assumed." [2]   What ordinary language assumes can only be discovered by systematic interpretation, and the ordinary man may often be led astray by false analogies. When he demands his rights, what he demands can be given to him ; but when he succumbs to Word-magic and adds, *qua* metaphysician, that rights are things, the Theory of Fictions steps in to disillusion him.   " There is many a man who could not endure patiently to sit and hear contested the reality of those objects which he is in the habit of speaking of as his rights." [3]   In *this* sense, therefore, something which the ordinary man assumes about the reality of the object is meant to be denied, and Bentham's aside might perhaps have been more carefully worded.

There is, however, no question of a confusion. Bentham is not contradicting himself as a result of some uncertainty in his own mind whether or in what sense there are such things as rights.[4]   " Altogether inevitable ", he says, " will this seeming contradiction be found. The root of it is in the nature of language." In this respect, when we return to the language of ordinary communication, it is much the same with rights as with qualities—whose status in this connexion we have already discussed. [5]

[1] *Works*, Vol. III, pp. 593–4.
[2] *Works*, Vol. VIII, p. 126 (= *Theory of Fictions*, p. 138).
[3] *Ibid.*, p. 328 (= *Theory of Fictions*, p. 60).
[4] *Contra* Wisdom, *Interpretation and Analysis*, pp. 104–6.
[5] Above, p. lx.

All predicative language, in Bentham's view, is fictional
and the ' qualities ' which make their entry at the lowest
level are near enough to ' reality ' to justify their claim
to be called, on occasion, relatively real.

As in the case of psychological descriptions, " this is
to misrepresent them. But very different from what it
is in most other cases, in this case misrepresentation is not
matter of blame. By it no deception is intended ; if to
a certain degree misconception be the result of it ", the
writer cannot, unless by accident, be held responsible.
In Psychology, moreover, " on no other terms can discourse be carried on ".[1] To Bentham's psychology we
may, therefore, with this methodological *caveat*, now
proceed.

PRINCIPLES OF PSYCHOLOGY

Bentham's chief concern with Psychology, apart from
its legal and medico-legal aspects, was the necessity for
an account of Volition which could serve as a basis
(*a*) for the study of motivation, and (*b*) for the theory of
fictions. His chief contention, that every sort of psychological description is fictional, might have saved much
subsequent confusion ; for it relegated the ' faculties ',
which dominated both the associationist and nineteenth-
century schools, to the position of mere heuristic con-
veniences which they occupy to-day,[2] and at the same
time gave the entire problem of symbolization a new
orientation.

[1] *Works*, Vol. VIII, p. 327 (=*Theory of Fictions*, p. 59).
We have seen that Bentham uses very similar language in discussing
the problem of ' rights ' and ' qualities '—both of which he is prepared,
on occasion, to justify at the level of ordinary discourse. " The word
right is the name of a fictitious entity ; one of those objects the existence
of which is feigned for the purpose of discourse—by a fiction so necessary
that without it human discourse could not be carried on ". And again,
" Though fictitious, the language cannot be termed *deceptious*—in
intention at least, whatsoever in some cases may without intention
be the result ". (*Works*, Vol. III, pp. 217–9=*Theory of Fictions*,
p. 118). Trouble only arises through false analogy and misinter-
pretation.
[2] Piéron, *Principles of Experimental Psychology*, 1929, Part IV,
Chapter II.

Here, too, the starting point is linguistic. "Words are the signs of ideas ; " and again, " language is the sign of thought, an instrument for the communication of thought from one mind to another." [1]

It may be the sign of other things ; it may stand indirectly for objects and facts in great variety : but the thought of the speaker is what is primarily symbolized— " of this object it is always the sign, and it is only through this that it becomes the sign of any other object ".[2]

Furthermore, the exterior objects about which discourse makes declarations " will belong either to the class of *persons*, or that of *things*, or to both these classes ". And as regards motion and rest, " the state in which, at any such given point of time, they are thus considered or spoken of as existing, will be either a quiescent state, *i.e.* a state of rest, or a moving state, *i.e.* a state of motion. . . . When considered as the result of motion, any state of things is termed an *event.*" Considered as the outcome of volition " an event is itself termed an *action*, or is considered as having action, an action, for its cause ". Finally, the existence of any expressible state of things (or persons) " whether it be quiescent, or motional, or both, at any given point or portion of time, is what is called a *fact*, or a *matter of fact* ".[3]

Bentham's own term for psychology, " in so far as pleasure or pain are taken for the subjects of it ", is *pathematology*. But for pre-established associations, *pathology* would have been preferable. " The appellative, however, has been employed by the art and science of medicine, and after being shorn of a great part of its import, confined to a corner of the field occupied by that science."

Pleasure and pain being the only objects possessed of intrinsic and independent value, " simple perceptions— perceptions, if any such there were, altogether unconnected with either pleasure or pain—would have no claim to

---

[1] *Works*, Vol. VIII, pp. 329 and 333.
[2] *Ibid.*, p. 329 (=*Theory of Fictions*, p. 70).   [3] *Ibid.*, p. 300.

f

attention, would not, in fact, engage attention, would not be comprehended within any part of the field of art and science ".

In general, pathematic feelings, *i.e.* pleasure or pain, and apathematic feelings, *i.e.* simple perceptions considered in so far as separable from pleasures and pains, are experienced together—are simultaneously concomitant. A simple perception, however, " which has neither pleasure nor pain for its contemporary adjunct, may, through the medium of attention, reflection, volition and transitive action ", so frequently include feelings of both sorts among its consequences, " that except for clearness of intellection, the distinction between pathematic and apathematic perception becomes void of practical use ".

Simple perception, simple remembrance, enjoyment, the sensation of pain, attention, reflection, examination, judgment or opinion or judicial determination, volition, volitional determination, internal action, external action— " all these, on one and the same occasion, indeed on most occasions, all these several accidents are taking place at the same time ; but, in the way of abstraction, for the purpose of science, any one of them, every one of them, may be, and has been, detached from the rest, and held up to view, and subjected to examination by itself. So many of these incidents as are capable of being distinguished from each other, so many compartments or separate fields are included within the vast all-comprehensive field of psychology." [1]

Every operation of the mind, and thence every operation of the body, is, according to Bentham, the result of an exercise of the will, or volitional faculty. " The volitional is a branch of the appetitive faculty, *i.e.* that faculty in which desire, in all its several modifications, has place. Desire has for its object either pleasure or pain, or, what is commonly the case, a mixture of both, in ever-varying and unascertainable proportions." [2]

A desire is termed a *motive*, when it is " considered as

[1] *Ibid.*, p. 228.   [2] *Ibid.*, p. 279.

having produced, or as being with more or less probability
of success operating towards the production of, the result
(viz. presence of pleasure, or absence of pain) which is
the object of it ".

An act of *will* [1] is said to take place " in so far as the
production of the state of things which is the immediate
object of the desire is considered as following immediately
and certainly upon the existence of the desire " ; and
the faculty " by which this effect is considered as produced
is termed the volitional, or volitive faculty, or, in one
word, the *will*. The volitional faculty is, therefore, a
branch of the appetitive."

An act of the will can only take place " in consequence
of a correspondent desire ; in consequence of the action
of a *desire* in the character of a motive." "Moreover, no
desire can have place unless when the idea of pleasure
or pain, in some shape or degree, has place. Minute, it
is true, minute in the extreme is the quantity of pleasure
or pain requisite and sufficient to the formation of a
desire " ; but it is none the less true that if all pleasure
and all pain are taken away there is no desire.

" Pleasure and pain, considered in themselves, belong to
the perceptive faculty, *i.e.* to the pathematic branch of it.

But pleasure and pain considered as operating, as
above, in the production of *desires*—operating, as above, in
the character of motives, and thus producing *volition*,
action, internal or external, corporeal, or purely mental—
belong to the appetitive faculty.

Pleasure and pain compose, therefore, as it were, the
bond of union and channel of communication between the
two faculties." [2]

The psychology of the Will, *thelematology* as Bentham
would call it, has pathematology for its basis. " It is by
the eventual expectation of pleasure or pain that in every
case the will, and thereby the agency, internal only or

[1] Those psychologists (cf. William James, *Principles*, Vol. II, p. 558)
who find a difficulty with this account may be reminded that Bentham
is primarily concerned with the practical or legal distinction between
e.g. wilful murder and manslaughter.
[2] *Works*, Vol. VIII, p. 280.

internal and external together, are determined. It is by
the idea of pleasure or of exemption from pain, considered
as about to result from the proposed act, that the volition
in pursuance of which the act is performed, and consequently the act itself, is produced."

It is clear that Bentham's account here applies rather
to processes of deliberate choice than to the operation of
such passions as would often be described as 'blind' or
'instinctive.' So Hume says, " though the satisfaction
of these passions gives us enjoyment, yet the prospect of
this enjoyment is not the cause of the passions, but, on
the contrary, the passion is antecedent to the enjoyment,
and without the former the latter could never possibly
exist." [1] But Bentham, who in many places recognizes
the force of habit, goes far to meet this objection with his
distinction between pleasure (and pain) as means and
as ends.

Both as means and as ends—" in that double character
it is that pleasures and pains or their respective negatives
are continually presenting themselves : not pain itself,
but its negative, *i.e.* exemption from pain, is the end ;
but in the character of a means, pain itself operates as
well as its negative—pain itself as well as pleasure ".
From which observation Bentham proceeds to a classification of psychology and its borderland sciences :—

" What dynamics is to somatology, the practical branch
of thelematology, or the art of giving direction to volition
and thereby to action, is to psychognosy or psychology ;
it may be termed *psychological dynamics.*

From somatology and psychology taken together, eudæ-
monics, or the art of applying life to the maximization of
well-being, derives its knowledge of the phenomena belonging
to human existence considered as applicable to that its
purpose. In the one word *Deontology* may be comprehended
the knowledge, in so far as by art it is attainable, of the
course by which, on each occasion those means may, with
most advantage, be rendered conducive to that common end.

In the field of Deontology, as thus explained, will be
found included the several fields of Ethics, meaning private

[1] *Essay,* "On the Different Species of Philosophy," § 1.

Ethics, or morals, internal Government, and International law." [1]

Finally, in this connexion, we may record a methodological observation of considerable interest. "By the name of *materialists*", says Bentham, "stand distinguished a set of philosophers, of whom Priestley was one, according to whom there exists not any such created being as a *mind* distinct from matter; for that *that* which is called *mind* is but an assemblage or collection, of the sort of fictitious entities called *properties*, with which certain species of *matter* are endowed." It would be a gross defect in any system, "if, by the unnecessary assumption of any proposition which by any class of men were regarded as false, the effect of it were to render itself so far, *i.e.* with reference to that class of men, unfit for use". In the case of pneumatology or psychology, the materialist may be readily accommodated if it is described, in fictional terms, as the science to which belongs "the consideration of such bodies or portions of matter as are endowed with the aggregate mass of properties collectively styled *mind*, considered in relation to those same peculiar properties ".[2]

THE DETECTION OF ELLIPSES

In view of his fictional approach both to Language and to Psychology, it could hardly be expected that Bentham would be satisfied with the relegation of Grammar to a consideration of the so-called parts of speech coupled with the conventional remarks on correctness of diction. What is really wanted, he says, is a new sort of work, "the object of which shall be to show the course best adapted to the purpose of rendering language—*i.e.* the particular language employed, whatsoever it be—in the highest practical degree well adapted to the *general* end or purpose of language, viz. *communication* of *thought*, abstraction made of the *particular* nature of the particular

[1] *Works*, Vol. VIII, p. 289.   [2] *Ibid.*, p. 84.

purpose to which on the particular *occasion* in question it
may happen to it to be employed. By the observation
of the rules, called *rules of grammar*, belonging to the
particular language in question, true it is, *that* general
purpose will in some measure be accomplished. But to
afford a complete direction of the complete accomplishment of it, will, it is believed, be found to require, in
addition to those at present designated by the appellation
of *grammatical rules*, others, in considerable numbers,
extent, and variety, which have not as yet been brought
to view." [1]

One of his most important rules is that which says—
" Prefer verbal substantives to verbs " ; as when, " instead
of *to apply*, the phrase *to make application* is used. From
this substitution convenience is frequently found to
result." This avoidance of verbs on account of their
elusive nature was characteristic of his own later style.

> " The noun from the same root is commonly a *verbal
> noun* ; a *verbal noun* of that sort which serves to designate,
> in the first place, the species of action for the designation
> of which the verb, including all the several adjuncts and
> modifications belonging to that complex part of speech, is
> used ; and thence, by an almost imperceptible transition,
> the state of things produced by that same act.
>
> This verbal noun—when thus obtained in a state of
> separation from these adjuncts, which form so many parts in
> the composition of the very complex part of speech called
> a verb ; and which, in this its separate state, becomes the
> name of a sort of fictitious entity, of a sort of fictitious
> body or substance—is, in this state, rendered more pre-
> hensible. Being thus prehensible, it is more easily and
> thence directly, brought to view ; and being thus brought
> to view, it is capable of being employed as a common
> subject to any number whatsoever of propositions that may
> be requisite for predicating, whatsoever the nature of the
> case requires to be predicated, of the sort of act in question,
> or of its result."

The treatment of Prepositions, Adverbs, and Conjunc-
tions, the explanation of which " constitutes the obscure,
the transcendental, the mysterious part of the art and

[1] *Ibid.*, p. 93.

science of universal grammar ", is equally indebted to the analysis of Fictions. " The relation they bear (*i.e.* which their imports respectively bear) to the imports of the other parts of speech (viz. the substantive, the adjective, and the verb) resembles that which, by the signs employed in algebra, is borne towards the signs employed in common arithmetic. When the signs employed in algebraic arithmetic are all of them translated into the signs employed in common arithmetic, those employed in common arithmetic being, at the same time, reduced to one simple uninterrupted line of numeral figures, the import of the algebraic signs is completely understood and the problem for the solution of which they have been employed is solved. In like manner, when of a sentence of which a preposition, an adverb, or a conjunction, makes a part, the equivalent is given in a sentence in which no part of speech other than a substantive, a verb, and an adjective, or some other substantive, is employed—then, and then only, is the import respectively attached to these mysterious parts of speech at once clear, correct, and complete."

Clearness, correctness, and completeness can be obtained only by the following technique :—

" 1. Denomination ; *i.e.* giving to them respectively, and to each separately, or to each aggregate composed of several together, an appropriate name of denomination.

2. Systematization ; *i.e.* placing the several denominations, when so constructed, as above, in systematic order ; *i.e.* by a division made of the respective universal *trunks* (being the names of the several *genera generalissima*, preposition, adverb, conjunction) performed, in each instance, as far as it can be pursued with advantage, in the exhaustive or bifurcate mode, whereby their several relations of agreement and disagreement to and with each other will be brought under the eye at one view.

3. Exemplification ; *i.e.* exhibiting a proposition or sentence of the sort of those in common use, in the texture of which several words, belonging respectively to the above-mentioned *genera generalissima*, shall respectively be employed.

4. Paraphrasis ; *i.e.* for the explanation or exposition

of each such proposition or sentence, exhibiting another which shall present exactly the same import, but without containing in it a word belonging to the part of speech thus undertaken to be expounded.

As in every instance in the paraphrasis, or paraphrastical proposition, or sentence thus brought to view, a more or less considerable number of words will be contained, while the word thus requiring to be expounded is but one (except in a few instances in which two are so put together as to form, as it were, but one)—on this consideration the paraphrasis may be termed the development." [1]

Phraseoplerosis, the filling in of such words as will serve to remove the oblique or elliptical element in a fictional statement, is also necessary before we can truly interpret many of the apparently straightforward normative utterances of everyday life. " In regard to some expressions, viz. course proper to be pursued, course not proper to be pursued ; one matter of fact there is, which, on every occasion, it may be of use to the reader to have in mind. This is, that everything, of which any such phrase can be, in an immediate way the expression, is a certain state of mind on the part of him by whom the expression is employed ; that state of his mind with relation to the subject-matter of the discourse, whatsoever it happens to be." The speaker himself is always involved. " The state of mind will be the state of one or more of his intellectual faculties, in one word, his understanding— or the state of his sensitive faculties, in one word, his feelings, or the state of his volitional faculties, in one word, his will, his desires, his wishes." [2]

That the proposition is the conventional unit of discourse must not be lost sight of when we come to interpret single words ; for the isolation of any part of such a unit will be liable to generate on its own account what may be called an elliptical fiction.[3] We do, however, communicate with some success ; and, in the circumstances, that is sufficiently surprising to require comment :—

[1] *Works*, Vol. VIII, p. 356.
[2] *Works*, Vol. XI, p. 4.
[3] *Theory of Fictions*, pp. 66 ff.

" In language are to be considered—
    1. The ideas designated ;
    2. The signs employed in the designation of those ideas.

As to the signs, they have been for the most part arbitrary, bearing no naturally characteristic analogy to the things respectively designated ; when considered apart from the ideas, no very considerable instruction, comparatively speaking, is accordingly derived from the consideration of them.

Being arbitrary, they have accordingly been infinitely diversified ; taking the human species in the aggregate, one and the same idea having found employment for signs to the number of some hundreds at least, not to say thousands, in the expression of it.

In a very different case are the ideas themselves. These being the furniture of the mind, and mind being, in fact, a property of the body—in the sort of fictitious language without which it cannot be spoken of—a sort of inmate of the body, the differences between minds (that is to say, the furniture of minds) are not greater than the differences between bodies.

Hence it is that, in the history of the formation of ideas, *i.e.* of the order in which the several ideas thus characterized by their several sets of signs have made their appearance, there must, throughout the whole human race, have been a considerable degree of sameness." [1]

COMPARATIVE PHILOLOGY

Hence the value of Comparative Philology to which Bentham, like Leibnitz, directed attention—particularly as regards field-work among those who still trail clouds of glottological glory. In a note dated 27th October 1826,[2] he wrote :—" *Spoken* words are the signs, the representation of ideas : *written* words, of spoken words. To class words we must class ideas. To give the origin of words, to show how words spring up, we must show how ideas spring up, and thence how spoken and written words spring up out of them. To give the history of language (the formation of language) we must give the history of ideas, of the formation of ideas."

[1] *Works*, Vol. VIII, p. 323.
[2] Univ. Coll. MSS. Box 102.

Such a comparative and historical study must, he agrees, be largely conjectural. " But in a considerable degree it will consist in a statement of unquestionable matters of fact ; it will be statistical, and of the conjectural parts the statistical will be the foundation." The analogy between time and space will afford great assistance here. " In one or other of the parts of the earth's surface may be seen at present the human species at all the different stages of civilization. In New South Wales there may be seen the immediate progeny of Adam and Eve. By their language no small light might be thrown upon the origin of language. By it would be exhibited the original stock —the scantiest stock possible of ideas and correspondent words," etc.

Meanwhile, whatever light may be shed on historical problems by the behaviour of his immediate progeny, we can form a tolerably clear idea of the linguistic procedure of a hypothetical angel. " While the human species contained but one individual, viz. Adam, individual designation was the only operation of this class which an intelligent and conversing being, such as an angel or devil, having occasion to designate him, could have occasion to employ in the designation of him ; but no sooner had Eve received a separate existence, than the occasion for *denomination, i.e.* collective designation or denomination, came into existence : a name such as should be capable of designating the species which by the addition of this second individual was now formed. One species was then already in existence ; at the same time, the two sorts of subordinate species, or rather two species at once (viz. the two species formed together by the difference in respect of *sex*), received already a sort of potential existence—were already formed *in potentia*. At the birth of Cain, the species corresponding to the male sex received an actual existence ; Adam and Cain the individuals. On the birth of Cain's eldest sister, the species corresponding to the female sex received the like existence ; Eve and her anonymous daughter, whoever she were, the individuals." [1]

DEAD LANGUAGES

It must not be supposed, however, that because comparative philology as such has strong claims, any particular advantage is to be derived from the maintenance of Latin and Greek in our educational system. For the purpose of the learned professions, such as Law or Medicine, an acquaintance with dead languages may, Bentham admits, have their value. But even here the case is too often overstated. " Though with a view to the bar or the pulpit, not to speak of the bed of sickness, the possession of a considerable acquaintance with the dead languages may, in a general view, be considered as necessary, this necessity, especially if comparison be had with the system of instruction here proposed, will hardly be regarded as having place, with relation to a yet more exalted theatre, the House of Commons. Take two men, one of them capable of rendering into English without premeditation (not perhaps that any such person ever had existence) any sentence whatsoever, in every one of the Greek and Latin classics extant, but unacquainted with any of the branches of art and science beyond common arithmetic included in this system—the other acquainted with every one of them, in the degree in which an average scholar may be generally expected to be acquainted with them, but unable to render into English any such sentence : which of these two men, on the occasion of the ordinary details of parliamentary business, will be likely to find himself most at home ? Without much danger of contradiction, the answer may surely be—he who passed through the proposed course of practically useful instruction. The classical scholar may be better qualified for decorating his speech with rhetorical flowers ; but the chrestomathic scholar, after

[1] *Works*, Vol. VIII, p. 226.

a familiar and thorough acquaintance has been con-
tracted with things, with things of all sorts, will be, in
a much more useful and efficient way, qualified for the
general course of parliamentary business."

The real question is not what the classical authors
knew, " but what, by the study of them, is at this time
of day to be learnt from them, more than is to be learnt
without reading them. Such is the question, and the
answer is—not anything." [1]

There is a finality about Bentham's views of the
theoretical value of a classical education for all but a
specialized few which must have endeared him to the
orthodox scholastic world of the early nineteenth century
hardly less than his entertaining assessment of its practical
achievements :—

" To the degree of inefficiency and slowness which, by
original weakness, the result of the immaturity and bar-
barism of the age—by original weakness, followed by
habitual and day-by-day more firmly rooted prejudice—
is capable of being established, there are absolutely no
limits. At Christ's Hospital, for example, to two or
three years consumed in learning the rudiments of Latin
grammar succeed two or three years which are employed
in forgetting those rudiments ; while, in addition to the
art of writing, the rudiments of arithmetic are endeavoured
to be learnt. After the course thus completed of learning
and forgetting, if a select few are applied to drawing, or
reapplied to grammar, and to Latin and Greek taught by
means of it—it were strange indeed, if in such a multitude,
a small number were not actually found who wrote well,
another small number who drew well, and another who,
with or without the benefit of being sent to the university,
to enjoy the provision attached to the school foundation,
acquire in a greater or less degree that sort of acquaintance
with the Greek and Latin classics which denominates a
man a good scholar.

But from the examples of inefficiency and tardiness,
were they even more egregious and numerous than they
are, the inference would be not less unreasonable than
discouraging if it were concluded that efficiency and despatch
are impossible. It would be as if, from the abundance of

[1] *Ibid.*, pp. 17–18.

snails and sloths, it were concluded that no such animal as a race-horse could have existence." [1]

In spite of his own sensitivity to verbal form and emotive nuance, Bentham's mistrust of linguistic accomplishment, which has so often proved prejudicial to linguistic reform, is consistently exhibited both in his attitude to poetry,[2] and in his treatment of the dead languages.[3] Science and curiosity are starved wherever the Classics are given undue prominence. In the study of language all is abstraction, there are no concrete objects to relieve the memory, and mental energy is consumed in the acquisition of words.

" The knowledge of languages is valuable only as a means of acquiring the information which may be obtained from conversation or books. For the purposes of conversation, the dead languages are useless ; and translations of all the books contained in them may be found in all the languages of modern Europe. What, then, remains to be obtained from them, not by the common people, but even by the most instructed ? I must confess, I can discover nothing but a fund of allusions wherewith to ornament their speeches, their conversations, and their books—too small a compensation for the false and narrow notions which custom continues to compel us to draw from these imperfect and deceptive sources. To prefer the study of these languages to the study of those useful truths which the more mature industry of the moderns has placed in their stead, is to make a dwelling-place of a scaffolding, instead of employing it in the erection of a building : it is as though, in his

[1] *Ibid.*, p. 19.
[2] *Works*, Vol. II, pp. 253–4.
" Between poetry and truth there is a natural opposition : false morals, fictitious nature. The poet always stands in need of something false. When he pretends to lay his foundations in truth, the ornaments of his superstructure are fictions ; his business consists in stimulating our passions, and exciting our prejudices. Truth, exactitude of every kind, is fatal to poetry. The poet must see everything through coloured media, and strive to make everyone else to do the same. It is true, there have been noble spirits, to whom poetry and philosophy have been equally indebted ; but these exceptions do not counteract the mischiefs which have resulted from this magic art. If poetry and music deserve to be preferred before a game of push-pin, it must be because they are calculated to gratify those individuals who are most difficult to be pleased."
[3] *Ibid.*, p. 258.

mature age, a man should continue to prattle like a child. Let those who are pleased with these studies continue to amuse themselves ; but let us cease to torment children with them, at least those children who will have to provide for their own subsistence, till such time as we have supplied them with the means of slaking their thirst for knowledge at these springs where pleasure is combined with immediate and incontestable utility."

THE NATURE OF MATHEMATICS

Though it was to a gradual realization of the nature of Fictions that Bentham looked for the progress of enlightenment in these various fields of human thought and activity, he was also influenced by the educative possibilities of science in general and of the physical sciences in particular. From this point of view he devoted special attention to the claims as well as to the technique of Mathematics. The relations between mathematical or other symbol systems and ordinary language occupied him particularly during the last thirty years of his life. So late as 1831 he makes a memorandum : " Arithmetical, algebraical, and musical notation are a portion of the quasi-universal written language ; while the correspondent spoken exists in all its varieties. An analogous case is that of the Chinese character, common to China, Japan, Cochin-China." [1]

Mathematics as such, he held, " otherwise than in so far as it is applicable to physics, Mathematics (except for amusement, as chess is useful) is neither useful nor so much as true. 1. That, except as excepted, it is not useful, is a proposition which, when clearly understood, will be seen to be identical ; a proposition disaffirming it would be a self-contradictory one. 2. That it is not so much as true, will, it is believed, be found, upon calm and careful reflection, to be little if anything different from an identical proposition ; a proposition contradicting it, little if anything different from a self-contradictory one."

[1] *Works*, Vol. XI, p. 72.

Apart from Geometry, a mathematical proposition is one " in which physical existences, *i.e.* bodies and portions of space, are considered in respect of their quantities and nothing else ".

A proposition in Geometry is one " in which physical existences, as above, are considered in respect of their figure, and thereby in respect of their quantity but in no other respect "—which leads to :—

" A proposition having for its subject the geometrical figure called a sphere is a proposition having for its subject all such bodies as can with propriety be termed spherical bodies, as likewise all such individual portions of space as can with propriety be termed spherical spaces ; and so in the case of a cone, a cube, and so forth.

In as far as any such individual portions of matter and space are actually in existence, the proposition is actually true. In as far as any such portions of matter or space may be considered as likely to come into existence, or as capable of coming into existence, it may be considered as having a sort of potential truth, which, as soon as any such portions of matter or space come into existence, would be converted into actual truth.

In point of fact, no portion, either of matter or space, such as agrees exactly with the description given by Mathematicians of the sort of figure called a sphere, ever has come into existence (there seems reason to believe). But, by this circumstance, though in a *strict sense*—that is, to the mere purpose of absolutely correct expression—*the truth* of all propositions concerning the sort of figure called a sphere is destroyed ; yet, in no degree is the utility of any of them either destroyed, or so much as lessened ; in no degree is the truth of them destroyed or lessened with reference to any *useful purpose*, with reference to any purpose, or in any sense, other than a perfectly useless one.

A general proposition which has no individual object to which it is truly applicable is not a true one. It is no more a true proposition than an army which has no soldier in it is a true army ; a faggot which has no stick in it, a true faggot." [1]

---

[1] *Works*, Vol. VIII, pp. 162–3. Bentham's distinction between truth and what he describes as 'potential' truth, on the one hand, and purely mathematical interpretable rules in an operational calculus, will be of interest to the modern mathematician.

All this, though largely admitted by modern mathematicians, was highly unacceptable to the expert of Bentham's day : " That before any such surface as a circular one had any existence, all its radii were equal is, in his creed, as in Montesquieu's, a fundamental article. That fluxions and equations should have had their origin in so impure a source as matter, is to an ardent-minded mathematician an idea no more to be endured than, by certain religionists it is, that moral evil should have no other source than physical ; or, by the sentimental poet, the sentimental orator, or the hypocritical politician, it is that sympathy (whether for the individual or the particular class of the community-political body he belongs to, the nation at large, or the human race) should have so unhonoured a parent or so despicable an antagonist as self-regard, either in his own pure bosom or that of any of his friends." [1]

In spite, however, of their lack of orthological orientation, mathematicians often get along remarkably well with their strange symbols. " What wonder if among those to whom, while not yet in possession of the key, the cypher comes to be pored over, the number of those to whose minds the words of the cypher have imparted clear ideas, is comparatively so inconsiderable."

By a small number of privileged minds, " to the constitution of which the subject happens to be in a peculiar degree adapted, at the end of a certain number of years thus employed, an acquaintance with the science—an acquaintance more or less clear, correct, and extensive—comes to have been attained. Attained ! but how ? by means of the cypher ? by means of the inapposite, the ill-constructed, the fictitious language ? No ; but in spite of it. Instead of being left to be drawn by abstraction, like Truth out of her well, from the bottom of an ocean of perturbers, had the key been conveyed in the first instance, and terms of compact texture constructed out of apposite, familiar, and unfictitious language, a

[1] *Ibid.*, p. 163.

small part of the time so unprofitably employed would have sufficed for extracting from the subject a set of conceptions much more clear, correct, and extensive than those obtained by a process so full of perplexity and inquietude." [1]

But all these wonders for which Algebra is responsible— " can it be that it is by mere *abbreviation*, by nothing but a particular species of *short-hand*, that they have been performed ? By the mere use of a set of *signs* or *characters*, by which the ideas in question are expressed in a less quantity of *space* and *time* than would have been necessary to the giving expression to them by the *signs* or *characters* of which *ordinary written* language is composed, and by which those sounds are designated of which the ordinary *spoken* language is composed ? Newton, Leibnitz, Euler, La Place, La Grange, etc., etc.—on this magnificent portion of the field of science, have they been nothing more than so many expert *short-hand writers* ? " The answer is that the system of abbreviated forms of expression is one thing, but the purpose for which they are employed is quite another. " The purpose to which, in the instance in question, this species of *short-hand* is applied comes, in every instance, within the description given above, viz. by *means of their relation to certain quantities that are known, the making known a certain quantity or certain quantities, which, in all other respects, are as yet unknown.*"

In order to determine this relation, " some *contrivance* in every instance (and, in some instances, abundance of very subtle contrivance) over and above the use of *short-hand* is, or at any rate originally was, necessary ; and from the *short-hand* itself, the system composed of these *contrivances* is in itself no less distinct than any one of the species of discourse (a *speech*, for instance, or the *evidence* of a *witness*) which *short-hand*, commonly so called, is employed in giving expression to, is distinct from the *short-hand*, the *mode of writing*, itself ".[2]

[1] *Ibid.*, p. 183. [2] *Ibid.*, p. 37.

g

The practical conclusion is that, for the convenience of learners, " it would probably be of no small use, if, in ordinary language—language clear from those *characters* and *formularies*, so appalling to every as yet uninitiated (and more particularly to the uninitiated juvenile) eye— explanations were given of the several *contrivances* in question ; or if, in this way, the explanation of the whole system, pursued to the length to which it has already been carried, would occupy too much space—at any rate, of such points as, by the joint consideration of *facility* and *utility* (*facility* in *acquisition*, and *utility* in *application*) should be found recommended for preference ".[1]

THE DIFFERENTIAL CALCULUS

To give the mathematical learner as complete an understanding as possible of what Mathematics is doing Bentham proposes a special technique.[2]

" A key should not only have the effect of letting the reader into the heart (so to speak) of the contrivance by which the proposed object is effected, the proposed advantage gained, but in the production of this effect the purely verbal mode of expression alone . . . should be employed : the *purely verbal* mode ; viz. in Geometry, to the exclusion of the diagrammatic, in Algebra to the exclusion of the Algebraic, characters and forms. . . .

The sort of intellectual instrument, the key thus proposed, or rather the apparatus or collection of keys, would, adds Bentham, "be very far from being complete, if in its purpose it did not include all the several fictions, which, in the framing of this branch of art and science, have been invented and employed." And for illustration, he mentions two such fictions—" the conversion of the algebraical method into geometrical, and the contrivance, called by its first inventor, Newton, and from him by British mathematicians, the method of *fluxions*, and by its second but not less original inventor, Leibnitz, and from him by the mathematicians of all other countries,

[1] *Ibid.*, p. 38.   [2] *Ibid.*, pp. 169 ff.

the *differential and integral calculus."* For the explanation
of these fictions, and, indeed, for the justification of the
use so copiously made of them, two operations would
require to be performed :

" One is, the indication of the really exemplified state of
things, to which the fiction is now wont to be applied, or
is considered as applicable, the other is the indication of the
advantage derived from the use of this the fictitious language,
in contradistinction to the language by which the state of
things in question would be expressed plainly and clearly
without having recourse to fiction.

1. As to the conversion of the forms of Algebra into those
of Geometry, or of the algebraic mode of expression into
the geometrical. If in a case in which figure has no place—
as in a case where the quantity of money to be paid or
received, or given under the name of interest for the use of
money during a certain time, is the subject of investigation
—the geometrical forms should be employed, or the subject
of investigation, thereby represented in the character of a
portion of matter or space, exhibiting a certain figure, here
a fiction is employed, figure is said to have place in a case
where it really has no place.

2. In cases where the geometrical form is the form in
which the subject presents itself in the first instance, and
the translation which is made is a translation from this
geometrical form into the algebraical, here in this case no
fiction has place : here what is done may be done, and is
done, without any recourse to fiction ; and as to the advantage looked for from this translation, an obvious one that
presents itself is the abbreviation which constitutes an
essential character of the algebraic form.   In the opposite
species of translation, viz. that from the algebraic form into
the geometrical, fiction is inseparable.   Why?—because
when by the supposition figure does not form part of the
case, figure is stated as forming part of the case.   But when
the translation is from the geometrical form into the
algebraical, neither in this, nor in any other shape, has
fiction any place.   Why ?—because, though in the case as
first stated, figure has place, yet if reference to the figure be
not necessary to the finding the answer which is sought, to
the doing what is required or proposed to be done, the
particular nature of the figure is a circumstance which,
without fiction, may be neglected, and left out of the
account."

So in the case of the method of fluxions, which is but a particular species of algebra distinguished by that name:

" Take some question for the solution of which this new method is wont to be employed. This question, could it be solved by ordinary algebra, or could it not ? If it could, then why is it that this new method is employed ? *i.e.* what is the advantage resulting from the employment of it ? If it could not, then what is the expedient which is supplied by fluxions, and which could not be supplied by algebra ?

In this method a fiction is employed : a point, or a line, or a surface, is said to have kept flowing where in truth there has been no flowing in the case. With this falsehood, how is it that mathematical truth, spoken of as truth by excellence, is compatible ?

The point here made is then illustrated in ordinary Geometry and Algebra :

" In the practice of mathematicians, propositions of the geometrical cast, and propositions of the algebraical cast, are, to an extent which seems not to have been as yet determined, considered as interconvertible ; employed indifferently, the one or the other, and upon occasion translated into each other. When, in the particular subject to which they are respectively applied, figure, although it have place, may, without inconvenience in the shape of error, or any other shape, be laid out of consideration—in this case, instead of geometry, which, in this case, seems the more apposite and natural form, algebra, if employed, is employed without fiction, and may, therefore, be employed without production of obscurity, without inconvenience in that shape ; and, in proportion as the sought-for result is arrived at with less labour and more promptitude, with clear, and peculiar, and net advantage.

But if, in a case in which figure cannot have place, as in the case of calculation concerning degrees of probability, as expressed by numbers, if any proposition be clothed in the geometrical form, so far will fiction have been employed; and with it, its never-failing accompaniment, obscurity, have been induced.

In the mind of him by whom they are employed, when the natural and individual ideas in which they have their source, and the individual or other particular objects, from which those ideas were drawn, are once lost sight of, all extensive general expressions soon become empty sounds.

In the use made of algebra, at any rate on the occasion

of instruction given in this art to learners, the particular application which, either at the time in question, was made, or at any future time, was proposed to be made of it, should never be out of sight."

Algebraical language, even where no fiction is involved, is, as previously explained, a sort of abbreviated or short-hand language :

" So far, and so far only, as the abbreviated expressions which it employed are, by him who employs them, capable of being, upon occasion, translated into propositions delivered at length, in the form of ordinary language ; so far, and so far only, as in the room of every such fiction as it employs, expressions by which nothing but the plain truth is asserted —expressions significative, in a direct way, of those ideas for the giving expression to which the fictitious language here employed—were capable of being substituted, and accordingly are substituted ; so far and so far only, are they in the mouth or pen of him by whom they are employed, of him by whom, or of him to whom, they are addressed, anything better than empty sounds.

It is for want of all regular recurrence to these sorts of intellection, it is for want of this undiscontinued reference to unabbreviated and unsophisticated language, that algebra is in so many minds a collection of signs, unaccompanied by the things signified, of words without import, and therefore without use."

Returning to the distinction between referential and fictional language, Bentham expands his views in relation to the work of the continental analysts.

" It was by an abstract consideration of the nature of the case (i.e. by a metaphysical view of the subject, as some mathematicians would incline to say, or a logical, as it might be more correct to say), that this notion of the natural distinctness between the contrivances for abbreviation on the one hand, and the contrivances for the actual solution of problems, though with the assistance afforded by those abbreviative contrivances on the other, were suggested to the writer of these pages. It was with no small satisfaction that, for this same idea, he found afterwards a confirmation, and a sort of sanction, in the writings of two first-rate mathematicians, viz. a passage in Euler, adopted and quoted with applause by Carnot (Euler, *Mémoires de l'Académie de Berlin*, Année 1754), *Reflexions sur la Métaphysique du Calcul infinitesimal*, Paris, 1813, p. 202—

" Persons there are, says he, in whose view of this matter, Geometry and Algebra (la géomètrie et l'analyse) do not require many reasonings (raisonnements) ; in their view, the *rules* (les règles) which these sciences prescribe to us, include already the points of knowledge (les connoissances) necessary to conduct us to the solution, so that all that we have to do is to perform the operations in conformity to those rules, without troubling ourselves with the reasonings on which those rules are grounded. This opinion, if it were well grounded, would be strongly in opposition to that almost general opinion, according to which Geometry and Algebra are regarded as the most appropriate instruments for cultivating the mental powers (l'esprit), and giving exercise to the faculty of ratiocination (la faculté de raisonner). Although the persons in question are not without a tincture of mathematical learning, yet surely they can have been but little habituated to the solution of problems in which any considerable degree of difficulty is involved : for soon would they have perceived that the mere habit of making application of those prescribed rules goes but a very little way towards enabling a man to resolve problems of this description ; and that, before application is actually made of them, it is necessary to bestow a very serious examination upon the several particular circumstances of the problem, and on this ground to carry on reasonings of this sort in abundance (faire la-dessus quantité de raisonnements) before he is in a condition to apply to it those general rules, in which are comprised that class of reasonings, of which, even during the time that, occupied in the calculation, we are reaping the benefit of them, scarce any distinct perception has place in our minds. This preparation, necessary as it is that it should be before the operation of calculation is so much as begun—this preparation it is, that requires very often a train of reasonings, longer, perhaps, than is ever requisite in any other branch of science ; a train, in the carrying on of which a man has this great advantage, that he may all along make sure of their correctness, while in every other branch of science he finds himself under the frequent necessity of taking up with such reasonings as are very far from being conclusive. Moreover, the very process of calculation itself, notwithstanding that, by Algebra, the rules of it are ready made to his hands (quoique l'analyse en préserve les règles), requires throughout to have for its support a solid body of reasoning (un raisonnement solide) without which he is, at every turn, liable to fall into some mistakes. The algebraist, therefore (*le géomètre* is the word, but it is in his algebraic, and not in his geometrical, capacity, that, on the present occasion, the mathematician is evidently meant to be brought to view)—the algebraist, then (concludes this Grand Master of the Order) finds, on every part of the field, occasion to keep his mind in exercise by the formation of those reasonings by which alone, if the problem be a difficult one, he can be conducted to the solution of it."

Thus far the illustrious pair. "Now," asks Bentham, "these reasonings (raisonnements) so often mentioned, and always as so many works or operations perfectly distinct from those which consist in the mere application of the algebraic formulæ, what are they?" His answer reverts once more to the distinction between references and fictions.

"Plainly the very things for the designation of which the words, contrivances for the coming at the solution of the problem, or some such words, have all along been employed. Thus much, then, is directly asserted, viz. that the operations which consist in the, as it were, mechanical application of this set of rules, which for all cases is the same, on the one hand, and, on the other hand, those which consist in the other more particular contrivances for solving the particular problem, or set of problems, in question, by the application of these same general rules, are two classes of operations perfectly distinct from each other. But, moreover, another thing which, if not directly asserted, seems all along to be implied, is that to one or other of these two heads everything that is or can be done in the way of algebra is referable. Of the descriptions given of these different contrivances and sets of contrivances, of this sort of materials it is, that, in as far as they apply to the algebraic (not to speak here of the geometric) method, all these *keys* and sets of *keys*, as employed by the hand of the mathematician, will have to be composed. But, these contrivances being in themselves thus distinct from the general formulæ, it follows that, for the explanation of them, language other than that in which these formulæ are delivered, may consequently be employed : other language, viz. (for there is no other) that language which is in common use. And thus it is that not only to Geometry, but to Algebra, may the purely verbal mode of designation be applied, to give to the several quantities which have place in the problem such a mode of expression as, by indicating the several relations they bear to each other, shall prepare them for being taken for the subjects of that sort of operation, which consists in the putting them in that point of view in which, by means of those relations, those quantities which at first were not known, but which it is desired to know, become known accordingly. This, when expressed in the most general terms of which it is susceptible, will, it is believed, be found to be a tolerably correct account of the sort of operation which, on each particular occasion, must proceed. No direct and, as it were, mechanical application of the set of general rules. Of what, then, is it that a sort of algebraic *key*, or *set of keys*, of the kind in question, must be composed ? Of a system of abbreviations or directions by which it shall be shown in what manner, in the several cases to which it is applicable, this sort of preliminary tactical operation may be performed, and to the best advantage.

As these two intimately connected yet distinguishable operations, viz. the application of the use-indicating and that of the key-presenting principle, went on together— the order of *invention, i.e.* the order in which the several propositions, or groups of propositions, come to be invented, would, in conjunction with the order of *demonstration, i.e.* the order in which, for the purpose of demonstration, it is either necessary or most convenient that they should be presented, be brought to light.

But in proportion as the order of invention came thus to be detected and displayed, in that same proportion would it be rendered manifest that theory was formed, and in what manner it was so formed, by abstraction, out of positive ideas ; more and more general out of particulars ; and, in a word, originally out of individual ones.

Supposing the whole field of Geometry, or, in a word, of Mathematics, measured and delineated upon this plan, what would, in that case, be signified by the word *understanding*, in such phrases as these, viz. ' he understands plain elementary geometry,' ' he understands conic sections,' or, in general, ' he understands the subject,' would be a state of mind considerably different from that which at present is indicated by these same phrases ; and accordingly, in the signification of the words *learning* and *teaching*, as applied to the same subject, the correspondent changes would be undergone." [1]

For the philosophical historian of mathematics these

[1] *Works*, Vol. VIII, pp. 176-7.

passages offer a most important clue for unravelling the symbolic tangles that accumulated for two hundred years around the notation for the derivative ; in fact this notation still haunts the modern mathematician in spite of the work of Weierstrass, Dedekind, and Cantor, who only obscurely see the part played by fictions in mathematical processes.

Bentham's rather oblique approach to the problem in this context presupposes that the reader accepts the earlier analysis of linguistic fictions ; and takes it for granted that the application to mathematical symbols follows as a matter of course. The case of the derivative, as it is presented in Carnot's *Reflexions sur la metaphysique du calcul infinitesimal*, then becomes a most elegant exemplification of fictional invention, and Carnot's analysis follows Bentham's method of archetypation and phraseoplerosis. The geometrical operation of finding the tangent at any point of a given curve is taken as the archetype, and the analytical formulation consists in adding to the fundamental algebraic operations—addition, subtraction, multiplication, division, involution, and evolution—a new operation on functions which will be analogous or isomorphic with the geometrical operation. The separation and formal consideration of these operational symbols, which are in themselves fictional and, as such, incitements to the hypostatization of mathematical entities, nevertheless throw their numerous applications in geometry and physics and also their previous partial formulations in the methods of exhaustions, indivisibles, indeterminates, prime and ultimate ratios, fluxions, vanishing quantities, and the calculus of derivations into a systematic analogical order ; and they themselves appear in their true light as shorthand notations with direct simple references to complicated things in geometry and physics and subtle connections with the other notations in higher branches of mathematics. The derivative and the integral are necessary fictions in that they cannot be reduced, and the attempt should not be made to reduce them, to the other mathematical operations ; but on the other hand their fictional and referential uses may be made clear as in Bentham's suggested interpretation of Carnot's exposition. There is an important suggestion in this for the current perturbations of pure mathematicians about the realities of the various infinities, those latest descendants of the antinomies of the infinitesimal calculus and fluxions of Bentham's time. The first step is the original invention of an operation to fit the archetypal problem ; the second step is the formulation of this new operation in a set of notations ; and the third step is the assimilation by analogy of the troublesome cases to the archetypal form—in short the disentangling of references after the manner of the analyses already indicated elsewhere.[1] This will be nothing new to the operating mathematician, but it will require a certain mental readjustment on the part of those mathematicians and scientists who have recently been aspiring towards what they still frequently regard as metaphysics.

TOWARDS A UNIVERSAL LANGUAGE

Passing now to the problem of universal grammar—what are the difficulties that have intimidated grammarians ? Admitting the reality of difficulties at some point in the inquiry, can we sidestep the ultimates, if any, and proceed with confidence in practice ? It is strange that the one thinker who was in a position to help us here has never been mentioned in this connexion. This is due in part to the inevitable tendency of historians to focus on their special interests ; and nothing could be more remote from the interests of social and political historians of today than the preoccupation of many of the world's greatest thinkers with apparently futile linguistic analysis.

Bentham has here suffered more than Locke, for although the third book of Locke's *Essay* ("On Words")

[1] See *op. cit.*, *The Meaning of Meaning*, Chap. IX, and I. A. Richards, *Mencius on the Mind*, 1932, Chap. IV.

is frequently dismissed with scant attention, his system can to some extent be discussed without it. In Bentham's case, however, the linguistic factor is paramount. His studies of language are both the key to his system and the foundation of his analytic and expository power.

It is unlikely that any writer has been less misled by words; and those who are concerned with the future of grammar will note especially that he avoided verbs wherever possible, employing a verbal substantive with an auxiliary, instead. "I use a verbal substantive," he says,[1] "where others use a verb. A verb slips through your fingers like an eel—it is evanescent: it cannot be made the subject of predication—for example, I say *to give motion* instead of *to move*. The word *motion* can thus be the subject of consideration and predication: so, the subject-matters are not crowded into the name sentence—when so crowded they are lost—they escape the attention as if they were not there."

In the practice of Nomography he had noted that where an idea is presented in the form of a verb, it is mixed up with other words in the form of a sentence, or proposition, more or less complex. "The import of it in such sort covered, disguised, and dunned that no separate nor continued view can be taken of it. Where, on the other hand, a substantive is employed the idea is stationed as it were upon a rock."[2] Bentham therefore advocated his "substantive-preferring principle," and sacrificed elegance of style to clarity on all occasions. He had no use for such an appeal "to the most miscellaneous and even the most fastidious societies" as he allowed to be an asset in his spiritual enemy, Blackstone, the merit of whose work he regards as primarily "the enchanting harmony of its numbers; a kind of merit that of itself is sufficient to give a certain degree of celebrity to a work devoid of every other. So much is man governed by the ear." Hence his concern with Grammar.

[1] *Works*, Vol. X, p. 569.
[2] *Works*, Vol. III, p. 268. Cf. Vol. VIII, pp. 315–6.

Grammar is defined by Bentham as " That branch of art and science in and by which the words of which language or discourse is composed are considered, without any regard to the subject or occasion of the discourse, but only with respect to the relations which the imports of the different classes of words of which it is composed bear to each other, these classes of words being the same whatsoever the subject of the discourse."

The differences between particular grammars may be considerable in regard to these classes, or ' parts of speech ', but the imports they designate (the ideas they symbolize) are, he holds, so similar that a *universal grammar* can be constructed from the study of a typical selection.   We can either study meaning and function abstracted from particular grammars or the concrete provisions made in practice.

The uses of *Universal Grammar* are that it helps us to study and understand any particular language or group of languages, to decide which language is most adequate for a given purpose, and to improve the psychology of thought.   " To give a clear, correct, comprehensive and instructive view of the field of universal grammar, it is not enough for a man to look into the books that are extant on the subject of grammar, whether particular or universal—he must look into his own mind." [1]

A fortiori any analysis based on Greek and Latin is vitiated from the outset.   " In both these languages, properties will be shown by which they are rendered in a high degree incompetent, and ill adapted for their purpose."

In addition to Greek and Latin, Bentham himself had a thorough knowledge of French and some acquaintance with Italian, Spanish and German ; and Brissot " saw him study Swedish and Russian ".[2]   He was perhaps the

---

[1] It is to be noted that Bentham did not devote attention to the question of an artificial language, not because he was not familiar with the controversy, but because he believed in the development of English for universal needs.

[2] *Works*, Vol. X, p. 193.

first writer to realize fully the advantages of the less inflected languages, not only in simplicity but in force [1]— though Comenius had explicitly corrected Bacon on this point in 1648. [2]

In English, the separate auxiliary verbs perform with great advantage " those functions in the performance of which terminations in prodigious number and variety are employed in the more inflected languages, viz. the Greek and Latin and their modern derivatives ".

A much higher degree of impressiveness is, he maintains, the result of this analytic process. " Witness the words *shall* and *will*; and the most imperiously *imperative* mood expressible by the word *shall*. Indeed, such is the quantity of verbal matter saved by the employing the word *shall* in its imperative sense that besides giving to the English, *pro tanto*, a degree of simplicity and force not possessed by any of those southernly derived languages, dead or living, it may almost be said to give to it a degree of copiousness equally peculiar. Why? Because in the expressing by means of the necessary circumlocution that the mind has not patience to draw them out, and so they remain unexhibited."

Bentham's analysis of the functions of the Indo-European verb, achieved in isolation over a hundred years ago, when read in conjunction with his theory of fictions, provides a basis for linguistic reconstruction that has not yet been superseded.[3] The next step, in accordance

[1] *Works*, Vol. VIII, p. 310. " The same modifications which, in the least inflected languages, are mostly expressed by separate words termed *auxiliaries*, are in the most inflected languages expressed by inseparable affixes, viz., prefixes and suffixes ; mostly by suffixes, more commonly styled terminations."

[2] Otakar Vočadlo, " Jespersen and Comenius ", *Xenia Pragensia*, 1931, p. 422.

[3] Cf. Sapir, *Language* (1921), p. 126, and Jespersen, *Philosophy of Grammar* (1924), pp. 91–2.

The reader who also takes into account such material as that collected in Sheffield's *Grammar and Thinking* (1912), pp. 87 ff. and 106 ff., and the Grammatical Appendix to *op. cit.*, *The Meaning of Meaning*, will find that he has at his disposal all that modern Linguistic has contributed to supplement Bentham's outline. Actually he regarded himself as a pioneer, doing the Grammarian's job for him, a job made possible by the discoveries of Horne Tooke (*Works*, Vol. VIII, pp. 187–8).

with Bentham's principles, was to inquire which, if any, of these functions is essential and which of practical convenience.[1] He was certainly in favour of the abolition of inflexions wherever possible, and the most recent findings of comparative philology would have delighted him.

' Though inflexional endings may seem too precious a possession for any language to get rid of them, the evolution of the European languages is steadily working for their entire abolition,'' writes Professor Karlgren.[2] In this, he adds, they are becoming more and more like Chinese, which is ahead of us in this respect. The Chinese, he explains, have no verbs, nor any parts of speech. They can say all that is said by the European language-forms without any formal word-classes to correspond to ' thing ' process, etc. Sheffield gives the following example :—

> *Ch'u mên pu tai ch'ien*
> *Pu ju chia li hsien*
> Go(ing) abroad without tak(ing) cash
> (is) not up-to loaf(ing) at home

Whether the Indo-European languages can dispense with verbs as readily as the Chinese dispensed with travel is another question. At a certain stage in teaching languages Bentham supposed the teacher to have introduced his charges to substantives and adjectives ; yet " without verbs no discourse can be held—no further exposition given, and consequently no clear ideas communicated ".[3] He further held that since the relations we wish to express are the same in all languages " the parts of speech are, therefore, the same in all languages, the scantiest and most inconveniently constructed as well as the richest and most cultivated—the Hottentot and Chinese as well as the Greek and English ".[4]

[1] L. W. Lockhart, *Word Economy*, 1931, pp. 24–37.
[2] *Sound and Symbol in Chinese*, 1923, p. 70.
[3] *Works*, Vol. I, p. 244.
[4] *Works*, Vol. VIII, p. 187. It is worth noting that Bentham devoted a great amount of thought to mathematical notations, which he regarded as " special signs,"—whose function is abbreviation and

This raises in an acute form one of those ultimates which have kept grammarians from interesting themselves in Universal Grammar. If we define our parts of speech in terms of the psychological, physical, and social requirements of communication, then we shall tend to find these parts of speech in all languages, however rudimentary their differentiation in terms of form and syntactic function. It might well be that the verb in Indo-European languages is a purely symbolic creation, completing a structural pattern ; and yet Bentham's view of its necessity, either by definition, or for practical purposes, might be valid. We must, in fact, always bear in mind that for one who realized that both *relations* and *qualities*, as well as all *mental phenomema* (in terms of which his definitions of the parts of speech are framed) are linguistic fictions,[1] any such conclusion was primarily pragmatic.[2]

Bentham believed that English used more " separate accessory words ", as distinguished from modifications or inflected words, than any other language. In connexion with the " substantive-preferring principle " already referred to, he had, as we have seen, made a special study of auxiliary verbs, on which simplification in the future chiefly depends. He strongly advocated a survey of their scope : " A catalogue of this species of auxiliary verbs, accompanied with a catalogue of the nouns substantive to which they are in use to be employed as auxiliaries is an instrument of elucidation that remains to be constructed, and by its usefulness may perhaps be found to pay for the trouble ".[3]   And though Chinese

condensation. A mathematical language, "except by means of the abbreviative and concentrative, cannot facilitate conceptions more than ordinary language, of which it is the sign, does." (*Works*, Vol. VIII, pp. 166–7).

[1] *Works*, Vol. VIII, pp. 129, 174, 189, 203. Cf. also his account of the language of algebra : " Reducing all styles to one, it places the most expert grammarian upon a level with the most inexpert."

[2] In other words, he is not necessarily discussing the problem at a level which would place him in conflict with such considerations as arise in Jespersen's survey of the Universal Grammar controversy, after a century of Comparative Philology, at pp. 45–71 of his *Philosophy of Grammar* (1924).

[3] *Works*, Vol. III, p. 268 ; cf. Vol. VIII, p. 316.

may have no verbs, defined as distinct language-forms, there is no doubt, as Karlgren himself has emphasized, that certain tonal equivalents of inflexion, and the use of auxiliaries as in *t'a yao lai*, " he will come," where there is a complete parallel with the auxiliary of the future, play a subordinate part ; so that, though an unambiguous word-order is the chief resource, a development of auxiliaries on European lines might well take place. This consideration is of importance to those who advocate a common technological language for East and West with a certain interchange of terms. The less the structural divergence the greater the hope of a *rapprochement*.

Hence the possibility of taking up the problem of Debabelization where Bentham left it.[1] His was the first important attempt to determine what we talk about, and his Theory of Fictions is basic for all classifications or evaluations of language forms, and of the Verb in particular, in terms of meaning, whether in relation to thoughts or things. His, too, was the first systematic analysis of the verb in terms of syntactic function. His own stylistic practice was the outcome of a personal interpretation of these achievements. If we do not admit its utility, it must be because we have other views of the best method of attaining clarity in communication and universality in form. Yet, after the lapse of a century, the case for a Back to Bentham movement in linguistic reform is at least as strong as in other fields of internationalism.

[1] See the writer's *Debabelization*, 1931 ; and *Basic English*, second edition, 1932, p. 19.

IV.—REMEDIES, LEGAL AND GENERAL

THE REFORM OF LEGAL JARGON

In the *Table of the Springs of Action* Bentham lays down the following propositions as relevant to all psychological, and *a fortiori* to all legal, discussion :—

"(a) The words here employed as leading terms, are names of so many *psychological entities*, mostly *fictitious*, framed by necessity for the purpose of *discourse*. Add, and even of *thought* : for, without corresponding words to clothe them in, ideas could no more be *fixed*, or so much as *fashioned*, than *communicated*.

(b) By habit, wherever a man sees a *name*, he is led to figure himself a corresponding object, of the reality of which the *name* is accepted by him, as it were of course, in the character of a *certificate*. From this delusion, endless is the confusion, the error, the dissension, the hostility, that has been derived." [1]

By this analysis of reference in terms of fictions, Bentham was enabled to avoid all discussion of ' incorporeal things '.[2]

"What shall we say of the famous division among the Romanists, of things *corporeal* and things *incorporeal* ; that is to say, of things which do not exist, which are not things ? It is a fiction which only serves to hide and to augment the confusion of ideas. All these incorporeal things are only rights either to the services of men, or of real things : this will be shown in treating of rights."

The fictional technique is invoked in every field with which the legislator or psychologist is called upon to deal. Thus *Security* may be considered with reference to the objects which are secured, and with reference to the objects against which they are secured :—

"Taking human beings individually considered, these are the only real entities considered as being secured. But

[1] *Works*, Vol. I, p. 205.   [2] *Works*, Vol. III, p. 177.

when a particular and practical application comes to be m^de of the word *security*, certain names of fictitious entities in common use must be employed to designate so many objects, to and for which the security is afforded. Person, reputation, property, condition in life—by these four names of fictitious entities, all the objects to which, in the case of an individual, the security afforded by government can apply itself, may be designated." [1]

Though legal fictions are only a particularly obvious form of linguistic compromise, it is commonly implied that Bentham's objections to their use was based on ignorance. Had he known what we know today he would have seen the folly of his tirades. Then comes a stock reference to Maine's *Ancient Law*. But what would Bentham have found in Maine to shake his conviction ? " At a particular stage of social progress they are invaluable expedients for overcoming the rigidity of law ; and, indeed, without one of them, the fiction of adoption which permits the family tie to be artificially created, it is difficult to understand how society would ever have escaped from its swaddling clothes, and taken its first steps towards civilization."

Exactly the same consideration presents itself to the historian of slavery or war. There is no reason, however, to suppose that Bentham was unaware of the historical value of primitive methods.

Just how, then, do modern jurists conceive that the polemic against fictions has been circumvented ? If we take Dicey's date, 1870, as that which marks the conclusion of a Benthamite era, the testimony of Professor Sheldon Amos is most relevant. He was born three years after Bentham's death, became Professor of Jurisprudence at University College, London, in 1869, and published his *Science of Law* in 1872. He there explains that by legal fictions " the imaginative reverence for old symbols and formalities is deferred to while more or less perceptible change is introduced into the substance of the law ". This practice " is now thoroughly understood, and has

---

[1] *Works*, Vol. IX, p. 11.

been fully commented upon ". By fictions, sometimes the legislature " is imposed upon ", generally the populace or the educated layman " is the object of the snare ", more frequently (*sic*) " the judges and all the ministers of the court who co-operate with them deceive themselves by tricks practised upon their own understanding ". Under the illusion that what is useful must be real, they innovate without feeling iconoclastic.

Instead of questioning the desirability of so ready a capitulation to Word-magic, Professor Amos passes on[1] to *equity* as another mode of altering laws without admitting it ; vouchsafing in extenuation that we are indebted to " a series of useful fictions for such benefits as the development of a large branch of the praetorian jurisdiction at Rome ", for the fact that " a variety of important doctrines —some useful, some pernicious—touching the prerogative of the English Crown, have taken symmetrical shape ", for encroachments of certain English Courts on the jurisdiction of others, and for a curtailment of inalienable entail.

Apart from fictions, equity is invoked to " get rid of the precise verbiage familiar to an older age " ; and the third way of securing legal reform without apparent change of front is by *interpretation*. Bentham, on the other hand, would have us endeavour to substitute for Fictions, Equity, and Interpretation—Candour, in relation to fact, Clarity, in the practice of nomography, and Codification, in the interests of the greatest happiness.

To realize the imperfections of English statute law, and of the language employed for the purpose of legislation by lawyers, it is only necessary, says Bentham, to sum up the points by which it is distinguished from the ordinary language of the multitude.

> " Wheresoever it is seen to differ, it will be seen to differ to its disadvantage—peculiar absurdity the immediate effect —peculiar mischief the result.

[1] In the following year, however, he made it clear (*An English Code, its Difficulties and the Modes of overcoming them*, 1873) that he himself was an advocate of Codification on Benthamic lines; cf. also his *Codification in England and the State of New York*, 1867.

This distinction from the ordinary language of the multitude is peculiar to the language of English statute law : foreign laws are clear from it.

It has been among the devices of lawyers to connect with everything that is justly dear to English hearts, the absurdities and the vices in and by which they reap their profit. Fiction—the vice which they are not ashamed to avow and magnify under that name—fiction has never been either more or less than lying, for the purpose of extortion and usurpation : yet men who ought to have known better have not been ashamed to stand up and speak of fiction as the foundation and efficient cause, *causa sine qua non* of everything that is most valuable in the fabric of the constitution, and the texture of the common law." [1]

And again :—

" With as much truth, and as much reason and sincerity, might a man slip in, along with the memorials usually buried with the first stone of an edifice, a bridge, or a court of justice—a rotten egg and a rotten apple, and then set up proclaiming the virtue of rotten eggs and rotten apples.

A rotten egg or a rotten apple is quite as necessary to the stability of a bridge for the convenience of passengers, or of the edifice in which justice, or what is called by that name, is to be administered, as fiction, legal fiction ever can have been or ever can be to any good work that may be attempted with it."

But nowhere did Bentham express himself more clearly on the whole subject of Legal Fictions than in Chapter XII of the little-known *Constitutional Code*. " By fiction ", he says, " in the sense in which it is used by lawyers, understand a false assertion of the privileged kind, and which, though acknowledged to be false, is at the same time argued from, and acted upon, as if true ". And he proceeds to enumerate its characteristic features :—

" It has never been employed but to a bad purpose. It has never been employed to any purpose but the affording a justification for something which otherwise would be unjustifiable. No man ever thought of employing false assertions where the purpose might equally have been fulfilled by true ones. By false assertions, a risk at least of disrepute is incurred : by true ones, no such risk.

[1] *Works*, Vol. III, p. 241.

It is capable of being employed to every bad purpose whatsoever.

It has never been employed but with a bad effect.

It affords presumptive and conclusive evidence of the mischievousness of the act of power in support of which it is employed.

It affords presumptive and conclusive evidence of the inaptitude of the form of government in support of which it is employed, or under which it is suffered to be employed.

It affords presumptive and conclusive evidence of moral turpitude in those by whom it was invented and first employed.

It affords presumptive and conclusive evidence of moral turpitude on the part of all those functionaries, and their supporters, by whom it continues to be employed.

It affords presumptive and conclusive evidence of intellectual weakness, stupidity, and servility, in every nation by which the use of it is quietly endured.

In regard to fiction, two sources of service require to be noted : one is the extent of the sinister service rendered ; the other is the extent of the class of persons to whom the service is rendered.

In respect of the extent of the service rendered, the use of fiction may be distinguished into general and particular.

By particular use, understand the particular benefit which, on the occasion of such fiction, results to the class or classes of persons served by it : by the general use, the benefit which accrues to all of them in the aggregate, from the general principle of demoralization which it contributes to establish : viz. that in regard to human action in general, right and wrong, proper ground for approbation and disapprobation depends, not on the influence of the action on the greatest happiness of the greatest number, but on the practice, consequently on the will, and thence on the interest, real or supposed, of the aggregate of those same particular classes. Of the establishment of this principle of demoralization, the object and the effect is— the causing men to behold, not merely with indifference, but even with approbation, in the first place, the perpetration of injustice, and in a word, of political evil in all its shapes; and in the next place, the employing, as an instrument in the commission of such mischief, wilful, deliberate, and self-conscious falsehood ; in a word, *mendacity* : the practising on this occasion and for this purpose, that vice which, when, by individuals not armed with power, it is employed to purposes much less extensively mischievous, is by these same men habitually and to a vast extent visited with the severest punishment.

Now as to the extent of the class of persons to whom the sinister service is rendered. In this respect, likewise, the service will require to be distinguished into particular and general. Of the wilful and mischievous falsehoods in question, some will be found in a more particular manner serviceable to the functionaries having the direction of that particular department of government, in the business of which they are employed to the giving augmentation to the arbitrary power of those same rulers : thus enabling them, with the greater efficiency, and to the greater extent, to make sacrifice of the universal interest to their several particular and sinister interests.

In every case, and throughout the whole field of government, these instruments of mis-rule have had, as they could not but have had, for their fabricators, the fraternity of lawyers : more particularly and obviously such of them as have been invested with official power, principally in the situation and under the name of judges : though, in the unofficial and less formidable characters of writers, authors of reports and treatises, men of the same class have not been wanting in contributing their share." [1]

THE PERSONIFICATION OF FICTIONS

Personification is usually regarded as a harmless literary device by which Ceres, for example, comes to the aid of the writer of Latin verse by deputizing for *corn*. Bentham, however, insists on its subtler uses :—

" Amongst the instruments of delusion employed for reconciling the people to the dominion of the one and the few, is the device of employing for the designations of persons, and classes of persons, instead of the ordinary and appropriate denominations, the names of so many abstract fictitious entities, contrived for the purpose. Take the following examples :—

Instead of Kings, or the King—the *Crown* and the *Throne*.

Instead of a Churchman—the *Church*, and sometimes the *Altar*.

[1] *Works*, Vol. IX, pp. 77-8.

Instead of Lawyers—the *Law*.
Instead of Judges, or a Judge—the *Court*.
Instead of Rich men, or the Rich—*Property*.
Of this device, the object and effect is, that any unpleasant idea that is in the mind of the hearer or reader
might happen to stand associated with the idea of the
person or the class, is disengaged from it : and in the
stead of the more or less obnoxious individual or individuals,
the object presented is a creature of the fancy, by the idea
of which, as in poetry, the imagination is tickled—a phantom
which, by means of the power with which the individual or
class is clothed, is constituted an object of respect and
veneration.
In the first four cases just mentioned, the nature of the
device is comparatively obvious.
In the last case, it seems scarcely to have been observed.
But perceived, or not perceived, such, by the speakers in
question, has been the motive and efficient cause of the
prodigious importance attached by so many to the term
property : as if the value of it were intrinsic, and nothing
else had any value : as if man were made for property,
not property for man. Many, indeed, have gravely asserted,
that the maintenance of property was the only end of
government." [1]

Having thus stigmatized the technique of the opponents
of linguistic reform in the legal field, Bentham proceeds
to the causes—" the moral, the inward, the secret causes,
in which this error, this pernicious mode of thinking,
appears to have had its source ". These, applied to the
field of thought and action taken in the aggregate, he
finds to be four in number :—

" 1. Aversion to depart from accustomed habits ; in
particular, the habit of regarding the stock of the matter
of language, as applied to the stock of ideas in question, as
being complete.
2. Love of ease, or say aversion to labour—aversion
to the labour of mind necessary to the forming therein,
with the requisite degree of intimacy, an association between
the idea in question, new or old, and the new word thus
introduced, or proposed to be introduced.
3. Where the word is such as appears to convey with it
a promise of being of use, more or less considerable, in that

[1] *Works*, Vol. IX, p. 76.

portion of the field into which it is thus proposed to be introduced, a sentiment of envy or jealousy, in relation to the individual, known or unknown, on whose part the endeavour thus to make a valuable addition to the stock of the language has been manifested.

4. Of the causes above mentioned, the application wants not much of being co-extensive with the whole field of human discourse : one cause yet remains, the influence of which will naturally be more powerful than that of all the others put together. This cause is confined in its operation to the field of morals and politics—taking, however, the field of opinion on the subject of religion as included in it.

It consists in the opposition made by every such new word—in the proportion to the tendency which it has to add to the stock of ideas conducive to the greatest happiness of the greatest number—to the particular and sinister interests of those by whom the sentiment of disapprobation, as towards the supposed effect and tendency of the new word in question, stands expressed, and is endeavoured to be propagated."

One of Bentham's most vigorous diatribes against the opposition to the reform of legal language follows an amusing passage in the *Nomography* on ' corruption of blood ' :—

" Within the memory of the author of these pages, the population of Great Britain, to the number of about twelve millions, was divided into two not very decidedly unequal halves : the one composed of those whose fondest wishes centred in the happiness of being slaves to a Scotchman of the name of Stuart :—the other of those whose wishes pointed in the same manner to a German of the name of Guelph. Of the twelve millions, six were devoted to extermination by the lawyers on one side :—the other six by the lawyers on the other side. In the aggregate mass of the blood of the whole population, not a drop that was not in those days in a state of corruption, actual or eventual, according to the system of physiology established for the benefit of most religious kings, by learned lords and learned gentlemen.

Scarcely of the whole number of those in whom, according to Blackstone's language, the capacity of committing crimes had place, would a single one have escaped the having his or her bowels torn out of his or her body, and burnt before his or her face, supposing execution and effect capable of being given, and given accordingly, to the laws made, under pretence of being found ready made, and declared for the more effectual preservation of loyalty and social order."

Language as we know it today is essentially the creation of savages—persons, no doubt, of broad minds and great ingenuity in some respects,[1] but holding less advanced views on the subtler aspects of science and jurisprudence. Science discovered their shortcomings several centuries ago, and in Bentham's view the legal profession would do well to follow scientific procedure.

" To whatsoever particular language the aggregate mass of discourse in question belongs, it will undeniably be in the greater degree apt with reference to the uses of human discourse taken in the aggregate, the more it abounds with words by which ambition and obscurity are excluded, or with words by means of which fresh and fresh degrees of conciseness are given to the body of the language.

Every language being the work of the human mind, at a stage of great immaturity, reference had to the present state of it, hence it is, that in every language, the most apt, or say the least unapt, not excepted, the demand for new words cannot but be great and urgent. In some of the departments of the field of language, including the field of thought and action, and the field of art and science, no reluctance at all as to this mode of enrichment has place :— on the other hand, in others such reluctance has place in a degree more or less considerable. Of this field, the portion in regard to which this reluctance seems to be most intense and extensive, is that which belongs to morals in general, and politics, including law and government, in particular :— of this reluctance, the inconsistency, and the evil effects that result from it to the uncontrovertible ends of human discourse, are apparent."

PURITY-INDIGENCE

And here Bentham makes use of his far-reaching analysis of *eulogistic* and *dyslogistic* terms, where a neutral nomenclature would usually deprive an argument of its popular appeal :—

[1] Malinowski, *The Sexual Life of Savages*, 1929.

" The opposite of that useful quality, the degree of which would be as the multitude of apt words associated with clear ideas—with ideas of unprecedented clearness, and introduced at a still maturer and maturer stage of the human mind, is a quality for the designation of which the word *purity* has commonly been employed.   No sooner is the idea for the designation of which this word is employed brought clearly to view, than it is seen to be that which is aptly and correctly designated by the word *indigence*.   This word *indigence*, wherefore then is it not employed—for what purpose is the word *purity* substituted to it ?   Answer : For this purpose, viz. the causing every endeavour to render the language more and more apt, with reference to the uncontrovertible ends of human discourse, to be regarded with an eye of disapprobation.   *Purity* is the number of those words to which an eulogistic sense has been attached—words under cover of which an ungrounded judgment is wont to be conveyed, and which are thence so many instruments in the hand of fallacy.

Of the use made of the word *purity*, the object, and to an unfortunate degree the effect, is to express, and, as it were by contagion, to produce and propagate, a sentiment of approbation towards the state of things, or the practice, in the designation of which it is employed—a sentiment of disapprobation towards the state of things or practice opposite.

On each occasion on which the word *purity*, is employed for the purpose of pointing a sentiment of disapprobation on the act of him by whom a new-coined word is introduced or employed, reference is explicitly or implicitly made to some period or point of time at which the stock of words belonging to that part of the language is regarded as being complete—insomuch that, of any additional word employed, the effect is, to render the aggregate stock—not the more apt but by so much the less apt, with reference to the ends of language : to wit, not on the score of its individual inaptitude (for that is an altogether different consideration) but on the mere ground of its being an additional word added to that stock of words which is found already complete —a word introduced at a time subsequent to that at which the language, it is assumed, had arrived at such a degree of perfection, that by any change produced by addition it could not be deteriorated—rendered less apt than it was with reference to the ends of language.

That as often as conveyed and adopted, any such

sentiment of disapprobation is not only ungrounded but groundless, and the effect of it, in so far as it has any, pernicious, seems already to have been, by this description of it, rendered as manifest as it is in the power of words to render it.

An assumption involved in it is, that so far as regards that part of the language, the perfection of human reason had, at the point of time in question, been already attained. Another assumption that seems likewise involved in it is—either that experience has never, from the beginning of things to the time in question, been the mother of wisdom, or that exactly at that same point of time, her capacity of producing the like offspring had somehow or other been made to cease." [1]

In the subsequent discussion of " the modes or sources of improvement of languages in respect of copiousness " the Purity *motif* is still prominent. Of single words, there are not many by which, in various ways, mischief to a greater amount has been done, than has been done by the word *purity*, with its conjugate *pure* : in the field of morals, of legislation, and of taste.

" In the fields of morals and legislation, purity has for another of its conjugates a word significative of the opposite quality, *impurity* :—to the field of language the application of this negative quality does not appear to have extended itself.

The grand mischief here is that which has been done by the inference that has been made of the existence of moral impurity from that of physical impurity—of impurity in a moral sense, from that of impurity in a physical sense.

In the field of taste, this word has been made the vehicle in and by which the notion is conveyed and endeavoured to be inculcated, that copiousness in language, instead of being a desirable is an undesirable quality—instead of a merit a blemish : purity, being interpreted, is the opposite of copiousness ; the less copious the language, the more pure. If ever there were a prejudice, this may assuredly be called one."

But it was left to Bentham himself to do the real work :—

" In the field of mechanics, when a workman has a new contrivance of any kind upon a pattern of his own to

[1] *Works*, Vol. III, pp. 273-4.

execute, a not uncommon preliminary is the having to contrive and execute accordingly a new tool or set of tools, likewise of his own contrivance, to assist him in the execution of the new work. Such, to no inconsiderable extent, has been the unavoidable task of the author with respect to legal language." [1]

FIXATION

We might have expected to find disquisitions on Language and Fictions in treatises on Political Economy or Codification, since in both fields the linguistic factor is of obvious importance,[2] but proposals for a Radical Reform Bill would at first sight seem less hopeful. Bentham, however, added an Appendix to his Bill,[3] dealing amongst other things with Fixation, Exposition, or Explanation (including Definition).

Fixation, deciding which meaning of a word is to be adopted, " has for its purpose the removal of *ambiguity* ; explanation, the clearing up of *obscurity* ". The distinction may not always be obvious ; sometimes both operations may be necessary. But between them the danger " that no object at all might present itself as clearly denominated " can be avoided. Elsewhere (in the *Nomography*) obscurity is referred to as " ambiguity taken at its maximum ".[4]

The form of exposition known as definition is usually understood as " the exhibition of some word of more extensive signification, within the signification of which that of the word in question is included—accompanied with the designation of some circumstance, whereby the object designated by it stands distinguished from all others that are in use to be distinguished by that more extensive appellative ". But though such a method—

---

[1] *Works*, Vol. III, p. 275.

[2] See " Bentham on Inventions ", *Psyche*, Vol. X, No. 2, October 1929, where the passages on language as a misleading factor in Economics are exhibited in their appropriate setting.

[3] *Works*, Vol. III, p. 592.

[4] *Ibid.*, p. 39 : " In the case of ambiguity, the mind is left to float between two or some other determinate number of determinate imports ; in the case of *obscurity*, the mind is left to float amongst an indeterminate, and it may be an infinite, number of imports."

of genus and differentia—is intended and supposed to þe employed, such words as *right, power,* and *obligation* cannot be so defined.[1]

On the other hand, as Bentham points out in his treatment of Power in the *Pannomial Fragments,*[2] it may sometimes be possible to give an orthodox definition of a fiction :—

> " Power may be defined to be the faculty[3] of giving determination either to the state of the passive faculties, or to that of the active faculties, of the subject in relation to and over which it is exercised :—say the correlative subject."

Bentham's theory of Definition has already been dealt with in sufficient detail ;[4] it is, however, worth while here to append the account of Dichotomy, as such, given by his Editor in the Introduction previously referred to :—

> " It is only by a division into two parts that logical definition *per genus et differentiam* can be accomplished. The species is marked off by its possessing the quality of the genus, and some differential quality which separates it from the other species of that genus. It is only by the expression of a difference as between two, and thought and language enable us to say whether the elements of the thing divided are exhausted in the condividends. We can only compare two things together—we cannot compare three or more at one time. In common language we do speak of comparing together more things than two ; but the operation by which we accomplish this end is compound, consisting of deductions drawn from a series of comparisons, each relating to only two things at a time. Com-

[1] See above, p. lxxvii ; and *Theory of Fictions,* pp. 86 ff.
[2] *Works,* Vol. III, p. 222.
[3] " In this form, the exposition is of the sort styled *definition,* in the narrowest sense of the word—*definitio per genus et differentiam :* exposition effected by indication given of the next superordinate class of objects in which the object in question is considered as comprehended, together with that of the qualities peculiar to it with reference to the other objects of that same class.
The import of the word *faculty* being still more extensive than that of the word power, as may be seen by its assuming the adjunct 'passive,' the word power is, in a certain sense, not unsusceptible of the definition *per genus et differentiam.* But to complete the exposition, an exposition by periphrasis may perhaps require to be added."
[4] Above, pp. lxxiii ff. ; cf. also *The Theory of Fictions,* pp. 84 ff.

parison is the estimate of differences ; and language, by giving us the word ' between ', as that by which we take the estimate, shows that we can only operate on two things at a time.   Thus, if we have a division of an aggregate into three, we cannot give such a nomenclature to these three elements as will show that they exhaust the aggregate. If we say law is divided into penal and non-penal, we feel certain, in the very form of the statement, that we include every sort of law under one or other of these designations ; but if we say that law is divided into real, personal, and penal, we cannot be, in the same manner, sure that we include every kind of law.   If we wish to proceed further in the division, and, after dividing the law into penal and non-penal, say the non-penal is divided into that which affects persons and that which does not affect persons, we are sure still to be exhaustive ; and this system we can continue with the same certainty *ad infinitum*.

The system is undoubtedly a laborious and a tedious one, when the subject is large, and the examination minute. The exemplifications which the Author has given in his tables are the produce of great labour, and cover but a limited extent of subject.   It was more as a test of the accuracy of the analysis made by the *mind* when proceeding with its ordinary abbreviated operations, than as an instrument to be actually used on all occasions, that the Author adopted the bifurcate system.   As a means of using it with more clearness and certainty, he recommended the adaptation to it of the Contradictory formula—viz., the use of a positive affirmation of a quality in one of the condividends, and the employment of the correspondent negative in the other.   The value of this test, as applicable to any description of argumentative statement, is, in bringing out intended contrasts with clearness and certainty.   It is not necessary that the Differential formula should be actually employed. In its constant use there would be an end to all freedom and variety in style.   But it is highly useful to take the statement to pieces, and try whether its various propositions contain within them the essence of the bifurcate system and the formula ; in other words, to see that when differences are explained, or contrasts made, they be clearly applied to only two things at a time, and that the phraseology, instead of implying vague elements of difference, explains distinctly what the one thing has, and what the other has not." [1]

[1] *Works*, Vol. I, pp. 82–3.

CLASSIFICATION

Natural Classification, we are told, in the *View of a Complete Code of Laws* [1] presents objects according to their most striking and interesting qualities, and " nothing is more interesting or striking to a sensible being than human actions considered in reference to the mischief which may result from them to himself or others ". Hence the merit of the classification of offences in the Nine Orders there adopted, which is moreover (2) *simple and uniform* and (3) best adapted *for discourse*, for the announcing of the truths connected with the subject :—

> " In every species of knowledge, disorder in language is at once the effect and the cause of ignorance and error. Nomenclature can only be perfected in proportion as truth is discovered. It is impossible to speak correctly, unless we think correctly ; and it is impossible to think correctly, whilst words are employed for registering our ideas, which words are so constituted that it is not possible to form them into propositions which shall not be false." [2]

The importance of a consistent nomenclature for the purposes of classification is again emphasized by Bentham in drawing up his Table of Rights.[3]

> " The preparation of a table of rights is a sufficiently dry and ungrateful task ; but such labours are required of those who would be of use to the science. It is necessary to distinguish one part of a subject from another, in order to be in a condition to establish true propositions respecting

---

[1] *Works*, Vol. III, p. 171.

[2] " When a nomenclature has been formed respecting a collection of things before their nature is known, it is impossible to draw from it any general propositions which will be true. Take *oils*, for example : under the same name of *oils* have been comprehended oil of olives and oil of almonds, sulphuric acid and carbonate of potass.—What true propositions can be deduced respecting the *delicta privata* and the *delicta publica*, the *delicta publica ordinaria* and the *delicta publica extraordinaria*, established by Heineccius in explaining the Roman laws ? What can be deduced from the *felonies*, the *praemunires*, the *misdemeanours* of the English Laws ?—from the *penal cases*, the *civil cases*, the *private* and the *public* offences of all laws ? These are objects composed of such disproportionate parts, of words referring to such heterogenous things, that it is impossible to form respecting them any general proposition."

[3] *Works*, Vol. III, p. 185.

them. Nothing can be asserted, nothing can be denied, respecting them, whilst objects are mixed *pell mell*, and form only heterogeneous masses. In order to make it understood that one plant is food, and another poison, the characters which distinguish them must be pointed out, and proper names must be assigned to them. So long as there are no names for expressing many rights, or that there is only one and the same name for expressing many dissimilar ones : so long as generic names are employed, without distinguishing the species included under them, it is impossible to avoid confusion—it is impossible to form general propositions which will be true. This observation has already been made, but it often presents itself in a science in which the greatest difficulties arise from a vicious nomenclature."

EXAMPLES

' RIGHTS '

The fictional treatment of rights in the two sections devoted to their analysis in the *View of a Complete Code of Laws* and in the more elaborate discussion of the *Pannomial Fragments*,[1] enables Bentham to restrict the term to a profitable field and divert attention from imaginary entities. The conclusion of the whole matter, from a legal standpoint, is as follows :—

" Rights are, then, the fruits of the law, and of the law alone. There are no rights without law—no rights contrary to the law—no rights anterior to the law. Before the existence of laws there may be reasons for wishing that there were laws—and doubtless such reasons cannot be wanting, and those of the strongest kind—but a reason for wishing that we possessed a right, does not constitute a right. To confound the existence of a reason for wishing that we possessed a right, with the existence of the right itself, is to confound the existence of a want with the means of relieving it. It is the same as if one should say : *Everybody is subject to hunger, therefore everybody has something to eat.*

There are no other legal rights—no natural rights, no rights of man, anterior or superior to those created by the laws. The assertion of such rights, absurd in logic, is pernicious in morals. A right without law is an effect

[1] *Works*, Vol. III, pp. 158–62, 181–6, and 217–21.

without a cause. We may feign a law in order to speak of this fiction—in order to feign a right as having been created ; but fiction is not truth.

We may feign laws of nature—rights of nature, in order to show the nullity of real laws, as contrary to these imaginary rights ; and it is with this view that recourse is had to this fiction—but the effect of these nullities can only be null."

Obligations and *rights* must be dealt with together. We require " an explanation of these moral, including political, fictitious entities, and of their relation to one another, by showing how they are constituted by the expectation of eventual good and evil, *i.e.* of pleasures and pains, or both, as the case may be, to be administered by the force of one or more of the five sanctions ". The political sanction, he explains, includes the legal, the religious, and the sympathetic.

" Of either the word *obligation* or the word *right*, if regarded as flowing from any other source, the sound is mere sound, without import or notion by which real existence in any shape is attributed to the things thus signified, or no better than an effusion of *ipse dixitism*." [1]

And here is perhaps the most characteristic passage in Bentham's many accounts of the word-cluster to which words like *right*, *obligation*, and *service* belong :—

" To declare by law that a certain act is prohibited, is to erect such act into a *crime*. To assure to individuals the possession of a certain good, is to confer *a right* upon them. To direct men to abstain from all acts which may disturb the enjoyment of certain others, is to impose *an obligation* on them. To make them liable to contribute by a certain act to the enjoyment of their fellows, is to subject them to *a service*. The ideas of *law, offence, right, obligation, service,* are therefore ideas which are born together, which exist together, and which are inseparably connected.

These objects are so simultaneous that each of these words may be substituted the one for the other. The law directs me to support you—it imposes upon me the *obligation* of supporting you—it grants you the *right* of being supported by me—it converts into an *offence* the negative act by

[1] *Works*, Vol. III, p. 293.

i

which I omit to support you—it obliges me to render you the *service* of supporting you. The law prohibits me from killing you—it imposes upon me the *obligation* not to kill you—it grants you the *right* not to be killed by me—it converts into an *offence* the positive act of killing you—it requires of me the negative *service* of abstaining from killing you. . . .

With respect to those actions which the law refrains from directing or prohibiting, it bestows a positive right,—the right of performing or not performing them without molestation from any one in the use of your liberty.

I may stand or sit down—I may go in or go out—I may eat or not eat, &c. : the law says nothing upon the matter. Still the right which I exercise in this respect I derive from the law, because it is the law which erects into an offence every species of violence by which any one may seek to prevent me from doing what I like.

This, then, is the connexion between these legal entities : they are only the law considered under different aspects ; they exist as long as it exists ; they are born and they die with it. There is nothing more simple, and mathematical propositions are not more certain. This is all that is necessary for obtaining clear ideas of the laws, and yet nothing of this is found in any book of jurisprudence ; the contrary is, however, everywhere found. There have been so many errors of this kind that it may be hoped that the sources of error are exhausted.

The words *rights* and *obligations* have raised those thick vapours which have intercepted the light : their origin has been unknown ; they have been lost in abstractions. These words have been the foundations of reasoning, as if they had been eternal entities which did not derive their birth from the law, but which, on the contrary, had given birth to it. They have never been considered as productions of the will of the legislator, but as the productions of a chimerical law—a law of nations—a law of nature." [1]

It follows from Bentham's account of Rights that when a right appears nominally to be conferred on a ┼hing it is really conferred on a person, which is " what the compilers of the Roman code never comprehended ". They were misled by grammar.

" According to them, all rights are divided into two masses, of which the one regards *persons*, the other *things*.

[1] *Works, Vol.* III, pp. 159–60.

They have set out with a false unintelligible division into two parts, which are not exclusive with regard to each other. *Jura personarum—Jura rerum.*

It may be said that they were led to take this division by a species of correspondence or grammatical symmetry ; for there is no correspondence between the two appellations except as to the form—there is none as to the sense. *Rights of persons*—what does it mean ? Rights belonging to persons, rights conferred by the law on persons, rights which persons may enjoy :—everything is clear. Transfer this explanation to *rights of things*, what is the result ? Things which have rights belonging to them, things on which the law has conferred rights, things which the law has wished to favour, things for whose happiness the law has provided :—it is the height of absurdity.

Instead of *rights of things*, it is proper to say *rights over things*. The change appears very slight : it, however, overthrows this nomenclature, this division of rights, all this pretended arrangement of the Romanists—since adopted by Blackstone, and according to which he has so badly classed the objects of the law."

In explaining the relations of *offence, right, obligation* and *service*, in the *View of a Complete Code of Laws*,[1] Bentham remarks that " the distinction between rights and offences is strictly verbal " ; and, as we have seen, he goes on to state that these legal entities " are only the law considered under different aspects ".

The problem of translation from one set of terms into another is thus raised, and Bentham refers to it specifically in distinguishing between the Civil and Penal Code. He will not allow that the civil code contains the descriptions of rights and obligations, the penal those of crimes and punishments—" There is no foundation for this distinction ". But the analysis in terms of offences does provide a solution.

" If you say that the right which you have to be supported by me belongs to a certain class of laws which ought to be called *civil*, and that the offence which I commit by neglecting to support you, belongs to a different class of laws which ought to be called *penal*, the distinction would be clear and intelligible.

[1] *Loc. cit.*, p. 159.

There exists between these two branches of jurisprudence a most intimate connexion ; they penetrate each other at all points. All these words—*rights, obligations, services, offences*—which necessarily enter into the civil laws, are equally to be found in the penal laws. But from considering the same objects in two points of view, they have come to be spoken of by two different sets of terms :— *obligations, rights, services,* such are the terms employed in the civil code : *injunction, prohibition, offence,* such are the terms of the penal code. To understand the relation between these codes, is to be able to translate the one set of terms into the other."

' TITLE '

As an example of the translation of a fiction in terms of ' real entities ', we may take the special case of *title*.[1] Bentham here requires the fundamental term *event* with which it " is possible to form a regular class of appellations ". These may have the double inconvenience of length and novelty, but—" I have tried to make use of the word *title*. I have found it equivocal, obscure, defective—spreading a mist over the whole field of jurisprudence ". It is especially defective when *obligations* are spoken of, but if we adopt the nomenclature of ' events ', *dispositive* events can be divided into *collative* and *ablative,* and we can then both classify and translate.

" There is here a series of names which have a reference to each other ; here is a generic name, and subordinate specific names. Take the word title, the logical ramification is stopped at the first step. There are no species of titles ; it is an absolutely barren trunk.

The radical objection against the word *title* is, that it is obscure—it does not exhibit things as they are. To say that an event has happened, is to speak the language of simple truth—is to announce a fact which presents an image to the mind—it is to present a picture which could be painted. To say you have a *title,* is to speak the language of fiction : it is to utter sounds which do not present any image, unless they are translated into other words, as we shall shortly see. To *possess,* to *have,* in a physical sense— here there is a real fact announced in a real manner ; for it

[1] *Works,* Vol. III, p. 189.

is to occupy the thing, or to be able to occupy it (*posse, potes,* to have power over it). To *possess* a thing in the legal sense, to *possess rights* over a thing—there is an equally real fact, but announced in a fictitious manner. To *have a title,* to *possess a title,* in relation to these rights— there is still a real fact, but announced in a manner still more fictitious—still more removed from presenting a real image.

I would not, therefore, employ the word *title* as a fundamental term, but as one translated from the language of fiction into the language of reality, I hesitate not to employ it. It is not luminous in itself, but when it has received light, if it be properly placed, it may serve either to reflect or to transmit it."

' Rule and Principle '

Another example of symbolic procedure is the verbal distinction which Bentham regards as preliminary to any inquiry into what is a law, and what laws are concerned with. Before this is explained, he says, the two mutually and intimately connected words *rule* and *principle* must be carefully defined :—

" Correspondent to every rule you may have a principle ; correspondent to every principle you may have a rule.

Of these two, a rule is the object which requires first to be taken into consideration and presented to view. Why ? Because it is only by means of a rule that any moving force can be applied to the active faculty, or any guide to the intellectual—any mandate can be issued—any instruction given.

A *rule* is a *proposition*—an entire proposition : a *principle* is but a *term.* True it is, that a principle instruction may be conveyed. Conveyed ? Yes : but how ? No otherwise than through the medium of a proposition—the corresponding proposition—the proposition which it has the effect of presenting to the mind. Of presenting ? Yes : and we may add, and of bringing back ; for only in so far as the rule has been at the time in question or in some anterior time, present to the mind, can any instruction, any clear idea be presented to the mind by a principle.

A principle, therefore, is as it were an abridgement of the corresponding rule :—in the compass of a single term, it serves to convey for some particular present use, to a

mind already in possession of the rule, the essence of it :
it is to the rule, what the essential oil is to the plant from
which it is distilled.

So it does but answer this purpose, its uses are great
and indisputable.

1. It saves words, and thereby time.

2. By consisting of nothing more than a single term,
and that term a noun-substantive, it presents an object
which, by an apt assortment of other words, is upon occasion
capable of being made up into another proposition.

So, it is true, may a rule—but only in a form comparatively embarrassing and inconvenient. This will appear
by taking in hand any sentence in which a principle has a
place, and instead of the principle employing the corresponding rule.

Upon occasion, into any one sentence principles in any
number may be inserted ; and the greater the number, the
stronger will be the impression of the embarrassment saved
by the substitution of the principles to the rules.

A principle, as above, is no more than a single term ;
but that term may as well be composite, a compound of
two or more words, as single. Of these words one must be
a noun-substantive ; the other may be either a noun-
adjective or a participle ; including under the appellation
of a noun-adjective, a noun-substantive employed in that
character, in the mode which is so happily in use in the
English language, and which gives it, in comparison with
every language in which this mode is not in use, a most
eminently and incontestably useful advantage." [1]

' FUNCTION '

Here, again, is his justification of the particular use
of the term *function*, at the beginning of the *Constitutional
Code* [2] :—

" The term *functions* has been employed for the sake of
conciseness, correctness, clearness, and symmetry. But for
this comprehensive denomination, where arrangements were
intended to be the same, assemblages of words, more or
less different from one another, would have been apt to
have been employed in giving expression to them ; and
from this diversity in expression, diversity of meaning
might, on each occasion, have naturally been inferred.

[1] *Pannomial Fragments*, Chapter II (*Works*, Vol. III, p. 215).
[2] *Works*, Vol. IX, p. 3.

But by a single word, with a few others, necessary to complete it into a proposition, less space by an indefinite amount will be occupied than would be occupied by any equivalent phrase of which this same word formed no part ...

If in any one of these instances, the word *function*, with the attribute connected with it, is the proper one, so by the supposition it is in every other : so much for correctness.

If in any one of these instances, the import meant to be conveyed is clear, so will it be in every other. For, there being no obscurity in it on the first that occurs of those occasions, so neither can there be on any other."

Another characteristic Benthamic Instrument (No. 12) relates to the special terminology, " the formation of an uniform and mutually correspondent set of terms ", which he adopted for " the several modifications of which the creation, extinction, and transfer of subjects of possession, whether considered as sources of benefit or as sources of burthen, are susceptible :—and thence of a mutually connected and correspondent cluster of offences, consisting of the several possible modes of dealing as above with such subjects of possession, in the case in which they are considered as wrongful, and as such prohibited by statute law, or considered and treated as prohibited by judiciary *alias* judge-made law ". These terms are, in the first instance, *Collation* and *Ablation*.

" In the case, and at the point of time, at which the subject-matter is for the first time brought into existence, collation has place without ablation : if it be already in existence, then collation and ablation have place together, and of their union *translation* is the result : in so far as ablation has place without collation, then not translation, but *extinction*, is the result.

Performed in favour of the collator himself, collation is *self-collation* :—if regarded as wrongful, it is *wrongful* self-collation ; or in one word, *usurpation* is the name by which it has been, and at any time may be, designated.

Performed by the ablator himself, ablation is *abdication* :—if by the laws regarded or treated as wrongful— wrongful abdication is accordingly the name by which it may be designated." [1]

[1] *Works*, Vol. III, p. 294.

FALLACIES

To rhetorical Fallacies Bentham devoted a special treatise ;[1] and he was able to show, in the words of his Editor, " that they consisted, to a great extent, in an ingenious perversion of the language of praise or blame, to make it comprehend that which did not properly come within the quality expressed : and the permanent evil to truth he found to consist in the circumstance, that by habitual use and reiteration, men came to associate the good or bad quality with the thing so spoken of, without examining it ". Thus the term ' old ', which, as applied to men, implies the probability of superior experience and sedateness, is nevertheless frequently used to characterize periods or states of society which had not the benefit of so long a lesson of experience as later times have had :—

> " It is singular that the persons who are most loud in magnifying the pretended advantage in point of wisdom of ancient over modern times, are the very same who are the most loud in proclaiming the superiority in the same respect of old men above young ones. What has governed them in both cases seems to have been the prejudice of names ; it is certain that, if there be some reasons why the old should have advantage over the young, there are at least the same reasons for times that are called modern having it over times that are called ancient. There are more : for decrepitude as applied to persons is real ; as applied to times it is imaginary. Men, as they acquire experience, lose the faculties that might enable them to turn it to account ; it is not so with times : the stock of wisdom acquired by ages is a stock transmitted through a vast number of generations, from men in the perfection of their faculties to others also in the perfection of their faculties ; the stock of knowledge transmitted from one period of a man's life to another period of the same man's life, is a stock from which, after a certain period, large defalcations are every minute making by the scythe of Time."

Unfortunately, the treatment is not generalized ; so a practical study of verbal fallacies as a whole is still a desideratum.

[1] *Works*, Vol. II, pp. 375 ff.

DARK SPOTS

To the objection that the sciences present too many
difficulties to be included in any system of elementary
education, Bentham replies with some force that " the
branches of knowledge which, by reason of the unfamiliarity
of their names, present this formidable aspect, are in
almost every instance less difficult to learn than those
dry and speculative *grammatical rules*, with their applications, and the tasks belonging to them, and the obligation
that arises out of them of penning discourses in prose and
verse in a dead language ; those tasks which, because it
has been the custom so to do, are, without a thought
about the difficulty, universally under the established
system put into the hands of children at ages less mature
than the earliest of those at which, under this new system,
it is proposed to apply to their youthful minds instruction
in various forms—selected on account of their simplicity
and of the promise they afford of converting the sort of
employment which hitherto has been the source of immediate and almost universal pain, into a source of
immediate and absolutely universal pleasure ".[1]

We must not allow ourselves to be horrified by a few
words, " which, because less familiar than those which
we are most accustomed to, are called hard names—
names without which the several branches of knowledge,
which are not only among the most useful but to a
greater or less extent even the most generally familiar,
could neither be distinguished from each other nor so
much as expressed. Let us not conclude, that because
without teaching, they are not to any extent generally
understood by grown men, therefore, *by* teaching, they
are not capable of being made to be understood by
children." [2]

The essential point for the educator is that there shall
be no ' dark spots ', and Bentham's graded technological
method was designed so to present matters that, " in the

[1] *Works*, Vol. VIII, p. 19.   [2] *Ibid.*, p. 24.

whole field of the language, there being no *hard words*
there shall be no absolutely *dark spots* ; nothing that
shall have the effect of casting a damp upon the mind,
by presenting to it the idea of its ignorance, and thence
of its weakness ". By means of his panoptic tables, he
hoped that from every part of the field of knowledge,
" through the medium of these appropriate denominations
(the relations of which, as well those to one another, as
to the matter of the body or branch of art and science,
are determined and brought to view) ideas, more or less
clear, correct, and *complete* ", would be " radiated to the
surveying eye ". By this means there would remain " no
absolutely *dark spots* ; no words that do not contribute
their share towards the production of so desirable an
effect as that of substituting the exhilarating perception
of mental strength to the humiliating consciousness of
ignorance and weakness ".[1]

He admitted, of course, that any word belonging to a
family of words of which no other member is as yet
known " constitutes, in every field over which it hangs, a
dark spot ; a spot to which no eye, among those in which
it excites the notion which that word is employed to
express, can turn itself without giving entrance to sentiments of humiliation and disgust ".[2] Here, however, in
addition to the advantages of a panoptic approach,
the educator can call to his aid two different sorts of
linguistic exercise :—

" 1. To render the scholar acquainted with the *structure*
of language in general, and that of his *own* language in
particular ; and thereby to qualify him for speaking and
writing on all subjects and occasions, with clearness, correctness and due effect—in his own language.

2. By familiarizing him with the greater part, in
number and importance, of those terms belonging to *foreign*
languages from which those belonging to his *own* are
derived, and in which the origin of their import, and the
families of words with which they are connected, are to be
found—to divest them of that repulsive and disheartening

---

[1] *Ibid.*, p. 101.   [2] *Ibid.*, p. 64.

quality of which so impressive an idea is conveyed by the appellation of *hard words*." [1]

Even so, certain technical terms, "words which, whether derived or not from foreign languages, appertain exclusively to particular trades and occupations, will of course continue to operate as so many incidental sources of the sensation of *ignorance*; to a person not correspondently conversant with the languages of those particular trades and occupations respectively, there must, in those several divisions of the language, be of course as many *dark spots* as there are of these peculiar words. But in these instances it will, by the context of the discourse, be sufficiently shown that by a want of acquaintance with the import of these particular words, nothing worse is indicated than a correspondent want of acquaintance with . . . the field of that *particular* trade or occupation ; not any want of acquaintance with any part of the general body of the language. The language of *seamanship* will afford an example." [2]

NEOLOGICAL EXPERIMENTS

Bentham himself was a linguistic innovator, but he had little hope that many of his recommendations would find acceptance. Specifically : if, in English, " *or*, being confined to the disjunctive, *or say* were the diction employed—and that exclusively, where the sense meant to be presented is the *sub-disjunctive*—a blemish, so incompatible with certainty and clearness of conception, might thus be removed. But supposing the improvement were ever so desirable, how the introduction of it could be effected seems not very easy to conceive. The inconvenience of departure from habit is an inconvenience which in such a case would be felt by everybody ", whether as speaker or writer, hearer or reader. " The uneasiness produced by a violation of the law of custom in matters of discourse is an inconvenience to which

[1] *Ibid.*, p. 33.   [2] *Ibid.*, p. 101.

everybody, without exception, is more or less sensible ;
want of precision—want of certainty—is an inconvenience
to which, though in many cases so much more serious
than the other is in any case, few indeed are sensible." [1]

Certain of his happiest creations, such as *international,
maximize, minimize, codification,* and so on, have become
part of the language. The case for another such neologism,
equally desirable perhaps but less seductive, is thus
stated. Hume, says Bentham, was the first to emphasize
" how apt men have been, on questions belonging to any
part of the field of Ethics, to shift backwards and forwards,
and apparently without their perceiving it, from the
question, what *has been done,* to the question, what
ought to be done, and *vice versa* ; more especially from the
former of these points to the other. Some five-and-
forty years ago, on reading that work—from which,
however, in proportion to the bulk of it, no great quantity
of useful instruction seemed derivable, that observation
presented itself to the writer of these pages as one of
cardinal importance." Unless such a distinction is clearly
made, the whole field of Ethics, must remain " a labyrinth
without a clue. Such it has been in general, for example,
to the writers on International Law ; witness Grotius
and Puffendorf. In their hands, and apparently without
their perceiving it, the question is continually either
floating between these two parts of the field of Ethics or
shifting from one to the other. In this state of things, a
name, which, such as *Deontology,* turns altogether upon
this distinction—suppose any such name to become
current, the separation is effectually made, and strong
and useful will be the light thus diffused for ever over
the whole field." [2]

In the choice of. words in general, appositeness is, of
course, purely a matter of association. Apart from
established associations one symbol has as much claim
as another ; but " with relation to the idea which for
the first time it is employed or about to be employed

[1] *Ibid.,* p. 85.   [2] *Ibid.,* p. 128.

to designate, a term is *apposite* when, in virtue of the family connexions with which it is already provided, it has a tendency, upon the first mention, to dispose the mind to ascribe to it properties, whatsoever they may be, by which that object is distinguished from other objects. It is inapposite when it tends " to dispose the mind to ascribe to it, instead of the properties which are thus peculiar to it, others which it is not possessed of, or at any rate which are not peculiar to it. Thus of apposite-ness on the part of the appellative, on the part of the mind to which it presents itself, correct at least, if not complete conception is at first sight the natural result : of in-appositeness, conception always more or less incomplete, and frequently altogether incorrect and erroneous." [1]

In connexion with Bentham's avoidance of grammatical forms which he considered dangerous, particularly the verb,[2] the following account of his peculiar use of the word *matter* is worth attention. He advocated its exten-sion from physics to the whole field of *psychics*, or *psychology*, including *ethics* and *politics* :—

" 1. In the higher, or more general quarter of them ; viz. in the phrases *matter of good, matter of evil.*

In the department of *law* in general, and of *penal* law in particular—*matter of satisfaction* or *compensation*, *matter of punishment*, *matter of reward* ; matter of punishment being neither more nor less than the matter of evil applied to a particular purpose ;—matter of reward, the matter of *good* applied to *one* particular purpose ;—matter of satis-faction, the matter of good applied to *another* particular purpose.

3. In political economy—matter of wealth and its modification ; viz. the matter of *subsistance,* and the matter of *opulence* or *abundance* ; each of these being neither more nor less than so many modifications of the matter of *wealth* ; and in so far as, through the medium of exchange, inter-convertibility as between them has place, with no other difference than what corresponds to the difference in the purposes to which that common matter comes to be applied.

Correctness, completeness, and consistency of the views taken of these large portions of the field of thought and

[1] *Ibid.,*, p. 290.   [2] See above, pp. cvii ff.

action—conciseness in the sketches made or to be made of them :—such are the desirable effects which this locution presented itself as capable of contributing in large proportion to the production of.

By this means, for the first time, were brought to view several analogies, which have been found of great use in practice—a clearer, as well as a more comprehensive view of all these objects having thereby been given, than in the nature of the case could, or can have been given by any other means.

The matter of *good*, as to one-half of it—one of the two modifications of which it is composed, viz. the negative—being the same as the matter of *evil*; one and the same object, viz. pain, having by its presence the effect of evil, by its absence or removal the effect of good : the matter of being good being, in its positive modification, composed of pleasures, and their respective causes—in its negative modification or form, of exemptions, *i.e.* exemptions from pain, and their respective causes.

In like manner, the matter of *evil* being as to one-half of it—as to one of the two portions of which it is composed, viz. the negative—the same thing as the matter of good, one and the same object, viz. pleasure, having by its presence the effect of good, by its *absence*, when considered as the result of loss, the effect of *evil* : the matter of evil being, in its positive form, composed of pains, and their respective causes—in its negative form, of losses corresponding to the different species of pleasure capable of being acquired and possessed, or lost, and their respective causes.

From this correspondency and interconvertibility, a practical result—in the hands of whosoever is able and willing to turn the observation to advantage—is the prevention of excess and waste in the application of both of these portions.

A position which by this means is placed in the clearest and strongest point of view, is—that by whatsoever is done in any shape, in and by the exercise of the powers of government, is so much certain evil done, that good may come.

Though the matter of reward, and the matter of satisfaction (viz. for injuries sustained) are in themselves so much of the matter of good, yet it is only by coercion, and that in a quantity proportioned to the extent to which that coercion is applied, that the matter of good thus applied can be extracted.

[When,] on the score of and in compensation for injury

sustained, the matter of good is, in the character of matter of satisfaction, extracted from the author of the injury, it operates, in and by the whole amount of it, in the character of punishment, on the person from whom it is extracted : and whatsoever may be the quantity of punishment inflicted in this shape, in that same proportion is the demand for punishment satisfied ; and whatsoever may be the amount of it in this shape, by so much less is the demand, if any, that remains for it in any other.

Operating in any such way as to produce, on the part of the party operated upon, an act or course of conduct adverse in any way upon the whole to the interest of the community in question—*e.g.* a particular class or district or other division of the political state, the whole of the political state in question, or mankind at large—the matter of good and evil becomes the matter of corruption.

It may either be the matter of *good* or the matter of *evil* : but it is the matter of good that most frequently presents itself in that character." [1]

In emphasizing the need for a new linguistic method, Bentham refers with admiration to the progress of Chemistry made possible by Lavoisier's improvements in its nomenclature.

" Not less extensive than just was the tribute of admiration and applause bestowed upon that illustrious man, and the no less illustrious partner of his bed, for that rich product of their conjoint labours in that branch of art and science.—Think of what chemistry was before that time—think of what it has become since !

Think of the plight that a natural history and natural philosophy would have been in, had a law of the public-opinion tribunal been in force, interdicting the addition of any terms belonging to these branches of art and science, to the stock in use at the time of Lord Bacon. But the employment of the terms then in use in the field of natural history and natural philosophy, is not more incompatible with the attainment and communication of true and useful knowledge in that field, than the employment of the terms now in use in the field of jurisprudence is with the attainment and communication of the conceptions and opinions necessary to the attainment of the only legitimate and defensible ends of government and legislation." [2]

[1] *Works*, Vol. III, pp. 287–8.
[2] *Nomography*, Chapter VII (*Works*, Vol. III, p. 273).

But the prospect of reform, however beneficial, is sufficiently remote. " What if, in this way and by these means, the import of all words, especially of all words belonging to the field of Ethics, including the field of Politics and therein the field of Political Religion, should one day become fixed ? What a source of perplexity, of error, of discord, and even of bloodshed, would be dried up ! Towards a consummation thus devoutly to be wished, there does seem to be a natural tendency. But, ere this auspicious tendency shall have been perfected into effect, how many centuries, not to say tens of centuries, must have passed away ? " [1]

THE SAD CASE OF MR. BEARDMORE

Finally, we must not overlook the effect of the enlightenment which might be derived by the public from a new approach to language. Is there not a risk of its proving what today would be termed ' mischievous ' by the elect ? " In the eyes of a class of persons, nor that an inconsiderable one, which always has existed nor will ever cease to exist, Religion, not only in the Church of England form, but in every form, is seen hanging on a thread—a thread which, by the blast of this or that speech or by the flutter of this or that pamphlet, is in continual danger of being cut ; while, without the support of their arm, the power of the Almighty is in continual danger of being overborne, his intentions defeated, his promises violated. To those to whom the promises of their God afford not any sufficient assurance, it were not to be expected that any firmer assurance should be afforded by any human promises." [2]

But, it may be asked, if in spite of all this intensive ratiocination there are to be yet other wars to end war, and the pious are still to be left more or less in the places in which they are found, what, apart from the diffusion of Truth, can be the advantage of educational reform ?

[1] *Works*, Vol. VIII, pp. 106–7.   [2] *Ibid.*, p. 42.

To such a question Bentham has a ready and characteristic answer. He was deeply interested in the prognosis
of a disease characterized by restlessness in retirement ;
a disease resulting from insufficient intellectual stimulus
in youth, maturity, and middle age ; a disease for which
modern methods of nomenclature would seem to indicate
the appellative, *Beardmore's Blues.*

> " For this sort of uneasy sensation, to which everywhere
> the human mind is exposed, the English language (in
> general, so much more copious than the French) affords no
> single-worded appellative. The word *ennui* expresses the
> species of uneasiness ; *désoeuvrement,* another word for
> which the English language furnishes no equivalent, ex-
> presses the cause of the uneasiness. Ennui is the state of
> uneasiness, felt by him whose mind unoccupied, but without
> reproach, is on the look out for pleasure—pleasure in some
> one or more of all shapes—and beholds at the time no
> source which promises to afford it : désoeuvrement is the
> state in which the mind, seeing before it nothing to be done,
> nothing in the shape of business or amusement which pro-
> mises either security against pain or possession of pleasure,
> is left a prey to the sort of uneasiness just designated." [1]

To this pain of ennui, which afflicts the man of industry
only towards the end of his career, " the man of hereditary
opulence stands exposed throughout the whole course of
it. It is the endemical disease that hovers over the
couch of him whose mind, though encompassed with the
elements of felicity in the richest profusion, allows them,
by neglecting them, to play a comparatively passive part.
From uneasiness of this sort, the mind of him who has
cultivated no more than a single branch of art or science,
possesses a rarely insufficient policy of insurance." And
in order to recommend his remedy—the cultivation of
the intellectual garden in general, and of the linguistic
and fictional in particular—Bentham treats us to the sad
story of one of the victims of its neglect,[2] as revealed in
the *Gentleman's Magazine* for February 1814 :—

[1] *Ibid.*, p. 8.
[2] *Ibid.*, pp. 8–9. In the first edition of the *Chrestomathia* the obituary
is taken from another source.

k

"𝔇𝔦𝔢𝔡, Feb. 13, of a gradual decline, after having passed his grand climacteric with less visitation from indisposition of mind or body than happens to mankind in general, at his house in Owen's Row, Islington ; calm from philosophical considerations, and resigned upon truly Christian principles ; beloved, esteemed, and regretted by all who knew his worth, John Beardmore, Esq., formerly of the great porter-brewing firm of Calvert and Co., in Redcross Street, London. A stronger evidence of the fallaciousness of human joys, and of the advantages resulting from honest employment, can scarcely be pointed out than the life, the illness, and the death of this good man exhibited. Mr. Beardmore was born in dependent circumstances, and of humble parentage, in the country. His constitution, naturally sound, was hardened by exercise ; his frame of body, naturally athletic, was braced by temperance ; his mind, naturally capacious, owed little to regular education. The theatre of life was his school and university, and in it he passed through all his degrees with increasing honours. For many years after his residence in London, Mr. Beardmore acted as a clerk in the brewery in which he finally became a distinguished partner. When it was deemed proper to transfer the concern from Redcross Street, and to consolidate it with that in Campion Lane, Upper Thames Street, Mr. Beardmore withdrew himself entirely from business, and retired to one of the houses which his brother William had left him at Islington, by will at his decease, some years before. From inclination active, and from habit indefatigably industrious, he had hitherto commanded such an exuberant flow of good spirits as made him the object of general remark among friends, whom his kindness and vivacity delighted. Early rising contributed much to the support of this happy and equable temperament. He preserved a memory richly stored with pleasant anecdotes, sprightly remarks, and useful information on a great variety of topics, derived not from books, but from living studies. He had acquired also a lively, popular facility of singing easy songs, to which a tuneful voice gave tolerable execution. For dull sedentary investigations of abstract science ; for . . . classical learning, or moral and theological knowledge, the gay, the heartsome John Beardmore, felt no wish, and avowed no relish. He was, as he often proudly declared, a ' true-born Englishman '. Humane by natural feelings, and charitable by a sense of religious duty, he passed through a life of honourable toil with a light heart. . . . From the fatal hour in which he quitted business, however, he grew insensibly more and more the victim of listlessness and ennui. With high animal spirits; with a mind still active, and a body still robust; with confirmed health, independent property, an amiable wife, a plentiful table, and a social neighbourhood, Mr. Beardmore was no longer 'at home' in his own house. The mainspring of action was now stopped. In all his pleasures, in all his engagements, for the day, for the week, or for the month, he was conscious of a vacuum, that, alas! his want of intellectual resources rendered him utterly unable to supply; he experienced now, perhaps for the first time, that intolerable *taedium vitae*, which, like hope deferred, 'maketh the heart sick'. The result is soon told. Long did he bear up against the clouds that obscured his little horizon of domestic repose; at times, indeed, transient flashes of cheerfulness still gleamed athwart the gathering gloom; but the intervals between these bright seasons grew longer, and even their short duration lessened. Want of customary application brought on relaxation of activity; want of exercise brought on langour of body and depression of spirits; a train of evils ensued, comprising loss of appetite, nervous affections, debility mental and corporeal, despondency, sleeplessness, decay of nature, difficulty of respiration, weariness, pain and death."

CONCLUSION

MUCH of Bentham's best work on language was done in the year of Waterloo ; all of it during the Napoleonic wars and the distressful years which followed. " In the storm of that eventful period ", wrote his Editor, the year Queen Victoria ascended her stable throne, " the small still voice of one weighing the meaning of words used was not heeded ".[1] Even less was it heeded when the storm had died down, however much the reformers may have profited by its practical suggestions. Yet as Bentham put it :—

> " In a play or a novel, an improper word is but a word : and the impropriety, whether noticed or not, is attended with no consequences. In a body of laws—especially of laws given as constitutional and fundamental ones—an improper word would be a national calamity : and civil war may be the consequence of it. Out of one foolish word may start a thousand daggers."

What, finally, are we, looking back on the controversies of a century, to think of this Theory of Fictions ? From the material here selected it is clear that he applied it consistently throughout his life and in all his writings ; that it arose from a series of personal adventures in the world of verbal illusion which began with the Word-magic of childhood and continued till the lonely clarity of his dotage found him writing for posterity alone ; and that both the formulation and the application were original to him and have been misunderstood by the posterity for whom he wrote no less than by his contemporaries.

Today a Philosophy of As-if dominates scientific thought —without the sound linguistic basis which Bentham gave it ; and an ingenious Logic of ' incomplete symbols ' has partly obscured the linguistic issues which he approached at the level of everyday practice. It is possible, as we have seen, to give a formal translation of part of his

[1] Introduction to Bentham's *Works*, Vol. I, p. 43.

doctrine in terms which a modern logician can recognize, if not as satisfactory, at least as intelligible. But it is doubtful what has been achieved thereby ; for the ' Logic ' of which the theory of ' incomplete symbols ' forms part is built on a verbal foundation as insecure as that of the lawyers whose ' rights ', the psychologists whose ' faculties ', the physicists whose ' qualities ' Bentham was at such pains to dethrone.

It was because it dissolved so much logical and metaphysical theory into Grammar on the one hand and Psycho-physiology on the other that the Theory of Fictions seemed to Bentham a powerful Instrument. But the dissolution and the disillusion in other fields than those which he so intensively cultivated have scarcely begun.[1]

If the Theory of Linguistic Fictions is to take the place of Philosophy, as he undoubtedly intended that it should, it must be developed as the nucleus of a complete theory of symbolism in every branch of human thought ; from the first mnemic reaction, through all forms of perception, interpretation, and eidetic projection, to the final achievements of grammatical accessories, abbreviations, and condensations, in notations as yet unborn. No wonder Bentham found the days too short and the nights too precious for sleep :—" O that I could decompose myself like a polypus. Could I make half a dozen selfs, I have work for all ".

---

[1] This Introduction has been reprinted as it appeared in 1932, with the correction of a few misprints. It is unlikely that any of the authors referred to on pp. xlvii–lii would now (June 1950) subscribe to the views they then held, or that the composite account of " incomplete symbols " there offered would be accepted as adequate by any contemporary analyst. The reader may gather something of more recent attempts to cultivate alternative fields from a study of M. Cornforth, *Science versus Idealism*, pp. 167–220 (1946), Yehoshua Bar-Hillel, " Analysis of ' Correct ' Language " (*Mind*, October, 1946), and A. C. Lloyd, " Empiricism, Sense Data and Scientific Languages " (*Mind*, January 1950). For contemporary contributions on the legal side, see the writer's second edition (1950) of Bentham's *Theory of Legislation*, pp. xxxix and 472.

NOTE

ON BENTHAM'S METHOD OF COMPOSITION

THE circumstances in which Bentham's MSS. were prepared require a few words of explanation.

His first printed contribution appeared when he was aged twenty-three, in the form of a letter to the *Gazetteer*. " Some will say it was better than anything I write now ", he said in later years. " I had not then invented any part of my new lingo." In those days, he adds, " composition was inconceivably difficult. I often commenced a sentence which I could not complete. I began to write fragments on blotting paper, and left them to be filled thereafter in happier vein. By hard labour, I subjugated difficulties ; and my example will show what hard labour will accomplish. I should be glad to see my earliest placed side by side with the latest compositions of my life. I used to put scraps into drawers, so that I could tumble them over and over ; to marginalize and make notes on cards, which I could shuffle about : but, at last, I took to arranging my thoughts. I had been in the habit of shifting my papers from shelf to shelf ; and well remember, when at Bowood, where I stayed two or three months at a time, that Lord Shelburne took Minister Pitt to see the strange way in which I worked, and arranged the many details of a complicated subject." [1]

By his ' new lingo ' Bentham meant the style which he adopted after the age of sixty, for the exposition of subjects in which clarity was more important than literary convention. Most of what he produced before the year 1808 and intended for publication is written in the best traditions of eighteenth century prose. Much of it is obviously the work of a stylist who has few equals in the history of English literature.

In 1810, he had been publishing for nearly forty years, his eyesight was beginning to give trouble, and though he was to continue his labours unremittingly for more than two decades he felt that Time was against him. There were certain major tasks, requiring concentration and experience, that only he—with the achievement of two lifetimes already behind him—was likely to face. The first was to develop the principles of Codification so that posterity might be able to make practical use of them ; the second was to give the Theory of Fictions a solid foundation in linguistic psychology.

---

[1] *Works*, Vol. X, p. 68. In the writer's *Jeremy Bentham, 1832–2032* (Appendices I and XII), the material in question is reproduced.

" It was his opinion ", says Burton, " that he would be occupied more profitably for mankind in keeping his mind constantly employed in that occupation to which it was supereminently fitted, and in which it seemed to find its chief enjoyment— ratiocination. He thought that while he lived in the possession of this faculty, he should give as much of the results of it to the world, as he could accomplish by a life of constant labour, temperance, and regularity ; and he left it to others to shape and adapt to use the fabric of thought which thus came out continuously from the manufactory of his brain. Laying his subject before him for the day, he thought on, and set down his thoughts in page after page of MS. To the sheets so filled he gave titles, marginal rubrics, and other facilities for reference, and then he set them aside in his repositories, never touching or seeing them again."

Moreover, throughout his life, unless he was writing deliberately with a view to publication, he adopted the unusual practice of starting afresh whenever he resumed the consideration of any subject from a different angle, or any new subdivision of a dichotomous table ; so that instead of removing an ambiguity or polishing a loose sentence he traverses the same ground, often in some detail, with whatever additions are suggested by the new approach. The whole mass of papers, with all their repetitions, was then handed to some editorial collaborator to be prepared for the press. In this way Dumont was able to make a readable synthesis of *The Theory of Legislation* (much of which, partly in order to prevent his thoughts from running in customary verbal grooves, Bentham had jotted down in French), and J. S. Mill a systematic treatise out of *The Rationale of Judicial Evidence*. But the material on Linguistic Psychology occupied a peculiar position, and its importance was not obvious to his younger collaborators. Not only was the subject matter somewhat difficult and outside the range of ordinary inquiry, but the entire technological approach was a century ahead of its time. His nephew George Bentham made a very creditable attempt to cope with such parts of the notes on Logic (twelve years after they were written) as could be related to contemporary doctrine, with elaborations of his own which evoked generous praise from the old man (Bentham was then in his eightieth year). He dealt briefly with the classificatory notes on Fictions (see Appendix B) ; but it was not till Bentham had been dead for more than a decade that the MSS. were printed by Bowring as he found them— though in such a form that their neglect by all subsequent writers is not altogether surprising.

In particular, Bentham's method of punctuation leaves much to be desired. Sometimes, especially in his first drafts, he seems to have punctuated as he breathed, but if so, his breathing was highly irregular ; and in any case the eighteenth century had a method of signalling by commas which is today no longer in vogue. Colons, semi-colons, and parentheses are interspersed with disturbing and unsystematic profusion. Such regularization

as has been attempted in these pages (with the occasional insertion
of a bracket, or the omission of a dash) will it is hoped render
their perusal less irksome to the modern eye.

A few general reference headings have been inserted to assist
the reader in identifying the main divisions—the sources of
which are in every case given in footnotes to the headings
themselves.

Otherwise, any minor editorial additions have been enclosed
in square brackets, and all omissions are indicated . . . as they
occur.

The printed text itself was transcribed by those responsible
for the official edition of Bentham's posthumous writings in a
manner far from satisfactory if judged by modern standards.
Fortunately the sense of the original has seldom been distorted.
Where, for example, Bentham writes that fictitious qualities (of
the second order) are " mere chimeras, mere creatures of the
imagination—mere nonentities ", the third ' mere ' is arbitrarily
omitted.[1] Where Bentham says, " Under yon tree, in that
hollow in the ground, lies an apple ", we find the text misprinted
' on the ground '. But thirteen lines lower, where the MS. reads :
" In this way it is, that we learn the import of this same word
in with reference to our two minds :—in a word, with reference
to *mind* in general. By no other means could we have learned
it "—the printed text [2] appears as follows :

> " In this way it is, that we learn the import of this same
> word *in* with reference to our two minds. In a word, with
> reference to *mind* in general, by no other means could we
> have learned it."

Here the careless alterations are at least confusing ; and
wherever doubt seemed justified, the original has been consulted.

[1] *Works*, Vol. VIII, p. 211.   [2] *Ibid.*, p. 329.

THE THEORY OF FICTIONS

BY

JEREMY BENTHAM

CONTENTS

PART I

GENERAL OUTLINE

3

PART II

SPECIAL PROBLEMS

APPENDIX A

APPENDIX B

The Theory of Fictions

Part I
GENERAL OUTLINE

I.—LINGUISTIC FICTIONS

A. Classification of Entities[1]

1. *Division of Entities*

An entity is a denomination in the import of which every subject matter of discourse, for the designation of which the grammatical part of speech called a noun-substantive is employed may be comprised.

Entities may be distinguished into *perceptible* and *inferential*.

An entity, whether perceptible or inferential, is either real or fictitious.

2. *Of Perceptible Entities*

A *perceptible* entity is every entity the existence of which is made known to human beings by the immediate testimony of their senses, without reasoning, *i.e.* without reflection. A perceptible real entity is, in one word, a body.[2]

The name *body* is the name of the genus generalissimum of that class of real entities. Under this genus generalissimum, a system of divisions which has for its limit the

---

[1] [*Works*, Vol. VIII, pp. 195–199.]
[2] The name *substance* has, by the logicians of former times, been used to comprise perceptible and inferential real entities : Souls, God, Angels, Devils have been designated by them by the appellation *substance*.

aggregate of all distinguishable individual bodies, may be pursued through as many stages as are found conducive to the purposes of discourse ; at any such stage, and at any number of such stages, the mode of division may be bifurcate[1] and exhaustive, *i.e.* all-comprehensive.

The division according to which bodies are spoken of as subjects of one or other of the three physical kingdoms, viz. animal, vegetable, and mineral, is a *trifurcate* division. By substituting to this one stage of division, two stages, each of them bifurcate, the division may be rendered, or rather shown to be, exhaustive ; as thus—

A body is either endued with life, or not endued with life.

A body endued with life, is either endued with sensitive life, or with life not sensitive.

A body endued with sensitive life, is an animal ; a body endued with a life not sensitive, is a vegetable ; a body not endued with life, is a mineral.

3. *Of Inferential Entities*

An *inferential* entity which, in these times at least, is not made known to human beings in general, by the testimony of sense, but of the existence of which the persuasion is produced by reflection—is inferred from a chain of reasoning.

An inferential entity is either, 1. human ; or, 2. super-human.

1. A human inferential entity is the soul considered as existing in a state of separation from the body.

Of a human soul, existing in a state of separation from the body, no man living will, it is believed, be found ready to aver himself to have had perception of any individual example ; or, at any rate, no man who, upon due and apposite interrogation, would be able to obtain credence.

---

[1] The use of the exhaustive mode of division, as contradistinguished from that which is not exhaustive, *i.e.* all-comprehensive, is to show that your conception and comprehension of the subject, in so far as the particulars comprehended in it are in view, is complete.

Considered as existing and visiting any part of our earth in a state of separation from the body, a human soul would be a ghost : and, at this time of day, *custom* scarcely does, *fashion* certainly does not command us to believe in ghosts.

Of this description of beings, the reality not being, in any instance, attested by *perception*, cannot therefore be considered any otherwise than as a matter of inference.[1]

2. A superhuman entity is either supreme or subordinate.

The supreme, superhuman, inferential entity is God : sanctioned by revelation ; sanctioned by the religion of Jesus, as delivered by the apostle Paul, is the proposition that no man has seen God at any time. If this proposition be correct, God not being consistently with the imperfection of the human senses capable of being referred to the class of perceptible real entities, cannot, in consequence of the imperfection under which human reason labours, cannot, any more than the soul of man considered as existing in a separate state, be referred by it to any other class than that of inferential real entities as above described.[2]

A subordinate superhuman entity is either *good* or *bad*. A good subordinate superhuman inferential entity is an angel ; a bad superhuman inferential entity is a devil.

By the learner as well as by the teacher of logic, all these

---

[1] Should there be any person in whose view the soul of man, considered in a state of separation from the body, should present itself as not capable of being, with propriety, aggregated to the class of real entities, to every such person, the class to which it belongs would naturally be that of fictitious entities ; in which case it would probably be considered as being that whole of which so many other psychical entities, none of which have ever been considered any otherwise than fictitious—such as the understanding, and the will, the perceptive faculty, the memory and the imagination—are so many parts.

[2] Should there be any person who, incapable of drawing those inferences by which the Creator and Preserver of all other entities is referred to the class of real ones, should refuse to him a place in that class, the class to which that person would find himself, in a manner, compelled to refer that invisible and mysterious being would be, not as in the case of the human soul to that of fictitious entities, but that of non-entities. [For Bentham's own views on Theism, see *The Memoirs of John Quincy Adams*, under date June 8, 1817.]

A

subjects of Ontology may, without much detriment, it is believed, to any other useful art, or any other useful science, be left in the places in which they are found.

4. *Of Real Entities*

A real entity is an entity to which, on the occasion and for the purpose of discourse, existence is really meant to be ascribed.

Under the head of perceptible real entities may be placed, without difficulty, individual perceptions of all sorts :[1] the impressions produced in groups by the application of sensible objects to the organs of sense : the ideas brought to view by the recollection of those same objects ; the new ideas produced under the influence of the imagination, by the decomposition and recomposition of those groups :—to none of these can the character, the denomination, of real entities be refused.

Faculties, powers of the mind, dispositions : all these are unreal ; all these are but so many fictitious entities. When a view of them comes to be given, it will be seen how perfectly distinguishable, among psychical entities, are those which are recognized in the character of real, from those which are here referred to the class of fictitious entities.

To some it may seem matter of doubt whether, to a perception of any kind, the appellation of a real entity can, with propriety, be applied.

Certain it is that it cannot, if either *solidity* or *permanence* be regarded as a quality belonging to the essence of reality.

But in neither of these instances can, it is believed, any sufficient or just reason be assigned, why the field of reality should be regarded as confined within the limits which, on that supposition, would be applied to it.

Whatsoever title an object belonging to the class of

---

[1] Pathematic, Apathematic, to one or other of these denominations may all imaginable sorts of perceptions be referred. *Pathematic*, viz. such as either themselves consist of or are accompanied by pleasure or pain ; *Apathematic*, such as have not any such accompaniment in any shape.

bodies may be considered as possessing to the attribute of reality, *i.e.* of existence, every object belonging to the class of *perceptions* will be found to possess, in still higher degree, a title established by more immediate evidence : it is only by the evidence afforded by perceptions that the reality of a body of any kind can be established.

Of *Ideas* our perception is still more direct and immediate than that which we have of corporeal substances : of their existence our persuasion is more necessary and irresistible than that which we have of the existence of corporeal substances.

Speaking of Entities, ideas might perhaps accordingly be spoken of as the *sole perceptible ones*, substances, those of the corporeal class, being, with reference, and in contradiction to them, no other than *inferential* ones.

But if substances themselves be the subject of the division, and for the designation of the two branches of the division the words *perceptible* and *inferential* be employed, it is to corporeal substances that the characteristic and differential attribute, perceptible, cannot but be applied : the term *inferential* being thereupon employed for the designation of incorporeal ones.

The more correct and complete the consideration bestowed, the more clearly will it be perceived, that from the existence of perceptions, viz. of sensible ones, the inference whereby the existence of corporeal entities, viz. the bodies from which these perceptions are respectively deduced, is much stronger, more necessary, and more irresistible, than the inference whereby the existence of incorporeal entities is inferred from the existence of perceptible entities, alias corporeal substances, alias bodies.

Suppose the non-existence of corporeal substances, of any hard corporeal substance that stands opposite to you, make this supposition, and as soon as you have made it, act upon it : pain, the perception of pain, will at once bear witness against you ; and that by your punishment, your condign punishment. Suppose the non-existence of any inferential incorporeal substances, of any one of them, or of all of them, and the supposition made, act upon it accordingly : be the supposition conformable or not conformable to the truth of the case, at any rate no such immediate counter-evidence, no such immediate punishment will follow.[1]

5. *Of Fictitious Entities*

A fictitious entity is an entity to which, though by the grammatical form of the discourse employed in speaking of it, existence be ascribed, yet in truth and reality existence is not meant to be ascribed.

Every noun-substantive which is not the name of a real entity, perceptible or inferential, is the name of a fictitious entity.

Every fictitious entity bears some relation to some real entity, and can no otherwise be understood than in so far as that relation is perceived—a conception of that relation is obtained.

Reckoning from the real entity to which it bears relation, a fictitious entity may be styled a fictitious entity of the first remove, a fictitious entity of the second remove, and so on.

A fictitious entity of the first remove is a fictitious entity, a conception of which may be obtained by the consideration of the relation borne by it to a real entity, without need of considering the relation borne by it to any other fictitious entity.

---

[1] In the works of the authors who now (anno 1813) are in vogue, not a few are the notions of which the appearance will, at this time of day, be apt to excite a sensation of surprise in an unexperienced, and, one day perhaps, even in an experienced mind.

Of this number are (1) The denial of the existence of bodies, (2) The denial of the existence of general or abstract ideas.

Of these kindred paradoxes—for such, in some sort, they will be found to be—who were the first persons by whom they were respectively broached is more than I recollect, if so it be that I ever knew ; nor, supposing it attainable, would the trouble of the search be paid for by the value of the thing found.

Of those by whom the notion of the non-existence of matter, including the several bodies that present themselves to our senses, is maintained, Bishop Berkeley, if not the first in point of time, is, at any rate, the most illustrious partisan.

A fictitious entity of the second remove is a fictitious entity, for obtaining a conception of which it is necessary to take into consideration some fictitious entity of the first remove.

Considered at any two contiguous points of time, every real entity is either in motion or at rest.

Now, when a real entity is said to be at rest, it is said to be so with reference to some other particular real entity or aggregate of real entities ; for so far as any part of the system of the universe is perceived by us, we at all times perceive it not to be at rest. Such, at least, is the case not only with the bodies called planets, but with one or more of the bodies called fixed stars ; and, by analogy, we infer this to be the case with all the rest.

This premised, considered with reference to any two contiguous points of time past, every perceptible real entity was, during that time, either in motion or not in motion ; if not in motion, it was at rest.

Here, then, we have two correspondent and opposite fictitious entities of the first remove, viz. a motion and a rest.

A motion is a mode of speech commonly employed ; *a rest* is a mode of speech not so commonly employed.

To be spoken of at all, every fictitious entity must be spoken of as if it were real. This, it will be seen, is the case with the above-mentioned pair of fictitious entities of the first remove.

A body is said to be in motion. This, taken in the literal sense, is as much as to say—Here is a larger body, called a motion ; in this larger body, the other body, namely, the really existing body, is contained.

So in regard to rest. To say this body is at rest is as much as to say—Here is a body, and it will naturally be supposed a fixed body, and here is another body, meaning the real existing body, which is *at* that first-mentioned body, *i.e.* attached to it, as if the fictitious body were a stake, and the real body a beast tied to it.

An instance of a fictitious entity of the second remove

is a quality. There are qualities that are qualities of real entities ; there are qualities that are qualities of the above-mentioned fictitious entities of the first remove. For example, of motion, rectilinearity, curvilinearity, slowness, quickness, and so on.[1]

6. *Uses of this Distinction between Names of Real and Names of Fictitious Entities*

These uses are, 1. Attaching, in the only way in which they can be attached, clear ideas to the several all-comprehensive and léading terms in question. 2. Obviating and excluding the multitudinous errors and disputes of which the want of such clear ideas has been the source : disputes, which, in many instances, have not terminated in words, but through words have produced antipathy, and through antipathy, war with all its miseries.

Fictitious entity, says some one—of such a locution where can be the sense or use ? By the word *entity* cannot but be represented something that has existence ; apply to the same subject the adjunct *fictitious*, the effect is to give instruction that it has not any existence. This, then, is a contradiction in terms, a species of locution from which, in proportion as it has any employment, confusion, and that alone, cannot but be the effect.

Entities are either real or fictitious, what can that mean ? What but that of entities there are two species or sorts : viz. one which is itself, and another which is neither itself nor anything else ? Instead of fictitious entity, or as synonymous with fictitious entity, why not here say, *non-entity* ?

Answer.—Altogether inevitable will this seeming contradiction be found. The root of it is in the nature of language : that instrument without which, though of

---

[1] The manuscript of this section finishes at this point, but the marginal note in pencil is—" Go on, bring to view the several other fictitious entities of the second remove, those of the third remove, if any, and so on."

itself it be nothing, nothing can be said, and scarcely can anything be done.

Of the nature of that instrument, of the various forms under which it has been seen to present itself among different tribes of men, of the indispensable parts (*i.e.* parts of speech) which may be seen to belong to it under every one of those forms, actual or possible, of the qualities desirable on the part of the collection of signs of which, under all these several forms, it is composed :—under all these several heads, sketches will be endeavoured to be given in another place.[1]

All this while, antecedently to the stage at which these topics will present themselves, use is however making, as it could not but be made, of this same instrument. At that future stage, it will not only be the *instrument*, but the *subject* also of inquiry : at present and until then, employing it in the character of an instrument, we must be content to take it in hand, and make use of it, in the state in which we find it.

In like manner, the several operations, which by the help of language, and under the direction of logic, are performed by human minds upon language and thereby upon minds—such as distinction, division, definition, and the several other modes of exposition, including those of methodization—must be performed at and from the very outset of a work of logic, antecedently to the stage at which the task of examining into their nature and origination will be entered upon and come to be performed.

To language, then—to language alone—it is, that fictitious entities owe their existence ; their impossible, yet indispensable, existence.[2]

In language, the words which present themselves, and are employed in the character of *names*, are, some of them, names of real entities ; others, names of fictitious entities : and to one or other of these classes may all

---

[1] [*Works*, Vol. VIII, pp. 295 ff.]

[2] The division of entities into real and fictitious is more properly the division of names into *names* of real and *names* of fictitious entities.

words which are employed in the character of *names* be referred.

What will, moreover, be seen is, that the Fiction—the mode of representation by which the fictitious entities thus created, in so far as fictitious entities can be created, are dressed up in the garb, and placed upon the level, of real ones—is a contrivance but for which language, or, at any rate, language in any form superior to that of the language of the brute creation, could not have existence.

And now, perhaps, may be seen the difference between a *fictitious entity* and a *non-entity* ; or, to speak more strictly, the difference between the import of the two words—a difference such, that when, with propriety and use, the one is, the other cannot be employed.

In the house designated by such a number (naming it), in such a street, in such a town, lives a being called the Devil, having a head, body, and limbs, like a man's, horns like a goat's, wings like a bat's, and a tail like a monkey's. Suppose this assertion made, the observation naturally might be, that the Devil, as thus described, is a non-entity. The averment made of it is, that an object of that description really exists. Of that averment, if seriously made, the object or end in view cannot but be to produce in the minds to which communication is thus made, a serious persuasion of the existence of an object conformable to the description thus expressed.

Thus much concerning a non-entity. Very different is the notion here meant to be presented by the term fictitious entity.

By this term is here meant to be designated one of those sorts of objects which in every language must, for the purpose of discourse, be spoken of as existing—be spoken of in the like manner as those objects which really have existence, and to which existence is seriously meant to be ascribed, are spoken of ; but without any such danger as that of producing any such persuasion as that of their possessing, each for itself, any separate, or strictly speaking, any real existence.

Take, for instances, the words *motion, relation, faculty, power*, and the like.

Real entities being the objects for the designation of which, in the first place, at the earliest stage of human intercourse, and in virtue of the most urgent necessity, words, in the character of names, were employed—between the idea of a name and that of the reality of the object to which it was applied, an association being thus formed, from a connexion thus intimate, sprung a very natural propensity, viz. that of attributing reality to every object thus designated ; in a word, of ascribing reality to the objects designated by words, which, upon due examination, would be found to be nothing but so many names of so many fictitious entities.

To distinguish them from those fictitious entities, which, so long as language is in use among human beings, never can be spared, *fabulous* may be the name employed for the designation of the other class of *unreal* entities.

Of fictitious entities, whatsoever is predicated is not, consistently with strict truth, predicated (it then appears) of anything but their respective names.

But forasmuch as by reason of its length and compoundedness, the use of the compound denomination, *name of a fictitious entity*, would frequently be found attended with inconvenience ; for the avoidance of this inconvenience, instead of this long denomination, the less long, though, unhappily, still compound denomination, fictitious entity, will commonly, after the above warning, be employed.

Of nothing that has place, or passes, in our minds can we give any account, any otherwise than by speaking of it as if it were a portion of space, with portions of matter, some of them at rest, others moving in it. Of nothing, therefore, that has place, or passes in our mind, can we speak, or so much as think, otherwise than in the way of *Fiction*. To this word Fiction we must not attach either those sentiments of pleasure, or those sentiments of displeasure, which, with so much propriety, attach themselves to it on the occasion in which it is most commonly in use. Very different in respect of purpose and necessity, very different is this logical species of Fiction from the poetical and political ; very different the Fiction of the Logician from the Fictions of poets, priests, and lawyers.

For their object and effect, the Fictions with which the Logician is conversant, without having been the author of them, have had neither more nor less than the carrying on of human converse ; such communication and interchange of thought as is capable of having place between man and man. The Fictions of the poet, whether in his character of historic fabulist or dramatic fabulist, putting or not putting the words of his discourse in metrical form, are pure of insincerity, and, neither for their object nor for their effect have anything but to amuse, unless it be in some cases to excite to action—to action in this or that particular direction for this or that particular purpose. By the priest and the lawyer, in whatsoever shape Fiction has been employed, it has had for its object or effect, or both, to deceive, and, by deception, to govern, and, by governing, to promote the interest, real or supposed, of the party addressing, at the expense of the party addressed. In the mind of all, Fiction, in the logical sense, has been the coin of necessity—in that of poets, of amusement—in that of the priest and the lawyer, of mischievous immorality in the shape of mischievous ambition ; and too often both priest and lawyer have framed or made in part this instrument.

B. Classification of Fictitious Entities[1]

1. *Names of Physical Fictitious Entities*

To this class belong all those entities which will be found included in Aristotle's list—included in his *Ten Predicaments*, the first excepted.

In the order in which he has placed and considered them, they stand as follows : 1. Substance. 2. Quantity. 3. Quality. 4. Relation. 5. Places. 6. Time. 7. Situation. 8. Possession. 9. Action. 10. Passion or Suffering.[2]

From this list of Aristotle's—the list of names of physical entities will, as here presented, be found to be in a considerable degree different : viz. in the first place, in respect of the particulars of which it is composed ; in the next place, in respect of the order in which they are brought to view. Of these differences the grounds will successively be brought to view as they arise.

1. *Quantity.* Quantity cannot exist without some substance of which it is the quantity. Of substance, no species, no individual can exist, without existing in some certain quantity.

2. *Quality.* Quality cannot exist without some substance of which it is the quality. Of substance, no species can exist without being of some quality ; of a multitude of qualities, of which the number is, in every instance, indeterminate, capable of receiving increase, and that to an indefinite degree, according to the purposes for which, and the occasions on which the several substances of which they are qualities, may come to be considered.

3. *Place.* Of place, the notion cannot be entertained

---

[1] [*Works*, Vol. VIII, pp. 199–211.]
[2] The enumeration is left blank in the original. Aristotle's own arrangement is filled in, in the printing, and not that of Sanderson, which the author generally employed as the text-book of the Aristotelian system.—*Ed.* [Ed.=editorial note in Bowring's edition.]

without the notion of some substance considered as *placed*, or capable of existing, or, as we say, being *placed* in it.

Place may be considered as *absolute* or relative. Supposing but one substance in existence, that substance would be in some place ; that place would be absolute place ; relative place there could be none. Suppose two substances—then, in addition to its own absolute place, each substance would have a *relative* place, a place constituted by the position occupied by it in relation to the other.

Of no individual substance is any notion commonly entertained without some notion of a place—a relative place as being occupied by it.

The place considered as occupied by an individual substance is different, according to the purpose for which, and the occasion on which, the substance is taken into consideration.

Expressive of the notion of place, in their original, physical, archetypal signification, are the several words termed prepositions of place and adverbs of place. These are—*In ; on,* or *upon ; under ; at ; above ; below ; round ; around ; out, out of ; from above ; from under ; from.*

4. *Time.* Time is, as it were, on an ulterior and double account, a fictitious entity ; its denominations so many names of fictitious entities.

Compared with substance, and, in particular, with body, place is, as hath been seen, a fictitious entity. Without some body *placed* in it, or considered as being capable of being placed in it, place would have no existence, or what, with reference to use, would amount to the same thing, there would be no purpose for which, no occasion on which, it could be considered as having existence.

But if, putting substance out of consideration, place be a Fiction, time is, so to speak, a still more fictitious Fiction, having nothing more substantial to lean upon than the Fiction of place.

To be capable of being spoken of, time itself must be,

cannot but be, spoken of as a modification of space. Witness the prepositions *in* and *at* : *in* such a portion of time—*at* such a portion of time ; *in* an hour—*at* 12 o'clock ; *in* such a year, month, day, *at* such an hour, *at* so many minutes after such an hour, *at* so many seconds after such a minute in such an hour.

Witness again, the common expressions, ' a short time ', ' a long time ', ' a space of time '.

By a line it is that every portion of time, every particular time, is conceived, represented, and spoken of ;— by a line, *i.e.* a body, of which the length alone, without breadth or depth, is considered.

5. *Motion.* 6. *Rest.* 7. *Action.* 8. *Passion.*

At every step the subject of consideration becomes more and more complicated.

Rest is the absence or negation of motion. Every body is either *in* motion or at rest. Here *place, i.e. relative space*, is still the archetype. Motion is a thing, an imaginary, an involuntarily imagined substance, *in* which the body is conceived as being placed. Rest a like body, *at* which the real body is considered as being placed.

In the idea of *motion* that of *time* is, moreover, involved ; and again, that of *place*—as being that in which the idea of time is, by the like necessity, involved.

In motion a body cannot have been but it must have been in two different places, at or in two different, which is as much as to say, in two successive portions of time.

For the space of time in question, *i.e.* for a portion of time composed of those same portions which were operative in the case of motion, the body has been at rest, in so far as in all that space or length of time it has not changed its place with reference to any others.

Taken in the aggregate, in so far as can be concluded, either from observation or from analogy in the way of inference, no body whatsoever is, or ever has been, or ever will be, absolutely in a state of rest, *i.e.* without being in motion with reference to some other body or bodies.

The earth which we inhabit is not at rest. The sun himself about which she moves is not at rest. The stars called *fixed*, being but so many suns, are themselves no more at rest than is he.

Considered as a *whole*, the parts of our earth are, as far as appears, with reference to one another, the greater part of them always at rest ; others, especially those near the surface, many of them occasionally *in* motion : and so in regard to the several separate bodies, consisting of such portions of the matter of which the earth is composed, as are detached and separate from one another, each of them having between itself and every other—with the exception of the base on which it stands, and upon which, by the principle of attraction under the several forms under which it operates, it is kept at that place—certain portions of intervening space.

Of such of them as are in a state of solidity, rest, relative rest, rest with relation to each other, in so far as they are in that state, is the naturally constant state. *In* motion they are not *put* but by some supervening accident operating from without. Of such of them as are in a state of fluidity, liquidity and gaseosity included, motion, relative motion is, in every instance, a natural state, exemplified to a greater or lesser extent, depending partly on the particular qualities of the several fluids, partly upon the accidents *ab extra* to which, individually taken, they happen to have been exposed.

In addition to the idea of motion, in the ideas of *action* and *passion*, the idea of causation or causality is involved. The body F is in motion :—of such motion, what is the cause ? Answer : The action of another body, the body S, which, by the influence or correspondent power which it possesses becomes productive of that effect.

In themselves the two fictitious entities, Action and Passion, are not only correspondent, but inseparable. No action without passion—no passion without action ;—no action on the one part without passion on the other.

In the case of action, and thereupon on the part of one

of two bodies, motion, perceptible motion :—on the part
of the other body, is relative motion, in every instance a
never failing consequence ?   To judge from analogy, the
probability seems to be in the affirmative.[1]

In so far as on the part of one of the two alone, any
motion is perceptible, on the part of the other, no motion
being perceptible, the one of which the motion is perceptible, is most commonly spoken of as the *agent*, the
other as the *patient* : a state of motion is the state in
which the former is said to be *in*, a state of passion the
state in which the other is said to be *in*.

9. *Relation.*   Under this head, such is its amplitude,
several of the others seem totally or partially to be included
—viz. 1. Quantity, all quantities bear some relation or
other to each other.   2. Quality.[2]

2. Absolute Fictitious Entities of the First Order
(Matter. Form. Quantity. Space)

No substance can exist but it must be itself *matter* ; be
of a certain determinate *form* ; be or exist in a certain
determinate *quantity* ; and, were there but one substance
in existence, all these three attributes would belong to it.

Matter, at first sight, may naturally enough be considered as exactly synonymous to the word *substance*.   It
may undoubtedly be with propriety employed instead of
substance on many of the occasions on which the word
substance may, with equal propriety, be employed.

But there are occasions on which, while substance may,
matter cannot, with propriety be employed.

By the word *substance*, substances incorporeal, as well
as corporeal, are wont to be designated ; the word matter
is wont to be employed to designa'e corporeal to the
exclusion of incorporeal substances.

On the other hand, neither are occasions wanting in

---

[1] 1. The earth and a projected stone.
   2. A larger and a lesser magnet.
   3. Liquids and gases.
[2] The MS. of this section here breaks off abruptly.—*Ed.*

which, while the word *matter* may, the word *substance* *cannot*, with propriety be employed.

Matter is wont to be employed in contradistinction to *form* ; and that, on occasions in which the word *substance* cannot, with propriety, be employed. Thus, in considering substance, any individual substance, consideration may be had of its matter, without any consideration had of its *form* ; and so *vice versa* of its *form* without its matter.

Thus it is, that, taken in that sense which is peculiar to it, the idea attached to the word *matter* cannot, by means of that word, be brought to view without bringing to view along with it the idea of another *entity* called form ; and this is the reason why, along with *form*, it has been considered as composing a group of entities distinct from the sort of entity for the designation of which the word substance has been employed.

The word *substance* is the name of a class of real entities, of the only class which has in it any corporeal entities.

The word *matter* is but the name of a class of fictitious entities, springing out of the sort of real entity distinguished by the word *substance*.

And so it is in regard to the word *form*.

The ideas respectively designated by these corresponding words are fractional results, produced from the decomposition of the word *substance*.

Every real physical entity, every corporeal substance, every sort of body has its matter and form ; and this its matter, and this its form are entities totally different from each other.

These names of entities possess, both of them, the characteristic properties of fictitious entities. It is by means of propositions designative of place, and, by that means, of a fictitious material image, that their images are connected with the name of the real entity substance.

In that substance exists such and such matter ; behold the matter of that substance ; behold all this matter from that substance. Here substance is a receptacle ; matter a fictitious entity, spoken of on one of these occasions as if it were a real entity contained within that receptacle ; on the others as one that had proceeded from it.

Behold the *form* in which that substance presents itself ; behold the form, the figure, the shape, the configuration *of* that substance.

Figure, configuration, shape, in these several words may be seen so many synonyms, or almost synonyms, to the word *form.*

Quantity has been distinguished into *continuous* and *discrete.*

Discrete quantity (it is commonly said) is number ; it should rather be said is *composed of numbers* ; viz. of numbers more than one, of separate entities.

It is only by means of discrete quantity, *i.e.* number, that continuous quantity can be measured by the mind, that any precise idea of any particular quantity can be formed.

To form an idea of any continuous quantity, *i.e.* of a body as existing in a certain quantity, one of two courses must be taken or conceived to be taken in relation to it. It must be divided, or conceived to be divided, into parts, *i.e.* into a determinate number of parts, or together with other similar bodies made up into a new, and artificial, and compounded whole.

To divide a body, or conceive a body to be divided into parts, it suffices not to divide it, or conceive it divided, into its constituent bodies, into any such smaller bodies as are contained in it. Either the entire body itself, or its parts respectively, must, by the mind, be conceived to be divided into its several *dimensions.*

Be the body what it may, not being boundless, it cannot but have some *bound* or *bounds* ; if one, it is a surface ; these *bounds*, if there be more than one, are surfaces : these surfaces again, not being boundless, have their bounds ; these bounds are lines.

The only bodies that have each of them but one uniform surface are spheres.[1]

[1] Here there is in the MS. a N.B., " Query as to Spheroids."—*Ed.*

B

Bodies are real entities. Surfaces and lines are but fictitious entities. A surface without depth, a line without thickness, was never seen by any man ; no, nor can any conception be seriously formed of its existence.

Space is the negation or absence of body.

Of any determinate individual portion of space, as clear an idea is capable of being formed as of any body, or of any portion of any body ; and besides, being equally determinate as that of body, the idea of space is much more simple.

To *space* it is difficult either to ascribe or to deny *existence*, without a contradiction in terms ; to consider it as nothing, òr as distinct from nothing.

Of body — that is, of all bodies whatsoever — the annihilation may be conceived without difficulty. Why ? Because, in whatsoever place—*i.e.* within whatsoever portion of space, within whatsoever receptacle, composed of mere space, any body is, at any given time conceived to be, it may thenceforward be conceived to be removed from that place, and so successively from any and every other portion of space.

Of space—*i.e.* of all portions of space whatever, indeed of so much as any one portion of space—the annihilation cannot be easily conceived. Why ? Because, in *mere* space there is nothing to remove ; nothing that can be conceived capable of being removed. In so far as matter is annihilated, there is less matter than there was before. But, suppose space to be annihilated ; is there less space than there was before ?

Hence, taken in the aggregate, no bounds, no limits can be assigned to space ; so neither can any *form* or any *quantity*. It cannot be removed ; it cannot be moved ; for there is nothing of it or in it to remove ; there is no place to which it can be removed.

So much for *space* taken in the *aggregate* ; but take this or that individual portion of space, the properties of it are very different. Conceive it, as in innumerable instances it really is, enclosed in bodies ; immediately it is, and unavoidably you conceive it to be, endowed with many of the properties of bodies. Of limits it is susceptible, as body is ; in point of fact it has limits : and, having these limits, it thereby has not only form but quantity. It not only has limits as truly as body has limits, but it has *the same limits.*

Having limits, it thereby has form, quantity, and even motion : along with the terraqueous globe—*i.e.* with the whole matter of it—all the portions of space enclosed in that matter describe round the sun, and with the sun, their continually repeated and ever varied round.

Substance being a real physical entity ; perceptions real psychical entities ; matter, form, quantity, and so on, so many fictitious entities : both descriptions being in part applicable to space, neither of them applicable entirely—space may be regarded and spoken of as a *semi-real entity.*

3. *Absolute Fictitious Entities of the Second Order* (*Quality. Modification*)

Matter, Form, Quantity—all these are susceptible of Quality. Matter, every portion of it, is capable of having its qualities, independently of those of its form and those of its quantity.

A body is said to be of such a *quality* ; such or such a quality is said to be *in* it, *resident, inherent,* in it. The matter, the form, the quantity of this body—in any one of these fictitious entities may this secondary fictitious entity be said to be resident, to be inherent.

Between quantity and quality, a sort of reciprocation, a sort of reciprocal intercommunion may be observed to have place. As we have the *quality* of a quantity—two qualities, for instance, vastness, minuteness, etc., so has a quality its quantities.

The *quantity* of a *quality* is termed a degree.

The term *modification* is nearly synonymous to the term quality.

Of modification it seems scarcely proper to speak, as constituting or being a fictitious entity different and distinct from *quality* : the difference between them is rather of a grammatical than of a logical nature. Yet, of the cases in which the word quality may be employed, there are some in which the word *modification* can scarcely, without impropriety, be employed. We may speak of a modification of this or that body, or of the matter, form, or quantity, as well as of a quality *of* that same body ; but we can scarcely, without impropriety, speak of a modification as being a thing *resident* or *inherent* in that same body.

By the word *quality* it is that are expressed all particulars whereby the condition of the body, or other object in question, is rendered similar or dissimilar—in the first place, to that of itself at different times, in the next place, to that of other bodies or objects, whether at a different, or at the same time.

Goodness and *badness* ; of all qualities experienced or imaginable, these are the very first that would present themselves to notice ; these are the very first that would obtain names. Interest, *i.e.* desire of pleasure and of exemption from pain, being, in some shape or other, the source of every thought as well as the cause of every action (and, in particular, amongst others of every action by which names are employed in the designation of persons and of things)—names plainly and immediately expressive of the two opposite modes of relation, in which those objects would be continually bearing relation to each man's interest, as above explained, would be among the very earliest to which the faculty of discourse would give existence.

Synonyms, or quasi-synonyms to quality ; in this character may be mentioned : 1. Nature ; 2. Sort ; 3. Kind ; 4. Mode ; 5. Complexion ; 6. Description ; 7. Character ; 8. Shape—viz. in a sense somewhat less extensive than that in which it is, as above, synonymous with Form.

4. *Fictitious Entities connected with Relation, enumerated*

No two entities of any kind can present themselves simultaneously to the mind—no, nor can so much as the same object present itself at different times—without presenting the idea of *Relation*. For relation is a fictitious entity, which is produced, and has place, as often as the mind, having perception of any one object, obtains, at the same, or at any immediately succeeding instant, perception of any other object, or even of that same object, if the perception be accompanied with the perception of its being the same : *Diversity* is, in the one case, the name of the relation, *Identity* in the other case. But, as identity is but the negation of diversity, thence if, on no occasion, diversity had ever been, neither, on any occasion, would any such idea as that of identity have come into existence.

Whatsoever two entities, real or fictitious, come to receive names, and thus to receive their nominal existence, *Relation* would be the third ; for, between the two—they being, by the supposition, different, and both of them actual objects of perception—the relation of difference or diversity would also become an object of perception, and in the character of a fictitious entity, a production of the acts of abstraction and denomination, acquire its nominal existence.

Next, after *matter* and *form*, the fictitious entity relation, or the class of fictitious entities called *Relations*, might, therefore, have been brought to view. But not only between matter and form, but also between the one and the other respectively, and the fictitious entities designated by the words *quantity*, *space*, and *quality*, so close seemed the connexion as not to be, without sensible inconvenience, broken by the interposition of any other.

Once introduced upon the carpet, the fictitious entity called relation swells into an extent such as to swallow up all the others. Every other fictitious entity is seen to be but a mode of this.

The most extensive, and, in its conception, simple of all relations—*i.e.* of all modes or modifications of the fictitious entity, denominated *relation*—is that of *place*, with its submodifications.

Next to that in the order of simplicity comes the modification of *time*, with its submodifications.

Next to them come successively the relations designated by the several words, *motion, rest, action, passion.* Subalternation, viz. logical subalternation, opposition, and connexion, or the relation between cause and effect.

Existence, with its several modifications, or correspondent fictitious entities—non-existence, futurity, actuality, potentiality, necessity, possibility, and impossibility—will, with most convenience, close the rear. Though still more extensive than even relation, they could not be brought to view before it, being applicable to all other relations—to relations of all sorts, and in a word, to entities, whether fictitious or real, of all sorts—no complete, or so much as correct view of their nature and character could be given, till these less extensive ones had been brought to view.

5. *Simple Fictitious Entities connected with Relation*

Place. Of the species of relation designated by the word *place*, the most perfect conception may be easily formed by taking into the account the species of relation designated by the word *time*.

Necessary altogether is the relation which the species of fictitious entity called *place* has, on the one hand, to the fictitious entity called *body*, on the other hand, to the fictitious entity called *space*.

Space may be distinguished into *absolute* and *relative*. To absolute space there are no conceivable bounds ; to relative space—*i.e.* to portions of space separated from one another by bodies — there *are*, in every instance, bounds, and those determinate ones.

As to the word *place*, whether it be considered as the

name of a real entity or as the name of a fictitious entity
would be a question of words, barely worth explanation,
and not at all worth debate.

Considered as a modification of space, it would, like
that, stand upon the footing of the name of a real entity ;
considered as a species of relation, it would stand upon the
footing of a fictitious entity. But in this latter case comes
an objection : viz. that the relations which on that
occasion are in question, are not place itself, or places
themselves, but such *relations as belong* to place.

Be this as it may, place is a relative portion of space,
considered either as actually occupied, or as capable of
being occupied, by some real entity of the class of bodies.

Portions of the earth's surface are considered and
denominated each of them *a place* ; but in this case, the
term *place* is used in the *physical* and *geographical* sense
of the word, not in an *ontological* sense.

Whether, in a *physical* sense, *place* be or be not the
name of a fictitious entity, that in every *psychical* sense
it is so, seems manifest beyond dispute. Take, for example,
the *place* occupied by such or such an idea in the mind,
by such or such a transaction in a narrative.

Time. Be it as it may in regard to place, that the
entity designated by the word *time* is but a fictitious
entity, will, it is believed, be sufficiently manifest.

Different altogether from each other are the perceptions
or ideas presented by the word *place* and the word *time*.
Yet as often as *time* is spoken of, it is spoken of as if it
were a modification of, or the same thing as, *place*.

Like place, time, or at least any given portion of time,
is spoken of in the character of a receptacle—as ' in such
or such a place things are done,' ' in such or such a time
things are done ' ; portions of *space* or place are long or
short, great or small—so are portions of *time*. In the
same sense we say ' a quantity of time ' or ' a space of
time '. As bodies are spoken of as going *to* or *from* such
or such a *place*, so operations are spoken of as going on
from and to such or such a portion of time.

But of every receptacle all the several parts are co-existent ; of any portion of *time*, no two parts, how small soever, are coexistent. Of any given portion of time, no two of the parts are coexistent ; with relation to each, all are successive. In the very import of the term *coexistent*, the idea of unity is implied in respect of the portion of time supposed to be occupied ; in the import of the term *succession*, that of diversity is of necessity implied.

Motion.   That the entity designated by the word *motion* is a fictitious entity seems at least equally beyond dispute.

A body, the body in question, is *in motion* : here, unless *in motion* be considered as an abbreviated expression substituted for *in a state of motion*, as we say, *in a state of rest*, motion is a receptacle in which the body is considered as stationed. *The motion of this body* is slow or is retrograde.   Here the body is a stationary object—a station or starting-post, of or from which the motion is considered as proceeding.

Necessarily included in the idea of *motion* is the idea of place and time. A body has been in motion.—When ? In what case ?   When having, at or in one point of time been in any one place, at another point of time it has been in any other.

Of any and every corporeal real entity, a similitude is capable of being exhibited as well in the form of a body, for instance a model, as in the form of a surface—as in painting, or drawing, or engraving ; which, in every case, is like the object represented, a stationary, permanent, and, unless by internal decay or external force, an unchanging and unmoving object.

But by no such graphical similitude, by no picture, by no model, by no stationary object, can any motion be represented.   A representation of the body as it appeared in the place occupied by it at a point of time anterior to that at which the motion commenced ; a representation of the same body as it appeared in the place occupied by it at a point of time posterior to that

at which the motion commenced : in these two repre-
sentations, conjoined or separate, may be seen all that
can be done towards the representation of motion by any
permanent imitative work.

Even on the table of the mind, in imagination, in idea,
in no other way can any motion be represented. There
not being any real entity to represent, the entity cannot
be any other than fictitious ; the name employed for the
purpose of representation cannot therefore be anything
else than the name of a fictitious entity.

Action. In the *idea* of action, the idea of motion is an
essential ingredient. But to *actual* action actual motion
can scarcely be regarded as necessary. Action is either
motion itself, or the tendency to motion. Under the
term *action*, besides motion, a tendency, though so it be
without actual motion, seems to be included. Held back
by strings, a magnet and a bar of iron, suspended at a
certain distance from each other, remain both of them
without motion : cut the strings of either of them, it
moves till it comes in contact with the other ; but for
the state of mutual action which preceded the cutting of
the strings no such motion would have taken place.

Passion, Reaction. Among all the bodies, large and
small, with which we have any the slightest acquaintance,
no instance, it is believed, can be found of action without
passion, nor of passion without reaction. But without
either of these accompaniments, a conception of action
may be entertained, at any rate attention may be applied
to it ; but if on either of two objects, attention be capable
of being bestowed without being bestowed upon the
other, the separate lot of attention thus bestowed affords
sufficient foundation for a separate name.

Here, then, are two more fictitious entities most nearly
related and intimately connected with the fictitious
entities action and motion, having all of them, for their
common archetype, the same image or set of images,
viz. that of a nutshell and nut, a starting-post and a
goal ; the representation of which is performed by the

prepositions *in*, *of*, *from*, etc., employed in connexion with their respective names.

6. *Fictitious Entities considered and denominated in respect of their Concomitancy*

(*Object. Subject. End in View*)

In the idea of an object, the idea of some action, or at any rate some motion, seems to be constantly and essentially involved. Where the object is a corporeal entity, it is a body towards which the body in motion moves: this body, whether permanently or momentarily, stands *objected*—*i.e. cast before* that other body which moves.

Even in the case of vision, in the instance of an object of sight, the relation is naturally the same; the only difference is that in the case of vision the moving bodies being the rays of light, the *object*, instead of being the body *towards* which, is the body *from* which the motion takes place.

In the picture, the tracing of which is the effect of the terms here in question, the *object* is either on the same level with the source of motion, or *above* it; the *subject*, as in its literal sense the word *subject* imports, is below and under it.

In the case of human action—a motion, real or fictitious, considered as being produced by an exercise of the faculty of the will on the part of a sensitive being—this action has in every instance for its cause the desire and expectation of some good, *i.e.* of some pleasure or exemption from some pain, and the entity, the good by which this desire has been produced, is in this case, if not the only object, an object, and, indeed, the ultimate *object*, the attainment of which is in the performance of the action aimed at.

Of entities thus intimately connected, it is not to be wondered at, if the conceptions formed, and the names bestowed in consequence, should frequently be indistinct.

In the designation of the same entity, in the designation

of which the word *subject* is employed, the word *object* is at other times employed ; and so also in the designation of the same entity in the designation of which the words *end in view* are employed, the word *object* is frequently also employed.

If, in a case by which a demand is presented for the mention of a subject and an object, so it happen that for the designation of the subject you employ the word *object*, then so it will be that for the designation of that which may with propriety be termed the object, but cannot with propriety be termed the subject, finding the only proper word preoccupied, you will naturally feel yourself at a loss.

In a case where the faculty of the will is not considered as having any part, the designation of *the end in view* is a function in which any occasion for the employment of the word object cannot have place ; in this case, therefore, neither has the uncertainty which, as above, is liable to be produced by that word.

In a case where the will is supposed to be employed, and in which there is accordingly an *end in view*—one single end to the attainment of which by the power and under the orders of the will the action is directed—in any such case-what may very well happen is that there shall be other entities to which, in the course of the action though not in the characters of *ends in view*, it may happen to the attention to be directed. Here, then, besides an object which may be, will be other objects no one of which can commodiously be, designated by the compound appellation, *end in view*.

In regard to the word *subject* (as well as the word *object*) one convenience is that it may be used in the plural number. This convenience belongs to them in contradistinction to the word *field*. For a group of numerous and comparatively small entities, the word *field* will not, either in the singular or in the plural, conveniently serve ; but to this same purpose the word *subject*, if employed in the plural, is perfectly well adapted.

If, beneath the imagined line of action, you have need to bring to view not merely one extensive fictitious immoveable body but a multitude of smaller moveable bodies lying on it, here comes an occasion for the use of both these terms—viz. *field* and *subject*, or *subjects* : the field is the extensive immoveable entity, the subjects the comparatively numerous and less extensive bodies, fixed or lying loose upon the surface of it.

In the place of the word *field*, as well as in place of the word *subject*, the words *subject-matter* may be employed ; so also the plural, *subject-matters*. But if, in addition to an extensive surface, you have to bring to view a multitude of smaller bodies stationed on it ; if, in that case, instead of the word *field*, you employ the words *subject-matters*, you will find that you cannot commodiously, after laying down your subject-matter, have subjects stationed on it.

In the case where the action in question is a physical, a corporeal one, a question might perhaps arise whether the entities respectively designated by the words *subject* and *object* belong to the class of real or fictitious entities : a platform on which you stand to shoot an arrow, a butt at which you shoot your arrow, to these could not be refused the appellation of real entities. But in so far as upon the *platform* you superinduce the character designated by the word *subject*, and upon the *butt* the character designated by the word *object*—of this subject and this object it might be insisted that they are but so many names of fictitious entities.

Not that for any practical purpose a question thus turning upon mere words would be in any considerable degree worthy of regard.

Be this as it may, in the case in which the action in question is an incorporeal, a psychical action, having no other field than the mind, or than what is in the mind— in this case the title of the words *subject* and *object*, as well as of the word *field*, to the appellation of fictitious entities will be seen to be clear of doubt.

7. Concomitant Fictitious Entities resulting from the Process of Logical Aggregation and Division, and Subalternation

It will be seen further on more at large how it is that when contemplating the qualities exhibited by individuals, by abstracting the attention successively from them, quality after quality, let the group of individuals—present, past, and future, contingent included—be ever so vast and multitudinous, there will, at last, be left some quality, or assemblage of qualities, which, being found all of them existing in a certain assemblage of individuals and not in any other, may serve for the foundation of a name by which that whole assemblage may be designated, without including in the designation any individual not included in that assemblage. The words, *mineral, vegetable, animal,* may serve for examples.

Wherever any such aggregate number of individuals can be found so connected with one another, so distinguished from all others, and, for the designation of the aggregate, the *fictitious* unit composed of that multitude, a name or appellation has been employed and appropriated by use, the fictitious unit thus formed will be found capable of being divided by the imagination into lesser component aggregates or units ; these again each of them into others : and, in this way, the largest and first divided all-comprehensive aggregate will be found capable of being divided and sub-divided into any number of aggregates not greater than the whole number of individuals, actual and conceivable, contained in the original factitious and fictitious whole ; the name of each one of these component aggregates constituting, as it were, a box for containing and keeping together the several aggregates comprised in it, the entire aggregate contained in each such box being characterized by some quality or qualities in respect of which, being agreed with one another, at the same time they disagree with and are therefore distinguished from all others.

Kingdom, class, order, genus, species, variety, have been

the names given to these boxes—to these factitious receptacles.

That it is to the class of fictitious and not to the class of real entities that these imaginary, however really useful, receptacles appertain is at this time of day sufficiently clear ; but the time has been when they have been mistaken for realities.

8. *Political and Quasi-Political Fictitious Entities*

I. EFFECTS. 1 .Obligation ; 2. Right ; 3. Exemption ; 4. Power ; 5. Privilege ; 6. Prerogative ; 7. Possession, physical ; 8. Possession, legal ; 9. Property.

II. CAUSES. 1. Command ; 2. Prohibition, Inhibition, etc. ; 3. Punishment ; 4. Pardon ; 5. License ; 6. Warrant ; 7. Judgment ; 8. Division.

All these have for their efficient causes pleasure and pain—but principally pain—in whatsoever shape and from whichsoever of the five sanctions or sources of pleasure or pain derived or expected, viz. 1. The physical sanction ; 2. The sympathetic sanction, or sanction of sympathy ; 3. The popular or moral sanction ; 4. The political, including the legal sanction ; 5. The religious sanction.

Obligation is the root out of which all these other fictitious entities take their rise.

Of all the sanctions or sources of pleasure and pain above brought to view, the political sanction being susceptible of being the strongest and surest in its operation, and, accordingly, the obligation derived from it the strongest and most effective, this is the sanction which it seems advisable to take for consideration in the first instance ; the correspondent obligations of the same name which may be considered as emanating from these other fictitious entities being, in the instance of some of these sanctions, of too weak a nature to act with any sufficient force capable of giving to any of those other productions any practical value.

An obligation—understand here that sort of obligation which, through the medium of the will, operates on the active faculty—takes its nature from some act to which it applies itself ; it is an obligation to perform or to abstain from performing a certain act.

A legal obligation to perform the act in question is said to attach upon a man, to be incumbent upon him, in so far as in the event of his performing the act (understand both at the time and place in question) he will not suffer any pain, but in the event of his not performing it he will suffer a certain pain, viz. the pain that corresponds to it, and by the virtue of which, applying itself eventually as above, the obligation is created.

9. *Fictitious Entities appertaining to Relation as between Cause and Effect*

In the idea of causation—in the idea of the relation as between cause and effect—in the idea of the operation or state of affairs by which that relation is produced, in which that relation takes its rise, the idea of motion is inseparably involved : take away motion, no causation can have place—no result, no effect, no *any*-thing can be produced.

In the idea of *motion*, the idea of a *moving body* is, with equal necessity, implied.

Of the cases in which the existence of motion, relative motion, is reported to us by our senses, there are some in which the commencement of the motion is, others in which it is not manifest to our senses.

Endless and *terminating*. Under one or other of these denominations may all motions, observed or observable, be included.

Endless motions are those which have place among the bodies (each of them considered in its totality) of which the visible universe is composed.

To the class of terminating or terminative motions belong all those which have place in our planet, and, to

judge from analogy, all those which have place in any
other of the celestial bodies.

So far as the motions in question belong to the endless
class, so far no such distinction, and therefore no such
relation as that of cause and effect, seems to have place.
Each body attracts towards it all the rest, and, were it to
have place singly, the attraction thus exercised might be
considered as if it operated in the character of a *cause* ;
but each body is attracted by every other, and, were it to
have place singly, the attraction thus suffered might be
considered in the character of an *effect*. But, in fact, the
two words are but two different names for one and the
same effect. In the case of motions that have place
among the distinct bodies with which the surface of our
earth is covered, action and causation are the phenomena
exhibited by different bodies in the character of agents
and patients. In the case of the celestial bodies, considered each in its totality, no such distinction has place.
No such character as that of agent, no such character as
that of patient, belongs separately to any one. They are
each one of them agent and patient at the same time.
No one exhibits more of agency, no one more of patiency,
than any other. Suppose that all these several bodies
having been created out of nothing at one and the same
instant, each with the same quantity of matter, and thence
with the same attractive power that appears to belong to
it at present, an impulse in a certain rectilinear direction
were to be given to each of them at the same time. On
this hypothesis it has been rendered, it is said, matter of
demonstration that the sort of intermediate motions
which would be the result would be exactly those which
these same bodies are found by observation to exhibit.

Here, then, we should have a beginning, but even here
we should not have an end. In the beginning, at a
determinate point of time, we should have a motion
operating in the character of a cause, but at no determinate point of time, to the exclusion of any other,
should we have either a motion or a new order of things

resulting from it, and produced by it, in the character of an effect.

Thelematic and *athelematic*. To one or other of these denominations will all motions of the terminative class be found referable. *Thelematic*, those in the production of which *volition*, in the mind of a sentient and self-moving being, is seen to be concerned. *Athelematic*, those in the production of which volition is not seen to have place.

In the case of a motion of the thelematic class, you have for the *cause* of the motion—meaning the *prime* cause of whatsoever motion happens in consequence to take place—the psychical act, the act of the will of the person by whose will the motion is produced ; you have that same person for the agent.

Fruitful or unfruitful, or, say *ergastic* or *unergastic*. To one or other of these denominations will all the motions of the thelematic class be found referable. *Ergastic* or fruitful, all those which have for their termination and result the production of a *work*. *Unergastic* or unfruitful all those which are not attended with any such result.

Between these two classes the line of separation, it will be manifest enough, cannot, in the nature of the case, be determinate.

A work has reference to human interests and exigencies. When, in consequence of a motion or set of motions of the thelematic kind, in the body or among the bodies in which the motion has terminated or those to which it has in the whole, or in any part, been communicated, any such change of condition has place, by which, for any considerable portion of time, they are or are not regarded as being rendered, in any fresh shape, subservient to human use, *a work* is spoken of as having thereby been produced.

In so far as a work is considered as having been produced, any agent who, in respect of his active talent, is regarded as having borne the principal part in the production of the work, is wont to be spoken of under the appellation of *an author* or *the author*.

In this same case any body which is regarded as having, in consequence of the motion communicated to it, been rendered contributory to the production of the work, is wont to be spoken of in the character, and by the name, of an instrument : any *body*, viz. inasmuch as considered as inanimate—an instrument in the *physical* sense ; if animated, or considered as animated, and, in particular, if regarded as rational—in the *psychical* sense ; if regarded as *simple*, a tool or implement ; if regarded as *complex*, an engine, a machine, a system of machinery.

To the case, and to that alone, in which the motion or motions, being of the *thelematic*, and therein, moreover, of the *ergastic* kind, have had for their prime mover or principal agent concerned, a rational, or at least a sentient, being, belong the words *end, operation, means, design*.

Of the word *end*, and its synonym the compound term *end in view*, the exposition has been already given. It consists in the idea of some good (*i.e.* pleasure, or exemption from pain in this or that shape or shapes) as about eventually to result to the agent in question from the proposed act in question.

Operation is a name given to any action in so far as it is considered as having been performed in the endeavour to produce a work.

The word *means* is a term alike applicable, with propriety, to the designation of body considered in the character of an *instrument*, or any *action* or *motion* considered in the character of an *operation*, tending to the production of *a work*, or any good looked to in the character of *an end*.

Productive and unproductive. Under one or other of these denominations, as the case may be, may be referred the action in question, in so far as where, being of the *thelematic*, and, moreover, of the *ergastic* kind, it has for its *end in view* the bringing into existence any intended result in the character of *a work*.

Productive and unproductive, whether in actual result or only in tendency, under one or other of these denominations may also be referred every motion, or set of motions, of the *athelematic* kind ; every motion, or set of motions, produced in, by, and upon, such agents as are of the purely physical kind.

This distinction is applicable to all the three physical kingdoms ; but, on the mention of it, the two living kingdoms, the vegetable and the animal, will be most apt to present themselves.

In the use frequently made of the word *cause,* may be seen an ambiguity, which, in respect of its incompatibility with any correct and clear view of the relation between cause and effect, there may be a practical use in endeavouring to remove from the field of thought and language.

On the one hand, *a motion, an action, an operation* ; on the other hand, *an agent, an operator, an author* ; to the designation of both these, in themselves, perfectly distinct objects, the words are wont to be indiscriminately applied.

Take, for example, the questions that used to be agitated in the logical schools. Is the moon, says one of them, the cause, or a cause, of the flux and reflux of the sea ? Here the moon, here the word *cause* is employed to designate a corporeal being considered in the character of an agent.

The cause (says a position of which frequent use was made in the same theatres of disputation), *the cause is always proportioned to its effect.* But, between the moon itself and the tide, *i.e.* the flux and reflux of the sea, there cannot be any proportion ; they are *disparate* entities, the one *the moon,* a real entity, the other, the flux and reflux, *i.e.* the motions of the sea, are but fictitious entities. Between the moon itself, and the water moved by it, *i.e.* between the quantity of both, proportion may have place ; between the motion, and thence the action of the moon, and the motion of the waters, a proportion may have place. But between the moon, a body, and the flux and reflux of the sea, no proportion can have place, neither can either be larger or smaller than the other.

In speaking of God, it has been common to speak of that inferential Being by such names as *the Cause of all things, the great, the universal Cause.* In this instance, the same sort of confusion, the same sort of indistinctness in the expression, the same consequent confusion in men's conception, as in the case mentioned, is apt to have place.

The *act* of God, the *will* of God—these are the entities, to the designation of which, and which alone, the term *cause* can, in the case in question, with propriety, and consistently with analogy, be employed; these, on the one hand, and the word *cause* on the other, are alike names of fictitious entities.

Author, and Creator—these alone, and not the word *cause*, can, with propriety, be employed in speaking of God. These, as well as God, are names of real entities, not names of fictitious entities: Author, a name applicable to men, or, in a word, to any being considered as susceptible of design; Creator, a term exclusively appropriated to the designation of God, considered with reference to his works.

In the use commonly made of the terms *work, cause, effect, instrument,* and in the habit of prefixing to them respectively the definitive article *the,* seems to be implied a notion of which the more closely it is examined the more plainly will the incorrectness be made to appear; this is, that where the effect is considered as one, there exists some one object, and no more than one, which, with propriety, can be considered as its cause. Of the exemplification and verification of this supposition, there exists not, perhaps, so much as a single instance.

Take, in the first place, an effect, any effect of the physical kind; no effect of this kind can, it is believed, be assigned that is not the result of a multitude of influencing circumstances; some always, in different ways, contributing to the production of it, viz. in the character of promoting and co-operating *causes*; others frequently contributing to the non-production of it, in the character of obstacles.

In relation to the result in question, considered in the character of an *effect*, suppose, at pleasure, any one body to be the *prime* or *principal* mover or agent, and the motion, the action, or the operation of it, to be the *prime* or principal *cause*.

In no instance can any such cause be in operation, but it will happen to it to be, on all sides, encompassed and surrounded by *circumstances*.

Those circumstances will consist of the state of the contiguous and surrounding bodies, in respect of motion or rest, form, colour, quantity, and the like.

Among these some will appear to be exercising on the result a material operative influence, others not to be exercising such influence. Influential or uninfluencing circumstances ; in one or other of these two classes of circumstances taken together, will every circumstance by which it can happen to the principal agent or agents to be encompassed, be comprised.

Promotive or *obstructive*—under one or other of these denominations may the whole assemblage of influential circumstances be comprised.

Any circumstances that act, that are considered as acting, in the character of *obstructive* circumstances are termed, in one word, *obstacles*.

Purely natural, purely factitious, and mixed—to one or other of these heads may every motion be referred, considered with reference to the part which the human will is capable of bearing in the production of it.

Solid, liquid, or gaseous—in one or other of these states, at the time of the motion, will the moving body be found.

The internal constitution of the moving body, the internal constitution of the unmoveable or non-moving bodies with which it comes in contact, and the configuration of these same bodies—upon all these several circumstances, or rather groups of circumstances, must the nature of the ultimate effect produced by the motion be dependent, whether that effect be a purely physical result, or a human work.

In so far then as, by the term *cause*, nothing more is meant to be designated than one alone of all those sets of co-operating circumstances ; be the effect what it may, the cause can never of itself be adequate to the production of it ; nor, between the quantum of the effect and the quantum of the cause, can any determinate proportion have place.

But, of the case in which, in the extent given to the import attributed to the word *cause*, the whole assemblage of these influencing circumstances is taken into the account and comprised, it seems questionable whether so much as a single example would be to be found.

Unless the above observations be altogether incorrect, it will appear but too manifest that, in the notions commonly attached to the word *cause*, much deficiency in respect of clearness and correctness as well as completeness cannot but have place ; and that, in the inferences made from either the one to the other, whether it be the cause that is deduced or supposed to be deduced from the effect, or the effect that is deduced or supposed to be deduced from the cause, much uncertainty and inconclusiveness cannot but be a frequent, not to say an almost constant and continual, result.

Seldom, indeed, does it happen that, of the co-influencing circumstances, the collection made for the purpose is complete ; nor is it always that, in such a collection, so much as the principally influencing circumstances are included.

In those cases in which the several influencing circumstances are, all of them, subject, not only to the observation, but to the powers of human agency, any such miscalculations and errors as from time to time happen to be made, may, when perceived from time to time, be corrected.

Thus it is, for example, in the case of observations that have for their field the anatomy and physiology of plants and animals.

Thus it is, moreover, with little exception in the instance

of the practical applications made of the respective theories of Chemistry and Mechanics, the influencing circumstances being for the most part or even altogether subject, and that, at all times, not only to our observations but to our command.

The cases in which our inferences from supposed causes to supposed effects, and from supposed effects to supposed causes, seem most precarious and exposed to error, are, on the one hand, cases belonging to the field of medicine, on the other hand, cases belonging to the field of naval architecture.

In cases belonging to the field of *medicine*, the influencing circumstances belonging principally to the class of chemical phenomena—to those phenomena by which particular sorts of bodies are distinguished from each other—lie, in a great degree, out of the reach of our observation.

In cases belonging to the field of naval architecture, the influencing circumstances, belonging principally to the class of mechanical phenomena—to those phenomena which belong in common to bodies in general—may, perhaps, in *specie* be, without much difficulty, comprehended in their totality by observation ; but, in respect of their *quantity*, lie in a great measure beyond even the reach of *observation*, and, in a still greater degree, are out of the reach of *command*.

Prone as is the human mind to the making of hasty and imperfectly-grounded inductions on the field of physical science, it cannot but be much more so in the fields of psychology and ethics, in which is included the field of politics. Commonly not only is the collection made of *influencing* circumstances incomplete, but *un-influencing* circumstances and even *obstacles* are placed in the station of, and held up to view in the character of, principally or even exclusively operating causes.

Thus superior is the density of the clouds which overhang the relation between cause and effect in the field of morals as compared with the field of physics. Two concurring considerations may help us to account for this difference ; I. The elements of calculation being in so large a proportion of the psychical class—such as intentions, affections, and motives—are, in a proportional degree, situated out of the reach of direct observation ; II. In the making of the calculation, the judgment is, in a peculiar degree, liable to be disturbed and led astray by the several sources of illusion—by original intellectual weakness, by sinister interest, by interest-begotten prejudice, and by adopted prejudice.

Material, formal, efficient, final—by these terms in the language of the Aristotelian schools, by these terms in the higher forms of common language, so many different species of causes are considered as designated.

Neither incapable of being applied to practice, nor of being ever applied with advantage, these distinctions present, in this place, a just claim to notice. The relation they bear to the foregoing exposition, will now be brought to view.

Matter and *form*—both these, it has been seen, are necessary to existence ; meaning, to real and that physical existence, the existence of a physical body.

1. By *material cause* is indicated the matter of the body in question, considered in so far as it is regarded as contributing to the production of the effect in question.

2. By *formal cause*, the form of the same body.

3. By *efficient cause* must be understood, in so far as any clear and distinct idea is attached to the term, the matter of some body or bodies : what is meant to be distinguished by it may, in general, be supposed to be the motion of that body, or assemblage of bodies, which is regarded as the principal motion—the motion which has the principal share in the production of the effect.

But to the production of the effect—meaning a physical effect—whatsoever it be, a correspondent and suitable disposition of the circumjacent non-moving bodies is not (it has been seen) less necessary than a correspondent and suitable motion, or aggregate of motions, on the part of the moving body.

To the designation of the *matter*, and of the *form*, that concurs in the production of the effect, the language here in question is, therefore, we see, adequate ; but, to the designation of the other influencing circumstances, we see how far it is from being adequate.

4. By *final cause*, is meant the *end* which the agent had in view ; meaning, as hath been seen, by the *end*, if anything at all be meant by it, the good to the attainment of which the act was directed ; the good, *i.e.* the pleasure, or pleasures, the exemption or security from such or such pain, or pains.

It is, therefore, only in so far as the effect is the result of design on the part of a sensitive being—a being susceptible of pains and pleasures, of those sensations which, by us, are experienced and known by the names of pleasures and pains—that the species of cause here called *final* can have place.

The doctrine of final causes supposes, therefore, on the part of the agent in question, the experience of pleasure and pain ; of pleasures and pains, the same as those of which we have experience—for us there are no others : employed in any such attempt as that of designating and bringing to view the idea of any others, they would be employed in designating and bringing to view so many non-entities.

10. *Existence, and the Classes of Fictitious Entities related to it*

Existence is a quality, the most extensively applicable and at the same time the most simple of all qualities actual or imaginable. Take away all other qualities, this remains : to speak more strictly, take any entity whatsoever, real or fictitious—abstract the attention from whatsoever other qualities may have been found belonging to it—this will still be left. *Existence* is predicable of naked *substance*.

Opposite to the idea of existence is that of non-existence. Non-existence is the negation of existence. Of every other entity, real or fictitious, either *existence* or *non-existence* is at all times predicable. Whether such other entity be real or fictitious, its existence is, of course, a fictitious entity ; *i.e.* the word existence is, in all cases, the name of a fictitious entity.

The idea of *non-existence* is the idea of *absence* extended. Take any *place*, and therewith any real entity—any body existing in that place, suppose it no longer existing in that place, you suppose its *absence*, its *relative* non-existence. Expel it in like manner from every, from all, place, you suppose its *absolute* non-existence.

It is through the medium of absence, the familiar and continually recurring idea of absence, that the idea of non-existence, the terrific, the transcendant, the awful, and imposing idea of non-existence is attained.

Existence being, as above, a species of quality, is itself a fictitious entity ; it is in every real entity ; every real entity is in it.

In it, the man, the object of whose appetite is the sublime and he the object of whose appetite is the ridiculous, may here find matter for their respective banquets. *Nothing* has been laughed at to satiety. The punster who has played with *nothing* till he is tired may renew the game with existence and non-existence.

At any point of time, in any place whatsoever, take any entity, any real entity whatsover, between its existence in that place and its non-existence in that same place, there is not any *alternative*, there is not any *medium* whatsoever.

Necessity, impossibility, certainty, uncertainty, probability, improbability, actuality, potentiality—whatsoever there is of reality correspondent to any of these names is nothing more or less than a disposition, a persuasion of the mind, on the part of him by whom these words are employed, in relation to the state of things, or the event or events to which these qualities are ascribed.

Down to the present·time, whatsoever be this present time, whether the time of writing this or the time of any one's reading it, whatsoever has existed has had existence, whatsoever has not existed has not had existence ; at this time, whatsoever does exist has existence, whatsoever does not exist has not existence ; and so at any and every future point of time, past, present, and future put together, where will room be found for anything real to answer to any of these names ?

Quality itself is but a fictitious entity, but these are all of them so many fictitious qualities. They do not, as real qualities—they do not, like gravity, solidity, roundness, hardness—belong to the objects themselves to which they are ascribed, in the character of attributes of the objects to which they are ascribed ; they are mere chimeras, mere creatures of the imagination, mere non-entities.

Yet, non-entities as they are, but too real is the mischief of which some of them, and, in particular, the word *necessity*, have been productive—antipathy, strife, persecution, murder upon a national, upon an international, scale.

The persuasion expressed by the word *certainty* has for its foundation the event itself simply. The persuasion indicated by the word *necessity* has for its object not only that event, but an infinity of other events, and states of things out of number, from the beginning of time, in the character of its *causes*.

Certainty, necessity, impossibility ; exhibited seriously in any other character than that of expressions of the degree of the persuasion entertained in relation to the subject in question by him whose words they are, in the use of these words is virtually involved the assumption of omniscience. All things that are possible are within my knowledge—this is not upon the list ; such being interpreted is the phrase, *this thing is impossible.*

The sort of occasion on which, without any such assumption, these terms can be applied, is that of a contradiction in terms—a self-contradictory proposition, or two mutually contradictory propositions issuing, at the same time, from the same mouth or the same pen. But here the objects to which these attributes are, with propriety, applicable, are not the objects for the designation of which the propositions are applied, but the propositions themselves. Propositions thus contradictory and incompatible cannot, with propriety, be applied to the same object. It is impossible that they should ; *i.e.* inconsistent with the notions entertained by the person in question, in relation to what is proper and what improper in language.

It is impossible that, among a multitude of bodies all equal to one another, four taken together should not be greater than two taken together. Why? Because, by the word *four* has, by every person, been designated a number greater than by the word *two*.

Yet, in affirmance of the truth of a proposition thus impossible, persuasion rising to the highest pitch of intensity has been entertained. Why? Because the human mind having it in its power to apply itself to any object, or to forbear to apply itself at pleasure, the person in question has exercised this power in relation to the import of the words in question, as above ; *i.e.* to the import which, according to his experience, all persons by whom they have been employed have been constantly in the habit of annexing to them. But against an object which the mind has contrived to exclude out of the field of its attention, no objection can, in that same field, be seen to bear. Whatsoever, therefore, were the considerations by which he was engaged to endeavour to persuade himself of the truth of the self-contradictory, and therefore impossible, propositions—remain without anything to counteract their force.

Of Improbability and Impossibility [1]

Improbability and impossibility are names, not for any qualities of the facts themselves but for our persuasion of their non-existence

Impossibility and Improbability are words that serve, to bring to view a particular, though very extensive modification of circumstantial evidence.

The occasion on which they are employed—the occasion, at least, on which, under the present head, I shall consider them as employed—is this : on one side, a fact is deposed to by a witness ; on the other side, the truth of it is denied —denied, not on the ground of any specific cause of untrustworthiness on the part of the witness, but because the fact is in its own nature *impossible* : impossible, or (what in practice comes to the same thing) too improbable to be believed on the strength of such testimony as is adduced in proof of it.

What is the nature and probative force of this modification of circumstantial evidence ? Is there any, and what, criterion, by which impossible facts, or facts which are to such a degree improbable as to be for practical purposes equivalent to impossible ones, may be distinguished from all others ?

If any such criterion existed, its use in judicature would be great indeed. By the help of it, a list of such impossible and quasi-impossible facts might in that case be made out by the legislator, and put into the hands of the judge. To know whether the probative force of the testimony in question were or were not destroyed by this modification of circumstantial disprobative evidence, the judge would have nothing more to do than to look into the list, and see whether the species of fact in question were to be found in it.

---

[1] [*Works*, Vol. VII, pp. 76–9.]

Unfortunately, there exists no such criterion—no *possibility* (if the word may here be employed without self-contradiction) of making up any such list. Not only would one man's list contain articles which another man would not admit into his ; but the same article which would be found in one man's list of impossibilities, would be found in another man's list of certainties.

From a man who sets out with this observation, no such list, nor any attempt to form one, can of course be expected. Yet, on the following questions, some light however faint, may be, and will here be endeavoured to be, reflected.

1. What it is men mean, when they speak of a fact as being impossible—intrinsically impossible ?

2. To what causes it is owing that one man's list of impossible facts will be so different from another's ?

3. Different modifications of impossibility ; different classes of facts which men in general—well-informed men in general—may be expected to concur in regarding as impossible.

4. Among facts likely to be, in general, considered as impossible, what classes are of a nature to be adduced in evidence ?

When, upon consideration given to a supposed matter of fact, a man feeling in himself a persuasion of its non-existence comes to give expression to that persuasion, he pronounces the matter of fact, according to the strength of such his persuasion, either more or less *improbable*, or *impossible*.

In and by the form of words thus employed for giving expression to that which is in truth nothing more than a psychological matter of fact, the scene of which lies in, and is confined to, his own breast—a sort of quality is thus ascribed to the external phenomenon, or supposed phenomenon ; viz. the matter of fact, or supposed matter of fact itself. Upon examination, this quality, it will be seen, is purely a fictitious one, a mere figment of the imagination ; and neither improbability and impossibility on the one hand, nor their opposites, probability and certainty, on the other, have any real place in the nature of the things themselves.

So far as concerns probability and improbability, the fictitiousness of this group of qualities will scarcely, when once suggested, appear exposed to doubt.

Take any supposed past matter of fact whatever, giving to it its situation in respect of place and time. At the time in question, in the place in question, either it had existence, or it had not : there is no medium. Between existence and non-existence, there is no medium, no other alternative. By probability—by improbability— by each of these a medium is supposed ; an indefinite number of alternatives is supposed.

At the same time the same matter of fact which to one man is probable, or (if such be his confidence) certain, is to another man improbable, or (if such be his confidence) impossible.

Often and often, even to one and the same man at different times, all this group of fictitious and mutually incompatible qualities have manifested themselves.

If his persuasion be felt to be of such a strength that no circumstance capable of being added to the supposed matter of fact could, in his view of the matter, make any addition to that strength ; or if, on looking round for other conceivable matters of fact, he fails of finding any one in relation to which his persuasion of its non-existence could be more intense—*impossible* is the epithet he attaches to the supposed matter of fact ; impossibility is the quality which he ascribes to it.

If, on the other hand, a circumstance presents itself by which in his view of the matter an addition might be made to the intensity of such disaffirmative persuasion ; or if the supposed matter of fact presents itself as one in relation to which his persuasion of its non-existence might be more intense ; in such case, not *impossible*, but *improbable*, is the epithet—not *impossibility*, but *improbability*, is the quality ascribed.

Certainty, which is the opposite to impossibility, or rather of which impossibility is the opposite, is applied to the persuasion, and from thence to the supposed matter of fact.   It is not, any more than impossibility, applied or applicable to testimony.

As certainty, so uncertainty, applies itself to the persuasion and the fact, and not to the testimony.   In the scale of persuasion, it embraces all degrees except the two extremes.   The existence of a fact is not matter of uncertainty to me, if the fact be regarded by me as impossible.

Certainty, therefore, has for its opposite, *uncertainty* in one way—*impossibility* in another.   Uncertainty, in the language of logicians, is its contradictory opposite—impossibility, its contrary opposite.

The fiction by which (in considering the strength of a man's *persuasion* in relation to this or that fact, and the probative force of any other matter of fact when viewed in the character of an evidentiary fact in relation to it) occasion is taken to ascribe a correspondent quality, indicated by some such words as *certainty* and *probability*, to the principal fact itself, appears to be, like so many other figments, among the offspring of the affections and passions incident to human nature.   It is among the contrivances a man employs to force other men to entertain, or appear to entertain, a persuasion which he himself entertains or appears to entertain, and to make a pretence or apparent justification for the pain which he would find a pleasure in inflicting on those whom a force so applied should have failed to be productive of such its intended effect.

Were it once allowed, that, as applied to the facts themselves which are in question, probability and certainty are mere fictions and modes of speaking ; that all of which, on any such occasion, a man can be assured is his own persuasion in relation to it ; that that persuasion will have had for its cause some article or articles of evidence, direct or circumstantial, real or personal, and will be the result of, and in its degree and magnitude proportioned to, the probative force of that evidence ; that, of such evidence, neither the probative force, nor consequently the strength of his persuasion, are at his command ; that it is not in the power of any article of evidence to have acted with any degree of probative force upon, nor consequently to have given existence to any persuasion in a mind to which it has not been applied ; and that therefore it is not in the power of any evidence to give either certainty or probability to any matter of fact (the matter of fact being, at the time in question, either in existence or not in existence, and neither the evidence nor the persuasion being capable of making any the slightest change in it) ; that it depends in a considerable degree upon the mental constitutions of A and B respectively, what sort of persuasion, if any, shall be produced in their minds by the application of any given article of evidence ; and that it is no more in the power of evidence applied to the mind of A, and not to that of B, to produce in the mind of B a persuasion of any kind, than it is in the power of evidence applied to the mind of B, and not of A, to produce a persuasion on the mind of A :—were all this to be duly considered and allowed, neither the existence nor the non-existence of a persuasion concerning a matter of fact of any sort would have the effect of presenting to any person any other person as a proper object of punishment, or so much as resentment.

But the certainty of this or that fact is assumed as perfect and indisputable ; and thus he of whom it is conceived that he fails of regarding, or of representing himself as regarding, that same fact in such its true light, is on no better foundation considered and treated as being either mendacious or perverse and obstinate : perverse and obstinate, if he fails of regarding it in that light ; mendacious, if, it being impossible to him to fail of regarding it in that light, he speaks of himself as if he did not.

D

When a man is himself persuaded—or though he does but, under the impulse of some interest by which he is actuated, appear to be, or profess to be, persuaded—of the existence of a fact, it is matter of pain and vexation to him to suppose that this same persuasion fails of being entertained, still more to observe that it is professed not to be entertained, by those with whom, on the occasion of it, he has to deal.

Hence it is that, in his mind and in his discourse, to entertain it is made matter of merit—to fail to entertain it, matter of demerit and blame, on the part of others with whom he has to do : and, to cause them to pursue that supposed meritorious line of conduct, the power of reward, if within his reach, is employed ; and to deter them from the opposite conduct, even the power of punishment : of both which powers, in the application thus made of them, mankind have been unhappily accustomed to see and to feel the exercise, carried to a pitch so repugnant to the dictates of humanity and reason.

II.—FICTIONS IN PSYCHOLOGY[1]

Necessity of Names of Material Objects for the Designation of Pneumatic or Immaterial Objects

All our psychological ideas are derived from physical ones—all mental from corporeal ones. When spoken of, mental ideas are spoken of as if they were corporeal ones. In no other manner can they be spoken of. But thus to speak of them is to give an erroneous, a false account of them, an account that agrees not with their nature; it is to misrepresent them. But very different from what it is in most other cases, in this case misrepresentation is not matter of blame. By it no deception is intended; if, to a certain degree, for want of sufficient explanation, misconception be the result of it, unless by accident, it is not among the results intended by him by whom the misrepresentation is made—the false account is delivered. From what there is of falsehood not only is pure good the result, but it is the work of invincible necessity; on no other terms can discourse be carried on.

Every noun-substantive is a name, a name either of an individual object, or of a sort or aggregate of objects. The name of an individual has, by all grammarians, been termed a *proper* name, the name of a sort or aggregate of objects, a *common* name; it being applied in common to each one of the individual objects which are regarded as belonging to that sort—as possessing certain properties supposed to belong in common to them all.

By this name an existence is ascribed to the individual object, or sort of object, of which it is the name. In the case where to the object thus spoken of, existence is actually an object of one of the five senses, and in par-

[1] [*Works*, Vol. VIII, pp. 327-9.]

ticular of the sense of touch or feeling—the only one without which man cannot exist—say, in a word, where the object is a tangible one ; here there is no fiction—as this man, this beast, this bird, this fish, this star ; or this sort of man, this sort of beast, this sort of bird, this sort of fish, this sort of star ; the object spoken of may be termed a real entity. On the other hand in the case in which the object is not a tangible one, the object, the existence of which is thus asserted, not being a real existing one, the object, if it must be termed an entity— as on pain of universal and perpetual non-intercourse between man and man, it must be—it may, for distinction's sake, be termed a fictitious entity. Take, for example, *this motion, this operation, this quality, this obligation, this right.* Thus then we have two sorts of names, with two corresponding sorts of entities. Names of real entities, names of fictitious entities.

Unfortunate it is, howsoever necessary and indispensable, that for speaking of fictitious entities there is no other possible mode than that of speaking of them as if they were so many real entities. This blameless falsehood being universally uttered, and remaining universally uncontradicted, is to a considerable extent taken for truth. With every *name* employed, an entity stands associated in the minds of the hearers as well as speakers, and that entity, though in one half of the whole number of instances no other than a fictitious one, is in all of them apt to be taken for a real one. To speak of an object by its name, its universally known name, is to ascribe existence to it :—out of this, error, misconception, obscurity, ambiguity, confusion, doubts, disagreement, angry passions, discord and hostility have, to no inconsiderable amount, had place. There is many a man who could not endure patiently to sit and hear contested the reality of those objects which he is in the habit of speaking of as being *his rights.* For the assertion of the existence of these fictitious objects, no small degree of merit has been ascribed—no small degree of praise has been given ; assertion has been taken for proof, and the stronger and more numerous the sets of words employed the more complete and conclusive has that proof been esteemed.

To such of the sources of perception as are of a material or corporeal nature, whether audible or visible, names are early attached ; by the presence of the object to both parties at once, by the addresser and the addressee— *i.e.* party addressed—at the time that, by the addresser, the sign is presented to the sense of the addressee, the individuality of the object, the idea of which is by that sign presented to notice, is continually established. Bring hither that loaf ; behold that apple ; at the time when the sign is thus presented to the sense, the thing signified —the portion of matter thus denominated—being at the same time presented to the senses of both parties, the import of the word loaf or apple is thus fixed, readily fixed, and beyond danger of mistake.

Objects of a corporeal nature may be designated and denominated in a direct way.

Not so in the case of an object of which the seat lies in the mind ; not so in the case of an immaterial being. For producing in any other mind any conception whatsoever of an object of this class, a man has absolutely but one means, and that is to speak of it as if it belonged to the other class—to speak of it as if it were a material object ; to present to the party addressed some sign or other with the signification of which he is acquainted, in the character of a sign of some material object—and upon the resemblance, or rather analogy, such as it is, which has place between the material object of which it was originally the sign and the immaterial object of which it is now employed as a sign, to depend for the chance of the sign's exciting in his mind the idea which, on the occasion, it is endeavoured to excite, viz. the idea of the immaterial object.

In saying, " Bring me that loaf, it lies in that pan ", if a pan with a loaf in it were accordingly existing in the presence of us both, I should raise up *in* your mind two ideas, that of a pan and that of a loaf. Correspondent to the portion of discourse having matter for its subject, here then is a portion of discourse having mind for its subject. By what means, then, is it that by words employed for that purpose I have succeeded in my endeavour to present to your own mind the general, in conjunction with the particular, idea of something which I have caused to have place in it ?

It is by causing you to consider your own mind under the image or similitude of a receptacle in which the idea has been made to have place, *as* in the material pan the material loaf is deposited. And here, after having officiated in the *material* sense, the preposition *in*, a preposition significative of *place*, officiates in the *immaterial* sense ; and it is by its material sense that it receives its explanation when employed in its immaterial sense, for from no other source could it receive its explanation.

Applied to the designation of any class of material objects a sign is, or may be, the sign of a real entity; applied to the purpose of designating any object of the class of immaterial objects a sign cannot, in that respect, be the sign of anything but a fictitious entity. The entity of which the sign in question is given as a sign— your mind, as in the above example—shall in the character of an immaterial substance have whatsoever reality it may be your pleasure to see ascribed to it. But in the phrase in question, in virtue of the preposition *in*, it is in the character of a material substance that it is spoken of, a receptacle in which an idea may have place, as a loaf may in a pan ; and in so far as *that* is the character in which it is spoken of, fiction is employed. So far, therefore, the name given to your mind is the name of a fictitious entity, and your mind itself a fictitious entity. If in the instance of your *mind* it be in any way displeasing to you to make this acknowledgement, take for the fictitious entity the idea spoken of as being lodged in it ;

or if that be not agreeable, let it be your understanding, your will, your conception, your imagination, considered in the character of so many separated existences capable of having objects lodged in them.

Of the origin of the import of the sign in some instances the materiality is, it is true, no longer visible. Take for example, as above, the word *mind* itself, and the word *will*. But in by far the greater number of instances it is plain enough. Take for example the words *understanding, conception,* and *imagination,* as above. Even in regard to *mind,* though of that word the root in material ideas is lost, in the French word, the import of which, though it coincide not with it, comes nearest to it, viz. *esprit,* the materiality is plain enough. Correspondent to, and derived from, that French word, or from the Latin word *spiritus,* is our word, *spirit*; and that spirit means originally breath, *i.e.* air discharged out of the lungs, is sufficiently notorious.

In so far as any origin at all can be found for it, it is in a material import that the origin of the import of every word possessing an immaterial import is to be found. Seeing that in the numerous instances in which both sorts of imports are attached to the same word, this rule is verified, we can do no otherwise than conclude that originally such was also the case in the instance of the comparatively small number of words in and for which no *material* import can at present be found.

Throughout the whole field of language, parallel to the line of what may be termed the material language, and expressed by the same words, runs a line of what may be termed the immaterial language. Not that to every word that has a material import there belongs also an immaterial one ; but that to every word that has an immaterial import there belongs, or at least did belong, a material one.

In a word, our ideas coming, all of them, from our senses, from what other source can the signs of them— from what other source can our language—come ?

Of one and the same thought, from mind to mind, by what means—through what channel—can *conveyance* be made ?   To no other man's is the *mind* of any man immediately present.   Matter, this or that portion of matter external to both, in this may be seen the only channel, the only medium which the nature of the case admits of.   Yonder stands a certain portion of matter. By that portion of matter feelings of a certain sort are produced in your mind : by that same portion of matter feelings of a sort, if not exactly the same, at least with reference to the purpose in question near enough to being the same, are produced at the same time in my mind. Here, then, is the channel of communication, and the only one.   Of that channel language takes possession and employs it.

Under yon tree, in that hollow on the ground, lies an apple ; in that same spot, while I am saying this to you, pointing at the same time to the spot, you are observing the same apple.   By this means, along with the signification of the words, *lies, ground, hollow,* etc. you and I learn the signification of the word *in.*

At and during the time we are thus conversing, the *ideas* of the *apple,* the *ground,* and the *hollow,* are *in* both our minds.   In this way it is, that we learn the import of this same word *in* with reference to our two *minds.*   In a word, with reference to *mind* in general, by no other means could we have learned it.   In no other way could the word *in*—add or *any other word*—have acquired a signification with reference to *mind.*

Unless it be the one expressed by the preposition *of,* taken as the sign of the possessive case, the material image, and thence the immaterial idea expressed by the preposition *in,* is the one the exemplification of which occurs with the greatest frequency.

By this example, the derivation of the immaterial idea from the material image, and the use thence made of the noun, considered as the name of the immaterial idea, from the use made of the same word in the character of the name of the material image, being once explained to anyone to whom the explanation thus given is clear and satisfactory ; of the two senses thus obtained by as many prepositions as the particular language, whatsoever it be, happens to furnish, the explanation may henceforward be despatched in a short formulary, and at the expense of a comparatively small number of words.

III—ELLIPTICAL FICTIONS[1]

Simple perception is not capable of erring; no, nor sensation neither. But judgment is, on the part of every person, and on almost every occasion, exposed to error.

A state or act of the mind in which judgment is continually included is apt to be considered as an exemplification of perception alone, or sensation alone. Such is the case with all instances of the exercise of the organs of sight and hearing. I see a hill, *i.e.* what appears to me a hill; but oftentimes when what a man sees is believed by him to be a hill, it is in reality a cloud. I hear the rain; but oftentimes when a man thinks he hears the rain falling, the cause of his perception is not rain but the wind whistling through certain trees.

When as above, desire (the state or act of the will) and simple perception or sensation (the state or act of the understanding) are excepted, all that the mind of man is capable of containing is an act of the judicial faculty—an opinion, a judgment; an opinion, entertained by himself, entertained in his own mind. This is the only immediate subject of any communication which, concerning the state of that faculty, can be made. Of no matter of fact, external to—of no matter other than that which passes in—his own mind, can any immediate communication be made by language. Opinion, an opinion entertained by the speaker, this is all of which, in any instance, communication can be made. Of an opinion thus expressed, any imaginable matter of fact, real or supposed, may have been taken for the object. But that to which expression is given, that of which communication is made, is always the man's opinion; *i.e.* that which, in so far as the expression answers its intended purpose, that which he

[1] [*Works*, Vol. VIII, pp. 320–3.]

wishes should be taken for his opinion in relation to the subject in question, nor anything more.

Be this as it may, the strictly logical consequences are the only ones that belong to the present purpose.

One is that in every portion of discourse which is not the expression of a desire, a simple sensation, or a perception—in every portion of discourse, for example, by which the existence of a matter of fact exterior to the person of the speaker is asserted—is included a communication made of the state of the judicial department of the speaker's mind, an opinion entertained in relation to that same matter of fact.

This being the case, a certain degree of complexity attaches to every proposition, the simplest imaginable not excepted, which has for its subject a matter of fact at large. . . .

The consequence is, that in saying, ' He is there ', the *proposition*, simple as it is in appearance, is in its import complex; and if it be considered as designating, expressing, communicating, the whole of the object of which it is employed as the sign (viz. the mode of *being* of my mind) it is *elliptical*. That to which it gives expression is the supposed matter of fact which (supposing me to speak truly) was the object of my thought ; that of which it does not contain the expression is that *thought* itself : the only matter of fact of which the discourse in question is strictly and immediately the assertion is left to be inferred from the context, from such words as are actually uttered. . . .

Of the above observations another logical consequence is this, viz. that for the giving expression and conveyance to any thought that ever was entertained, so far as

[1] From this observation various practical inferences of the moral class may be seen to follow :

(a) All reliance on the opinion as supposed of others is in fact reliance upon a man's own opinion ; viz. upon his opinion concerning the credit due to the opinion which in the instance in question is attributed to those others.

(b) That, in other words, all bigotry is grounded in, includes in it, self-conceit.

concerns *import* and not *discourse*, nothing less than the *import* of an entire proposition, and that, as above, a complex one, ever was, or ever could be made to serve.

Not but that in many instances, for the making communication of thought, even a single word is made to serve. But then it is by means of other words—which, according to the occasion, the single word in question may have the effect of suggesting as effectually as by this same single word—that the ideas constantly associated with it are suggested.

And thus it is by bringing to view other words, in the character of words of which, though not pronounced, the import was meant to be conveyed by the word which was pronounced, that a single word may be made to have the effect, and thus, as it were, comprise the import, of an indefinite number of other words—of a discourse of an indefinite length.

This being the case, if nothing less than the import of an entire proposition be sufficient for the giving full expression to any the most simple thought, it follows that, no word being anything more than a fragment of a proposition, no word is of itself the complete sign of any thought.

It was in the form of entire propositions that when first uttered, discourse was uttered. Of these integers, words were but so many fragments ; as afterwards *in written discourse* letters were of words. Words may be considered as the result of a sort of analysis—a chemicological process for which, till at a comparatively much later period than that which gave birth to propositions, the powers of the mind were not ripe.

With a view, however, to save the words which would be required to point out this complexity, such propositions as are *only in this way complex* may, for some purposes and on some occasions, be considered and spoken of as *simple*.

Upon this field of observation the logic of Aristotle and his followers did not penetrate. The subjects it began with were *terms*, *i.e.* words of a certain description ; and beginning with the consideration of these terms, it went on to the consideration of propositions in the character of compounds capable of being composed out of these elements.

Antecedently to all particular inquiry, in an inquiry the subject of which was confined to the signs of thought —in an inquiry in which no attempt was made to look into the thoughts signified—in the conception entertained in relation to the nature of thought and of the diversification of which it is susceptible, much clearness, correctness, or advance to completeness could not naturally be expected.

These terms are accordingly spoken of as possessing of themselves an original and independent signification, as having existence before anything of the nature of a proposition came to be in existence ; as if finding these terms endowed, each of them, somehow or other, with a signification of its own, at a subsequent period some ingenious persons took them in hand and formed them into propositions. . . .

IV.—FICTION AND METAPHOR [1]

Subjects of Discourse, immediate and ulterior

Language is the sign of thought, an instrument for the communication of thought from one mind to another.

Language is the sign of thought, of the thought which is in the mind of him by whom the discourse is uttered.

It may be the sign of other things and other objects in infinite variety, but of this object it is always a sign, and it is only through this that it becomes the sign of any other object.

On this occasion, and for this purpose, the whole of the mind of man may be considered as distinguishable into two parts, the purely passive and the active. In the passive is included the intellectual; the active may also be styled the concupiscible. The passive, the seat of perception, memory, and judgment, in so far as it is capable (as in *seeing*) of being exercised without any consciousness of the intervention of the *will*—the active the seat of desire, and thence of violition, and thence of external action.

The object for the designation of which a class of words, termed by grammarians a verb in the imperative mood, is employed, is one example out of several modifications, of the state of which the concupiscible part of the mind is susceptible. . . .

Thus far, then, are we advanced. The immediate subject of a communication made by language is always the state of the speaker's mind; the state of the *passive* or *receptive* part of it, or the state of the *active* or *concupiscible* part.

[1] [*Works*, Vol. VIII, pp. 329–31.]

Now then, in the case where it is the state of the receptive part, what is, or may be, the *ulterior* subject of the communication thus made ?

Answer. It will be, in some respect or other, the state (viz. meaning the supposed or alleged state) either of the corporeal part of the speaker's frame or the state of some object other than, and exterior to, the speaker.

Of the corporeal part of the speaker's frame. Examples : *I am weary, I am hungry, I am dry.*

Of the state of some object other than and exterior to the speaker. Examples :—*That apple is ripe, Apples are sweet, Apples are good.*

In both these cases, an object other than the state of my own mind is the subject of the discourse held by me, but in neither of them is it the immediate subject.

In both of them the immediate subject is no other than the state of my own mind—an opinion entertained by me in relation to the ulterior object or subject.

In the one case it is an opinion of which the subject is the state of my own body.

In the other it is an opinion concerning the state of a body exterior to my own body.

In the first case, the opinion, though it be but an opinion, is not, as the case is here put, much in danger of being erroneous. In respect of the actual state of my sensations, meaning the sensations themselves, I am scarcely liable to be in an error. But beyond that point no sooner do I advance but a single step, if I undertake to pronounce an opinion relative to the cause of any of those sensations, from that moment I am liable to fall. I here launch into the ocean of art and science. I here commence physician ; and, in the field of the physician the dominion of error is but too severely felt.

Speaking of the state of my own body, am I thus exposed to error ?—Much more so am I in speaking of the state of any other.[1]

---

[1] From these speculative observations practical inferences of no small importance might be deduced :

(*a*) Avoid dogmativeness. (*b*) Still more avoid intolerance. In both

The sort of infirmity just noticed, being common to all discourse in the composition of which an assertion of the state of the speaker's mind intervenes, precedes, introduces, and weakens the ulterior assertion which lies beyond it, the consideration of the intervening assertion may, in every case but the present (in which, for the purpose of explanation, it has been necessary thus, for once, to bring it to view) be dropped, and the subject of the discourse may be stated as being, except in the particular case where it is the state of the speaker's body, the state of some exterior *entity* or assemblage of entities.

But now already comes the stage at which it will become necessary to launch into the track of fiction, at which, by an irresistible voice, and on pain of leaving everything unexplained and misconceived, the land of fiction calls upon us to visit it.

That apple is ripe. Apples are sweet. Apples are good. An apple is a real entity ; in saying, *That apple exists,* the existence of which I express my opinion is a real entity. But *That apple is ripe ;* of what is it that, in addition to that of the apple, I express my opinion of the existence ? It is of the existence of the quality of ripeness in the apple.

But the quality of ripeness, is it a real entity ? Different from apples, and everything else that is susceptible to it, has this quality, or any quality, any separate existence ? If there were no other apple in the world than that which I have in my hand, this apple would not the less be possessed of existence ; but if there were nothing in the world that were susceptible of being ripe, where would be the quality of ripeness ? Nowhere.

In saying " This apple is ripe ", what is it that I affirm ? It is, that *in* this apple is the quality of ripeness. The two expressions are equivalent. But, " In this apple is the quality of ripeness ", in the assertion thus made,

cases never cease to bear in mind how slippery and hollow the ground on which your opinion, and consequently the utmost value of any expression which you can give to it, rests.

what is the image that I bring to view ? It is that the apple is a receptacle ; and that, in this receptacle, the quality of ripeness—the imaginary, the fictitious entity called a *quality*—is lodged. For, of the preposition *in* this is the import. Witness the apple which I am supposing myself to have in my hand ; witness the pen which, at this moment, I actually have in my hand.

Thus it is that, in the use made of language, fiction, at the very first step that can be taken in the field of language, fiction, in the simplest, or almost the simplest, case in which language can be employed, becomes a necessary resource.

Coeval with the very first steps that can be taken in the endeavour to give a clear explanation of the nature of language, must be the intimation given of the distinction between real and fictitious entities, and the correspondent distinction between names of real and names of fictitious entities.

Though to the development, and thus to the explanation of the import of the word *ripe*, the word *ripeness* may thus be rendered subservient, it follows not that of the two the word *ripeness* was first in use. From the use which (in and for the developing the texture of the import of the verb) of the word quality, in the character of a generic name, and of the names of the several sorts of qualities distinguishable in the several sorts of substances in the character of so many specific names, may now be made, it follows not that words of this description were in use before the verb—before that complex species of verb, in every individual of which the import of some species may be found contained. On the contrary, the contrary course seems even by much the most natural and probable to have taken place.

In the earlier stages of society, all conceptions, and, consequently, all expressions, were generally indistinct ; it is only by long-continued courses of attention that distinctness in conception and expression have been produced.

E

It seems probable that it was in the shape of entire propositions that the sounds of which audible language was composed, first presented themselves ; witness those words which, under the name of *interjections*, are by grammarians numbered among the parts of speech, and which may be considered as so many fragments of language as it showed itself in its earliest state.

As it was with the audible, so it appears to have been with the visible signs of language ; and as words were formed by the decomposition of propositions, so were letters by the decomposition of words.

If all language be thus figurative, how then (it may be asked), how then is it that the character, and, in so important a class of instances the reproach, of figurativeness, is cast upon the use made of it in particular instances ?

To this it may be answered :   The discourse that, in this particular sense, is *not* figurative, is the discourse in which, for the conveyance of the immaterial part of the stock of ideas conveyed, no other fictions—no other figures—are employed than what are absolutely necessary to, and which, consequently, are universally employed in, the conveyance of the import intended to be conveyed.

When a discourse is figurative, in lieu of those, or in addition to those, other images not necessary to, and thence not universally employed in, the conveyance of the import in question, are employed.

V.—EXPOSITION[1]

1. *Seats of Unclearness. The Words or their Connexion.
Exposition what ?*

A sentence, in the grammatical sense of the word
sentence, consists either of a *single proposition,* in the
logical sense of the word proposition, or of a number of
such propositions ; if of one only, it may be termed a
simple sentence—if of more than one, a *compound* sentence.

A proposition is *clear,* in proportion as it is *clear*—that
is, *free*—at the same time from *ambiguity* and *obscurity.*

Clearness is, on every occasion, relative ; relation being
had to the person considered in the character of hearer
or reader.

There exists not, nor ever will exist, any proposition
that is perfectly clear to every hearer and reader. There
exist but too many that neither will be, nor ever have
been to any one ; not so much as to those by whom they
were respectively framed.

Instances are not, however, uncommon where ideas,
which in the mind of him, by whom the discourse meant
for the communication of them, was uttered, were perfectly clear, are expressed in such a manner as not to be
clear to anyone else. Clear in the conception—clear in
the expression—clear in neither—clear in the conception
alone, not in the expression ; if in the conception a set
of ideas were not clear, it is not natural that they should
be clear in the expression—yet by accident it may happen
to them so to be.

Where *unclearness* (why not ' unclearness ' as well as

'uncleanness') has place in a discourse, the seat of it will be either in the *words* or in the *syntax* :—in some one word, or number of words, each taken singly, *i.e.* without regard to the mode of their connexion, or in that mode itself ; in the state of their mutual relations with reference to the import of each other.

In so far as the seat of the unclearness is in the words taken singly, *clearness* has for its *instrument, exposition.* Exposition is a name which may, with propriety, be applied to the designation of every operation which has for its object, or end in view, the exclusion or expulsion of unclearness in any shape ; to the operation, and thereby (for such on the present occasion is the poverty, and thence the ambiguity, of language) to the portion of discourse by which the end is endeavoured to be accomplished, and by which the operation of accomplishing it is considered as performed.

Of the two cases which follow, for the purpose of this inquiry, convenience seems to require that the first place should be allotted to the case where the exposition takes for its subject an object proposed to be expounded, as well as the word with the assistance of which, in the character of its sign, the object is proposed to be expounded ; the second place to the case where, without reference to any particular object or class of objects, the exposition takes for its subject a word considered in the character of a sign, which, for the designation of some object or class of objects, is wont to be employed.

2. *Subjects to which Exposition is applicable*

Be the exposition itself what it may, a *subject* it cannot but have—a subject to which it is applicable.

This subject, what may it be ?   What are the diversifications of which it is susceptible ?   Questions to which, in the first place an answer must be provided.   Why ? because, on the nature of the subject will depend the nature of the mode of exposition of which it is susceptible.

In relation to the subject of this instrument of clearness, two observations require to be brought to view in the first place.

(*a*) The subject of exposition, viz., the immediate and only immediate subject is in every case a *word*.

(*b*) That word is in every case a *name* : *i.e.* a word considered in the character of a name.

Exposition supposes *thought*. A word is a *sign of thought*. How imperfectly soever—in a manner how deficient soever in respect of *clearness*—*thought*, it is true, may be expressed by *signs* other than words ; by inarticulate sounds, by gestures, by deportment. But as often as any object has been considered in the character of a subject of or for exposition, that object has been a word[1]—the immediate subject of exposition has been a word ; whatsoever else may have been brought to view, the signification of a *word*—of the word in question—has been brought to view : the word is not only a subject, but the only physically sensible subject, upon and in relation to which the *operation* called exposition has been performed.

3. *Mode of Exposition where the Thing which is the Subject is an Individual. Individuation. Individual and Generic.*

Thus much being premised, the word in question is either the name of an *individual* object or the name of a *species* or sort of objects.

[1] On this subject, for the purpose of exposition, *i.e.* for the purpose of ensuring clearness, the Aristotelians have given us a distinction which may be seen to be itself a source of unclearness—viz. of that sort which is termed obscurity. For the purpose of exposition, one of the instruments or operations they employ is *definition*, to which again they apply another instrument, viz. *division*. A definition (say they) is either a definition of the *name*, or a definition of the *thing* ; meaning evidently of the thing—of the object—of which the word is employed as a name. Now, in the account thus given of the matter, a proposition is implied which is not true ; viz. that where the definition is a definition of a thing, it never is the definition of the name ; whereas in truth it always is.

Of the distinction which they had in view, the form they should have employed seems to be this : a definition is either a definition of the word alone, or a definition of the thing by means of the word. A definition of the thing signified meant to be expressed by it.

If it be the name of an individual object, *individualization* is the general name [for] the only mode of *exposition* of which (regard being had at the same time to the subject) the name of an individual object is susceptible.

Individual individualization, or say, *individuation—generic*, or *specific individuation*—by these two denominations may be distinguished two modes of individuation which for practical purposes may require to be distinguished.

Individual individuation is where, in relation to an individual object, an indication is endeavoured to be given, whereby, or by the help of which, an individual object may be distinguished from any or all other individual objects wherewith it is regarded as being liable to be confounded.

Take for instance, on the surface of the earth, the designation of the several distinguishable portions which it contains ; and into which, physically or psychically speaking, it is capable of being divided. In so far as the portion in question is considered as relatively large, geography is the portion of art and science to which, with the help of astronomy, the individuation of the object is considered as appertaining ; topography, in so far as it is considered as relatively small. From geography will be sought, on the surface of the terraqueous globe, the portion distinguished by the name of Europe ; from geography, again, in Europe, England—in England, London, and Westminster ; [from topography] in London and Westminster, Queen's Square, Westminster, and Queen's Square Place.

Generic, or *Specific Individuation*. By this appellative may be distinguished the operation which has place in the case where, regard being had to a genus of objects, as distinguished by a generic name, instructions are given, having for their object the causing men to be agreed in determining within what limits or bounds an individual, when designated by and under that name, shall be considered as limited, so as to be distinguished from all objects which are regarded as liable to be confounded with it ; or, in relation to any individual aggregate likely to be considered as designated by that name, of what elements that aggregate shall be considered as composed.

The field of *law* is the field in which the demand for this mode of individuation, for this mode of exposition, is most copious and most urgent, and the use of it most conspicuous and incontestable.

In the individuation of moveable physical objects, the instruments are conjunct portions of time and space. *Axiom.*—No two portions of matter can exist at the same portion of time in the same portion of space.

4. *Mode of Exposition where the Teacher and Learner have no Common Language*

1. *Representation.* If all words were significative of real entities, and if these were all objects which might at all times be brought within the reach of the perception both of the learner and the teacher, exposition would be easy and consist in the pointing to the object in question and pronouncing at the same time the word which it is wished to attach to it as its name. This is exposition by signs, and may be termed *representation.* Among persons who have no common language by which they can communicate their ideas this is at first the only practicable method ; and we see it continually exemplified when a child is taught to speak or a foreigner who understands no words with which we are acquainted, or who cannot make use of dictionaries or any other written explanations of our words, is instructed in our language.

Next to these names of real entities, perceptible and present, those which are the most readily expounded by representation are names of collective fictitious entities. By representing successively a number of objects comprehended in the collective fictitious entities—book, plant, etc.—we may easily succeed in attaching to those words in the learner's mind a general idea of the sense we attach to them, and which, though at first very vague and imperfect, will at any rate serve as the groundwork of the discourse by which a clearer and more correct exposition may subsequently be given.

A generic idea once formed, the meaning of words indicative of specific differences may be deduced from it ; still, by mere representation, not perhaps the *substantive names* of that class of fictitious entities called *relations*, but those abbreviative words called *adjectives*, which designate at once the relation or property and the fact of its being attributed to the object represented. A *great book*, a *little book*, a *yellow flower*, a *red flower* etc. may be thus expounded, whilst the explanation of the words *greatness* and *smallness, colour*, etc., may require one or other of the species of discourse which are comprehended among the ensuing modes of exposition.

As yet, however, we have but *substantives* and *adjectives*, and without *verbs* no discourse can be held, no further exposition given, and consequently no clear ideas communicated ; we must again have recourse to representation, but in a manner far more complicated. Taking verbs expressive of operations as the most simple, it will be necessary to repeat the operation in question, within the reach of the senses of the learner, a number of times more or less considerable, according to his intellectual powers, before we can have any security for his attaching to the word the idea we wish to convey.

Thus, by taking successively a variety of things, and alternately putting them in motion, and pointing to them whilst at rest, and pronouncing on each occasion either the words *I move* (naming the thing whatever it may be) or the name of the thing with the words *at rest*, the constant repetition of the same word will soon cause the mind of the learner to attach to it the idea required. A phenomenon which appears to depend particularly on that passive property of the mind which may be designated by the name of *habit*. It is evident, however, that great mistakes may frequently occur in the learner's mind in these cases ; if, for instance, all the things represented as being *in motion* happen to be *red*, and all these which are spoken of as being *at rest* are *white*, he may just as well attach to the words *I move* the meaning *red*, and to these *at rest* the meaning *white*, as the signification intended to be conveyed.

The exposition by representation of the substantive verbs *to be* and *to have*, and of prepositions and other expletives necessary in the composition of discourse, must then be undertaken. But it will in most cases be still more complicated, and consequently still more liable to misconception. As soon, however, as any tolerable degree of certainty is obtained of the having conveyed a sufficiently adequate idea of the signification of these several classes of words, extensive enough to form a connected discourse, a more exact exposition may then be undertaken in that one of the other modes which may be found most suited to the object in question.

5. *Modes of Exposition, by Comparison with Words, intelligible to both Teacher and Learner*

The two modes comprehended under this head are Translation and Etymologization.

1. *Translation.* Exposition by translation is performed by mentioning a word already known to and understood by the learner, and by giving it as expressive of the same idea or image as the one represented by the word to be expounded. The proposition, " *Man* is what you, a Spaniard, call *hombre* ; *Oxide of hydrogen* is what you, in ordinary conversation, call *water* " are expositions by translation of the words *man* and *oxide of hydrogen*.

This operation supposes the ideas represented by the word in question to be equally well known to both learner and teacher ; and in that case only will this mode suffice. If the idea entertained by the learner with reference to the words *hombre* or *water* be not exactly the same as that of the teacher (as will frequently be the case), a further exposition is necessary by some other mode.

From the two examples given above, it may be inferred that exposition by translation may be usefully employed for two distinct purposes : (1) for teaching words in the same language more convenient for particular purposes, because they are those made use of by this author, or that practitioner, with whom it is the learner's interest to become conversant ; or (2) because the word is more convenient for use than the one the learner is already acquainted with.

Sets of words thus translated for the use of particular classes of learners, and arranged in an order convenient for reference, are compiled under the name of *Dictionaries of Languages*,[1] *Dictionaries of Technical Terms, Dictionaries of Synonyms ;* and may furnish examples of the very extensive use of the mode of exposition. In the case of the two latter dictionaries, however, very few expositions are by mere explanation, particularly in the case of synonyms—this name having been unfortunately given sometimes to words which have exactly the same meaning, sometimes to those which have *nearly* the same meaning, an inconvenience which I shall more fully expose under the head of synonymation.

In physical sciences, where the use of exact exposition has been so much felt of late, the word *synonym* has retained its correct signification, and the name of *synonomy* is given to a collection of results of translation, and may serve as an excellent example of this mode of exposition, applied to the second of its two above-mentioned purposes. A similar synonymy or translation of the leading words of many ethical, neological, or pathological works, would throw a singular light upon many subjects of controversy between authors hitherto irreconcileable.

2. *Etymologization.* By etymologization I do not mean to indicate that long and uncertain investigation of the

---

[1] *Dictionaries of Languages*, that is, where the words of one language are expounded by giving the corresponding words of another. Dictionaries in a single language generally comprehend almost every species of exposition.

various changes and transformations of sense and sound which a word has undergone in the course of time—that search after etymology which leads into so many blunders, and which, though sometimes productive of a certain degree of advantage to the study of some sciences, is more frequently of no other use than mere momentary amusement. The operation I have now in view is the exposition of *inflected words* and *conjugates* by the exhibition of the *root* from which they are derived.

The distinction between *inflection* and *conjugation* will be more fully given when we come to the analysis of language. In the meantime, for the understanding of the above definition, I shall only mention that I comprehend under the terms inflected words and conjugates all such words as are modified in part so as to change their signification, corresponding modifications being applicable, with the same effect, to a number of other words. The original words thus to be modified go under the name of *roots*. Thus from the root *rego* are derived the several inflected words and conjugates *rexi, rectum, regnans, regnum, interregnum, rex, regalis, etc., etc.*

In all cases where each inflection has a particular name, which, as well as the root, is equally well understood by both learner and teacher, exposition by etymologization will suffice, and should be preferred to any of the succeeding ones as being next in simplicity to translation. Thus the expression *rexi* is the first person singular, perfect tense, and indicative mood of the verb *rego—children's* is the genitive case, plural number, of the substantive *child—reader* is the name of the operator that relates to the operation to *read*—will immediately give a clear and correct idea of their meaning to one who understands already the names of the classes of inflection, *first person, plural number, perfect tense, indicative mood, genitive case, operator relating to an operation,* and of the roots *rego, child,* to *read.*

Whenever this is not the case, etymologization will not suffice : but even then, whenever an inflected word occurs, it is almost always more advantageous to reduce it to its root, to expound that root, and to explain the class to which the inflection belongs. As a general rule, we may say that exposition by etymologization, as well as by translation, should be given whenever the case admits of it, either alone or in conjunction with any of the other modes.

6. *Modes of Exposition where the subject is a Class*

1. Definition ; meaning the sort of operation and correspondent work ordinarily understood by that name. 2. Operations and works incidentally employed as preliminary and preparatory to that of definition ; say preparatory operations. 3. Operations incidentally employed as subsequential and supplementary to that of definition ; say supplementary operations. 4. Operations which, in certain cases in which the purpose cannot be accomplished by definition—understand by definition in that same form—require to be performed in lieu of it ; say succedaneous operations. By one or other of these subordinate appellations may the operation of exposition, in every shape of which it is susceptible, it is believed, be designated.

To *define* a word is to give indication of some aggregate in which the object of which it is the sign is comprehended, together with an indication of some quality or property which is possessed by that same object, but is not possessed by any other object included in that same aggregate.

Elliptically but more familiarly, to *define* a word is to *expound* it by indication of the genus and the difference —*per genus et differentiam*, say the Aristotelians.

In this account of the matter, two things, it may be observed, are, howsoever inexplicitly, assumed ; viz. (1) That the object in question belongs to some nest of aggregates. (2) That it is not itself the highest, the most capacious, the all-comprehending aggregate of the nest : in other terms, that the word is not of the number of those the import of which is not included in the import of any other of the words employed in giving names to aggregates :—

that it belongs to some nest of aggregates, and that it is not itself the most comprehensive and all-comprehensive aggregate of the nest.

The genus represented by a word which is the name of that aggregate, in which all the other aggregates of the nest to which it belongs are contained and included, has no genus which is superior to it : it is, therefore, in its nature incapable of receiving a definition ; meaning always that mode of exposition which, in modern practice, seems to be universally understood by that name.[1]

Meantime the class of words which are in this sense of the word incapable of receiving exposition in that shape are among those in the instance of which the demand for exposition is the most imperious. For these then that mode of exposition is necessary to which, by the description of succedaneous modes of exposition, reference has just been made, and of which an account will presently be endeavoured to be rendered.[2]

Yet of these words which are all of them incapable of receiving a definition, in effect definitions are very generally, not to say universally, wont to be given with a degree of unconcern and confidence not inferior to that with which the operation is attended when the subject upon which it is performed is with the strictest propriety susceptible of operation in that mode.

[1] An excellent illustration of definition, in contradistinction to other modes of exposition, is afforded by the characteristic phrases of writers on the physical sciences, in which those characters alone are given which are *necessary* to distinguish the species from all others in the same genus ; or, in other words, which *constitute* the species. All other properties, the knowledge of which may assist the learner in the formation of the idea he is intended to receive, being referred to *description*—of which I shall speak further on

A great light would be thrown on the pneumatological branches of science were the like exactness to be given to the definition of words in use, wherever definition may be employed with advantage. In the case of all terms of very general import, it will be found much more useful to consider them as genera generalissima and expound them by other means ; but when once the import of these genera is fixed, definition should be applied to, and persevered in to the greatest extent possible. The advantage of this will appear in a clearer light when I speak of methodization, an operation with which definition is intimately connected.

[2] See Section 8.

7. *Of Exposition by Paraphrasis, with its Subsidiary Operations, viz. Phraseoplerosis and Archetypation*

I. EXPLANATION OF THESE MODES OF EXPOSITION, AND
OF THE CASE IN WHICH THEY ARE NECESSARY

Paraphrasis is that mode of exposition which is the only instructive mode where the thing expressed, being the name of a fictitious entity, has not any superior in the scale of logical subalternation.

Connected, and that necessarily, with paraphrasis, is an operation for the designation of which the word *Phraseoplerosis* (*i.e.* the filling up of the phrase) may be employed.

By the word *paraphrasis* may be designated that sort of exposition which may be afforded by transmuting into a proposition, having for its subject some real entity, a proposition which has not for its subject any other than a fictitious entity.

Nothing has no properties. A fictitious entity, being, as this its name imports—being, by the very supposition —a mere nothing, cannot of itself have any properties : no proposition by which any property is ascribed to it can, therefore, be, in itself and of itself, a true one ; nor, therefore, an instructive one. Whatsoever of truth is capable of belonging to it cannot belong to it in any other character than that of the representative—of the intended and supposed equivalent and adequate succedaneum—of some proposition having for its subject some real entity.

Of any such fictitious entity, or fictitious entities, the real entity with which the import of their respective appellatives is connected, and on the import of which their import depends, may be termed the real source, efficient cause, or connecting principle.

In every proposition by which a property or affection of any kind is ascribed to an entity of any kind, real or fictitious, three parts or members are necessarily either expressly or virtually included, viz. (1) A *subject*, being the name of the real or fictitious entity in question ; (2) A *predicate* by which is designated the property or affection attributed or ascribed to that subject ; and (3) The *copula*, or sign of the act of the mind by which the attribution or ascription is performed.

By the sort of proposition here in question, viz. a proposition which has for its subject some fictitious entity, and for its predicate the name of an attribute attributed to that fictitious entity, some sort of image— the image of some real action or state of things—in every instance is presented to the mind. This image may be termed the *archetype, emblem,* or *archetypal image* appertaining to the fictitious proposition of which the name of the characteristic fictitious entity constitutes a part.

In so far as of this emblematic image indication is given, the act or operation by which such indication is given may be termed *Archetypation*.

To a considerable extent Archetypation—*i.e.* the origin of the psychological in some physical idea—is often, in a manner, lost ; its physical marks being more or less obliterated by the frequency of its use on psychological ground, while it is little, if at all, in use on the original physical ground.

Such psychological expressions, of which, as above, the physical origin is lost, are the most commodious for psychological use. Why ?—Because in proportion as it is put out of sight, two psychological expressions, derived from two disparate and incongruous physical sources, are capable of being conjoined without bringing the incongruity to view.

When the expression applied to a psychological purpose is one of which the physical origin remains still prominent and conspicuous, it presents itself to view in the character of a figurative expression ; for instance, a *metaphor*. Carried for any considerable length through its connexions and dependencies, the metaphor becomes an allegory—

a figure of speech, the unsuitableness of which, to serious and instructive discourse, is generally recognized. But the great inconvenience is that it is seldom that for any considerable length of time, if any, the physical idea can be moulded and adapted to the psychological purpose.

In the case of a fictitious proposition which, for the exposition of it, requires a paraphrasis, having for its subject a real entity (which paraphrasis, when exhibited, performs, in relation to the name of the fictitious subject, the same sort of office which, for the name of a real entity, is performed by a definition of the ordinary stamp, viz., a definition *per genus et differentiam*), the name forms but a part of the fictitious proposition for the explanation of which the sort of proposition having for its subject a real entity is, in the character of a paraphrastically-expository proposition, required. To compose and constitute such a proposition as shall be ripe and qualified for the receiving for itself, and thereby for its subject, an exposition by *paraphrasis*, the addition of other matter is required, viz. besides the name of the subject, the name of the predicate, together with some sign performing the office of the copula ; the operation by which this completion of the phrase is performed, may be termed *phraseoplerosis*.

Phraseoplerosis is thus another of the operations connected with, and subservient to, the main or principal operation, paraphrasis.

2. EXEMPLIFICATION IN THE CASE OF THE FICTITIOUS ENTITY, OBLIGATION

For exposition and explanation of Paraphrasis, and of the other modes connected with it and subsidiary to it, that which presents itself as the most instructive of all examples which the nature of the case affords is that which is afforded by the group of ethical fictitious entities, viz. *Obligations*, rights, and the other advantages dependent on obligation.

The fictitious entities which compose this group have all of them, for their real *source*, one and the same sort of real entity, viz. *sensation* ; the word being taken in that sense in which it is significative not merely of perception but of perception considered as productive of pain alone, of pleasure alone, or of both.

Pain (it is here to be observed) may have for its equivalent, loss of pleasure ; pleasure, again, may have for its equivalent, exemption from pain.

An obligation (viz. the obligation of conducting himself in a certain manner) is incumbent on a man (*i.e.* is spoken of as incumbent on a man) in so far as, in the event of his failing to conduct himself in that manner, pain, or loss of pleasure, is considered as about to be experienced by him.[1]

In this example—

1. The exponend, or say the word to be expounded, is an *obligation*.

2. It being the name not of a real, but only of a fictitious entity, and that fictitious entity not having any superior genus, it is considered as not susceptible of a definition in the ordinary shape, *per genus et differentiam*, but only of an exposition in the way of paraphrasis.

3. To fit it for receiving exposition in this shape, it is in the character of the subject of a proposition, by the help of the requisite complements, made up into a fictitious proposition.   These complements are (1) the predicate, *incumbent on a man* ; (2) the copula *is* : and of these, when thus added to the name of the subject, viz. *obligation*, the fictitious proposition which requires to be expounded by paraphrasis, viz. the proposition, *An obligation is incumbent on a man*, is composed.

4. Taking the name of the subject for the *basis*, by the addition of this predicate, *incumbent on a man*, and the copula *is*, the phrase is completed—the operation called

---

[1] It is, however, only in so far as a man is aware of the probability that in the event in question the unpleasant consequence in question will befall him, that the obligation can possess any probability of proving an effective one.

phraseoplerosis, i.e. completion of the phrase, is performed.

5. The source of the explanation thus given by paraphrasis is the idea of eventual sensation, as expressed by the names of the different and opposite modes of sensation —viz. pain and pleasure, with their respective equivalents —and the designation of the event on the happening of which such sensation is considered as being about to take place.

6. For the formation of the variety of fictitious propositions of which the fictitious entity in question, viz. obligation, or an obligation, is in use to constitute the subject, the emblematical, or archetypal image, is that of a man lying down, with a heavy body pressing upon him ; to wit, in such sort as either to prevent him from acting at all, or so ordering matters that if so it be that he does act, it cannot be in any other direction or manner than the direction or manner in question—the direction or manner requisite.

The several distinguishable sources from any or all of which the pain and pleasure constitutive of the obligation in question may be expected to be received—viz. the several sanctions, distinguished by the names of the physical sanction, the popular, or moral, sanction, the political (including the legal) sanction, and the religious sanction—these particulars belong to another part of the field, and have received explanation in another place.[1]

To that other place it also belongs to bring to view the causes by which the attention and perception of mankind have to so great an extent been kept averted from the only true and intelligible source of obligation—from the only true and intelligible explanation of its nature, as thus indicated.

On the exposition thus given of the term obligation may be built those other expositions of which it will form the basis, viz. of rights, quasi-rights or advantages

[1] See *Principles of Morals and Legislation,* Chapter III.

analogous to rights, and their respective modifications, as well as of the several modifications of which the ficti- tious entity, *obligation*, is itself susceptible.

8. *Of Modes of Exposition subsidiary to Definition and Paraphrasis*

1. *Synonymation.* Indication of some other word or words, the import of which coincides or agrees with the term to be expounded, more or less correctly.

The use to be derived from the employment of synony- mation consists in maximizing the number of the persons by whom conception, clear of obscurity and ambiguity and incorrectness, may on each occasion be collected from the several expressions.

It is not, however, without great danger of error that any two words can be stated as synonymous.

2. *Antithesis.* Indication of some other word, or words, the import of which is opposite to that of the word in question.

3. *Illustration.* Bringing to view some word or words, by which, in any one or more of the above ways or in any other way or ways, *light* may be thrown upon the import of the word in question, *i.e.* the import of it may, in some way or other, be rendered clearer—*i.e.* more surely clear as well of obscurity as of ambiguity.

4. *Exemplification.* Indication of some individual, or of some lesser aggregate, as being included in the name of the aggregate in question.

Without any difference, or at any rate without any difference worth remarking, all these subsidiary modes of exposition seem capable of being applied with equal propriety and utility, whether the main mode of exposi- tion be in the form of a *definition* or in the form of a *paraphrasis*.

5. *Description* is a detailed exposition of those properties the exhibition of which is not necessary in order to distinguish the object in question from all such which

are not designated by the same name. It may, accordingly, be more and more ample to an indefinite degree. A definition is a concise description, a description is an enlarged definition.

Description may be considered as referring to an individual, in which case it may be termed *individual* description ; or as referring to the name of a collective entity, in which case it may be termed *specific*.

The differences, in use and importance, between individual and collective description are analogous to those which distinguish the corresponding operations of individuation and definition. Definition applies to an indefinite number of individuals connected together only by those properties exhibited by that operation ; and therefore, by means of it, whensoever any individual is brought to view, a decision may be formed whether it does or does not belong to the aggregate in question. The individual characterized by individuation is unique ; being unique, every property described as belonging to him must have belonged to him at the time and place of his individuation ; but the greater the number of properties enumerated, the less chance is there of their aggregate being possessed in common by other individuals, or of their not having undergone any change other than such as may be accounted for, and calculated upon, during the change from the time and place fixed by the individuation. Description, therefore, though itself uncertain as to answering the purpose intended, is the only mode of exposition which can efficiently be adopted in such cases.

6. *Parallelism* is the pointing out of certain particular properties of a thing, with a view to the showing the resemblance it has to some other thing. Its use is to resolve any doubts which may arise, either from imperfect conception or imperfect expression, whether the object in question does or does not belong to the class of objects expounded.

Comparison is an act by which Distinction and Parallelism may be indifferently carried on.

7. *Enumeration* is the exhibiting the nature of the class of things characterized by any name, by bringing to view the names of certain subordinate sorts of things or even certain individual things which it is meant to signify. It may be complete or incomplete.

Enumeration is arithmetical or systematical. Systematical enumeration is by division, or rather is accompanied with, and performed by division. It is the gathering up and naming of the parts which result from the division of the whole.

8. *Ampliation* is the declaring concerning any word that it has been, or that it is intended that it should be, understood to have a more extensive meaning than, on certain occasions, people, it is supposed, might be likely to attribute to it ; that is, to comprehend such and such objects over and above those objects which they, it is supposed, would be apt to understand it to comprehend.

9. *Restriction* is the declaring concerning any word that it has been, or that it is intended it should be, understood not to have so extensive a meaning as, on certain occasions, people, it is supposed, might be likely to attribute to it ; that is, not to comprehend such and such objects of the number of these which they (it is supposed) would be apt to understand it to comprehend.

9. *Distinction and Disambiguation what ?—in what Cases employed*

Distinction, or real Antithesis, is the pointing out of certain particular properties of a thing, with the view of showing its dissimilarity to some other particular thing with which it is apprehended it may be confounded in such manner as to be deemed either the same with it, or more similar to it than it is in reality.

Distinction precedes division in the scale ; distinction exhibits the relation of the object to the equally ample objects, its congeners—division breaks it down into its component species ; distinction is a fragment of a supposed preceding division of an ampler term, bearing the ratio of a genus to that in question.

Disambiguation is distinction applied to words.

Such is the imperfection of language : instances are numerous in which the same words have the same audible with their attendant visible signs ; and, in the same language, have been employed to designate objects that have nothing in common.

Be the word what it may, if so it be that it is wont to be employed in more senses than one, between or among which no coincidence either total or partial is perceptible—when, at the same time, while by one person it is received in one sense, by another person it is received in another different sense—an operation, necessarily preliminary to definition, is distinction or disambiguation ; in other words, when so it happens that the word in question has been employed in the character of a sign for the designation of several objects, insomuch that, without further explanation, it may happen to it to be taken as indicative of one object, when, by the author of the discourse, it was meant to be indicative, not of that, but of a different one, what for the exclusion of such misconception may every now and then be necessary is— an intimation, making known which of all these several objects the word is, in the case in question, meant to designate, and what other, or others, it is not meant to designate.[1]

Take, for example, the English word *Church* ; this English word is uniformly considered and employed as the correct and complete representative of the Latin word *Ecclesia*, which, in other letters somewhat different in appearance, serves for the designation of the same sound as the correspondent Greek word ; in French, *Eglise*.

1. Among the Greeks, in its original acceptation,

---

[1] Multisensual, by accident and without analogy ; multisensual, by reason of analogy ; under one or other of these heads, may all the cases in which it can happen to a word to stand in need of *distinction* be comprised.

Ecclesia was employed to signify an assembly of any kind ; it was manifestly from the union of two words which signified to call out, viz. for the purpose of a joint meeting, and more particularly of a joint meeting for a public, for a political purpose.

2. Thence, among such of the first Christians whose language was Greek, it came to signify, in particular, such assemblies as were held by these religionists, as such, whether for the purpose of devotion or conjunct economical management.

3. In an association of this kind there was commonly, at least, one member whose occupation consisted in taking the lead in their common exercises of divine worship, and by the exposition of that book, or collection of books, which, by all of them, was recognized as constituting the standard of their faith and action, to administer instruction to the rest. The operations thus performed being considered as *serviceable*, with reference to the persons at whose desire they were performed, the persons by whom they were performed were, accordingly, sometimes designated, in consideration of such their services, *ministers*, the Latin word for servants ; sometimes, in consideration of their age, *Presbyters*, from the Greek word for Elders, *i.e.* for men of any description when advanced in age (from which word *Presbyter*, the French word *Prestre* and the English word *Priest*) ; sometimes in consideration of their acting as overseers or overlookers—overlooking and overseeing, in relation to deportment, the behaviour of their disciples, the members of the association at large, *Episcopi*, whence the English word *Bishop*.

In process of time, those members of the association whose occupation, originally with or without pay, consisted, on the occasion in question, in acting as the servants of all came to act as rulers over the members at large, at first on this or that particular occasion, at length upon all occasions.

At this time, besides the other senses of which mention

will require to be made presently, the word *Church* came to signify, according to the purpose which, by those who were employing it it was designed to serve, three very different assemblages of persons : viz. (1) The whole body of the persons thus governed ; (2) The whole body of the persons thus employed in the government of the rest ; and (3) The all-comprehensive body, or grand total, composed of governed and governors taken together.

When the persons in question were to be spoken of in the character of persons bound to pay obedience, then by the word *Church* was meant to be designated these subordinate subject-members of the association, in a word the *subject many*. When the persons in question were to be spoken of in the character of persons to whom the others were bound to pay obedience, then by the same word were designated the *ruling few*. When, for the purpose of securing in favour of both parties, and especially of the ruling few, the affections of respect and fear, then would the import of the word open itself, and to such an extent as to include under one denomination the two parties whose situations and interests were thus opposite.

4. From designating, first, the act of calling together an assembly, then the assembly composed of all persons, and no other than all persons, actually assembled together at one and the same time in a particular place, and then all the persons who were regarded as entitled so to assemble at that place, it came also to be employed to designate the place itself at or in which such assembly was wont to be held ; the *place* consisting of the *soil*, the portion of the earth's surface, on which, for containing and protecting the assembly from the occasional injuries of the weather, a *building* was erected, and such building itself when erected.

Such as above being the purpose for which the sort of building in question was erected, viz. the paying homage to God, God, although present at all times in all places, was regarded as being in a more particular manner present at and in all places of this sort ; attentive to whatsoever was passing at all other places, but still more attentive to whatsoever was passing in these places.

Being thus as it were the dwelling-places of God, these places became to the members of the association objects of particular awe and reverence, of a mixture of respect and terror—they became, in one word, holy ; whereupon by an easy and insensible transition, this mixture of respect and terror came to extend itself to, upon, and to the benefit of, the class of persons in whose hands was reposed the management of whatsoever was done in these holy places : holy functions made holy places, holy places and functions made holy persons.

On the score of beauty, admiration ; on the score of kindness and tenderness, love ; on the score of fitness for domestic management and rule, respect : these affections are in use to find their joint object in the character or relation designated by the word *mother*. Admiration, love, and respect, on the one part ; all these are on the other part so many instruments of governance. The servants of the subject many had their assemblies for acting in such their capacity, and securing to themselves the faculty of continuing so to do. Of these assemblies, the members were some young, some middle-aged, some elderly men. Upon contemplating themselves altogether in the mirror of rhetoric, it was found that of all these males put together was composed one beautiful female, the worthy object of the associated affections of admiration, love, and respect—the Holy Mother Church.

Besides this, this holy female was seen to possess a still greater quantity of holiness than could have entered into the composition of the aggregate mass of holiness composed of the separate holiness of the several holy males of which she was composed, had they not in the above-mentioned holy place been thus assembled and met together. By ordinances issued by this holy female, a greater and surer measure of admiration, respect, and consequent obedience, was obtained than would have been obtained by the assembly in its plain and original character of an assembly of males, notwithstanding all their holiness.

By this combination thus happily accomplished, an effect no less felicitous and convenient than it was holy, was produced ; in the holy compound, while all the perfections of which both sexes are susceptible were found united, all imperfection, as if by chemical precipitation, were found to have been excluded. The holy men might, notwithstanding their holiness, have remained fallible ; the Holy Mother was found to be infallible. Her title to implicit confidence, and its naturally inseparable consequence implicit obedience, became at once placed upon the firmest ground, and raised to the highest pitch.

Great is the scandal, great to all well-disposed eyes the offence, if to her own children, or any of them, a mother has been an object of contempt ; proportioned to the enormity of the offence is the indignation of all well-disposed spectators, the magnitude of the punishment which they are content to see inflicted on the score of it, and the alacrity with which they are ready to concur in promoting the infliction of such punishment.

How much more intense that indignation, should any such indignity be offered to that holy character—should her servants or even her ordinances be violated. Flowing from the maternity of this *holy*, this *sanctified*, this *sacred* character—to all these epithets the same venerated import belongs ; they deserve the same respect : how convenient and useful the result !

When an edifice of the holy class has been erected and duly consecrated, proportioned to the holiness, the sanctity, the sacredness bestowed upon it in and by its consecration, is the enormity of any offence by which it has been profaned and its sanctity violated.

When, again, an edifice of the holy class has been erected and duly consecrated, the more sumptuous, the more magnificent, the more lofty, the more admirable, the more venerable the structure, the greater the calamity, the wider the ruin, the more intense the shock arising from its being subverted, the more intolerable the apprehension of the danger of its being subverted, the more intense and implacable the indignation excited towards and pointed against all persons regarded or considered as capable of being the authors or promoters of so shocking a catastrophe.

Already has been seen the advantage derivable and derived by and to the rulers of the Church, themselves being that Church, by the creation of a Church capable of being violated.

Here may now be seen the advantage producible and produced by and to the same rulers of the Church from the creation of a Church, themselves being that Church, capable of being subverted.

By any unholy person is this holy will in any particular opposed or threatened to be opposed—that same sacrilegious, unholy, profane, unbelieving infidel, miscreant, reprobate person is already a violator, and, in intention, a subverter of the Church, worthy of all indignation, all horror, all punishment, all vengeance, which it is in the power of any dutiful and worthy son of the Church to contribute to pour down upon his devoted head.

In the above example may be seen an instance of that impracticability which is liable to have place—the impracticability of exhibiting a definition of the term in question, where the import of the term is such that, antecedently to any such operation, a division of the contents of such its import requires to be made—its imports being in such sort compound and diverse that no one exposition, which shall at the same time be complete and correct, can be given of it.

In the particular instance here in question, although before any correct definition could be given it was necessary that an apt division should be made, yet, when once such division has been made, the need of any ulterior exposition in the shape of a definition may, perhaps, be seen or supposed to be, pretty effectually superseded ; other instances might, perhaps, be found in which such ulterior exposition might still be requisite.

Beard. Do you mean the beard of a *man* ? Beard ! Do you mean the beard of a *plant* ?—for example, barley or wheat. By these questions *division* is already made : and then for the instruction of any one to whom (he being acquainted with other sorts of wheat) it had not happened to him to have heard of the sort called *bearded wheat*, some sort of an *exposition*, in the shape of a definition, might be necessary.

In the above instance the imports, how widely and materially soever different, might, however, be seen to be connected with each other by a principle or chain of association. But the more important, especially in respect of practical purposes, the difference is, as also, the more liable the several senses are to be mistaken for each other—and that which, in one sense, is not true, however in another sense it may be true, to be understood in the sense in which it is not true—the more material is it that whatsoever distinction has place should be brought to light, and held up to view.

In all matters relative to the Church in so far as concerns the interests of the members of the Church, the good of the Church ought to be the object pursued in preference to any other. By each of two persons this proposition may, with perfect sincerity, have been subscribed. But according as to the word Church, the one or other of two very different, and in respect of practical consequences, opposite imports, has been annexed, their conduct may, on every occasion, be with perfect consistency exactly opposite ; one meaning by the word church *the subject many*—the other, by the same word, the *ruling few*.

At the same time, the number of pronounceable changes of which the letters of the alphabet are susceptible being, how ample soever, not altogether unlimited, instances cannot but have place in which to one and the same word divers imports, altogether uninterconnected by any such bond of association, may have happened to be attached.

Many, however, are the instances in which, of two or more in appearance widely different imports, the connexion, though real, may not be generally perceptible.

In French, by one and the same word, *worms* and *verses* are designated. Between two objects so widely dissimilar in any mind would there have existed any principle of connexion ?—Possibly not : in this instance possibly no such connexion has had place ; but neither is the contrary impossible. The French *vers* is from the Latin *versus* a verse ; but, in Latin, *vermes* is the name of a worm ; in the same language *verto* is ' to turn ' : and, who can say but that of *versus* and *vermes*, this verb *verto* may have been the common root. " Tread upon a worm and it will turn ", says an English proverb ; and, in the construction of verses, how much of turning the stock of words of which the language is composed requires is no secret to any person by whom a copy of verses has ever been made or read.

10. *Modes of Exposition employed by the Aristotelians*

In the preceding sections we have seen what the species of discourse, called an exposition, is, and of what modifications it is susceptible. Of some of these no conception appears to have been entertained by the Aristotelians. Others, it will now be seen, have been noticed by them, and stand comprised under the head of *definitio*, definition.

Of these modes, by far the most important is the one styled in the language of ancient Logic, *definitio per genus et differentiam.*

It consists in an indication given of a certain class of objects to which the object in question is declared to belong—that class being designated by a denomination styled a generic name. But the case being such that the object in question is not the only object which belongs to that class, some mark is at the same time attached as indicative of some property which is possessed by the object in question, and not possessed by any other individual or sub-class of objects included in that same class.[1]

Here, then, it may be seen already to what a degree the ancient Logic—for these 2000 years the only Logic—has in this by far the most useful track of it, the *tactic* branch, been all this while deficient. Its defectiveness of arrangement forms a sort of counterpart to its defectiveness in respect of argument, as exemplified in its list of Fallacies.[2]

To objects in general the system of division has never yet been applied, though, towards exhibiting the indefinite chain of divisions, one other advance, it is true, had been made by the ancient Logic. This advance consists in the use of the term *genus generalissimum*. By this term intimation, how obscure soever, was given of these links—of the three highest links in this chain. By the term *genus generalissimum* was designated the first class ; by the genus which was not the *genus generalissimum*, but of narrower extent and comprised within it, the next class ; and, by the term *species*, a class which was to the genus what the genus was to the *genus generalissimum*—a bi-sub-class.

Assigning the appropriate genus being one of the two operations included in the idea of a definition, according to this exclusively common acceptation of the word, the consequence was that whatsoever names were of such sort that no genus, in the import of which the classes respectively indicated by them were contained, was afforded by the language in use, of the words so circumstanced no such exposition as a definition, properly so called, could be furnished.

Susceptible of receiving a definition, in this usual and indeed only sense of the word *definition*, a *term* cannot be,

---

[1] Here, by the by, we have two sub-classes formed by the division of any one class ; of the one class in question, whatever it be. But as this class is divisible into two classes, say, sub-classes ; so may each of these sub-classes be divided each into two bi-sub-classes, each bi-sub-class into tri-sub-classes, and so on without end.

[2] See *Book of Fallacies*, Introduction, section 2.

unless it belong to and form a step in some assignable scale of aggregates, related to each other in the way of logical subalternation.

This word definition has, in many cases, been used as the collective designation for all modes of exposition. Sanderson does not, however, appear to have fallen into this error ; he always using *definitio* alone as the name of the genus and *definitio per genus et differentiam*, as the name of the particular species. In the foregoing chapter his example in this respect has not been followed, both on account of the difficulty there would be in finding a more appropriate single-worded denomination for the species, and on account of the more expressive nature of the word *exposition* as the name of the genus.

The Bishop has certainly not succeeded so well in the very first exposition he had occasion to give. In his chapter on the subject of the very word *definition*,[1] *Definitio*, he says, *est definiti explicatio*. And what, we may ask, is *explicatio* ? The answer might with equal clearness be : *Explicatio est explicati definitio*. The words employed are synonymous ; and the one as easy to be understood as the other. Not one of the rules of exposition laid down on the next 'page are followed in this case ; in fact, no new idea is at all conveyed. If any tolerably correct conception can be formed of what he meant by *definitio*, it must be gathered from the subsequent enumeration of its species, and not from the professed exposition.

His first division of the subject nearly coincides with its division into the exposition of *words alone*, and of objects connected with words ; but he falls into an error by giving to the results of this division the designations of *definitio nominis* and *definitio rei* ; every exposition being the exposition of a name, the difference consisting in this—that in one case we consider the name alone, in the other, the object in conjunction with that name

[1] Book I, Chap. 17, *De Definitione* [Sanderson says, " Definitio est Definiti *(sive nominis sive rei)* explicatio.—*Ed.*]

without which we cannot speak, nor perhaps think, of any fictitious entity, or of any real one, which is not present to our perception.

No mention is made of exposition by representation—the only mode that can be employed where the parties in question have no common language.

The division of *definitio nominis* would appear to comprehend the modes of *translation* and *etymologization*, whilst *definitio rei* may have been intended to mark the distinction made above into necessary and subsidiary modes of exposition : by the first, such properties only being exhibited as are necessary for exact exposition ; by the latter, other properties being presented to view for the purpose of facilitating comprehension. Exposition by paraphrasis, for want of a due conception of its nature, is put into the latter class ; the genera generalissima, and those fictitious entities to which that mode applies, being designated as things not susceptible of a perfect exposition. Of definition they certainly are not susceptible ; but the exposition of them by paraphrasis may be quite as perfectly applied as definition to real entities.

Of modes of description, the enumeration, or rather exemplification, is very imperfect. The first and last examples are alone applicable. *Frui est uti cum voluptate,* is a definition ; *Sol est mundi oculus* belongs to archetypation ; *Frigus est absentia caloris* is mere translation.

The four *canones definitionis* correspond with the four properties desirable in discourse :—

1. *Definitio verbis propriis, perspicuis, usitatis, et ab omni ambiguitate liberis, exprimatur* refers to clearness of expression ; *Nihil contineat superflui,* to conciseness ; *Nihil desit,* to completeness ; *Sit adequata definitio* to correctness. How far the author has himself followed these rules has already appeared in an instance derived from this chapter.

The *modus investigandi rerum definitiones,* detailed in the fifth paragraph, are sources of classification and belong to that head. His division of *Definitio,* lib. III. cap. 16, refers also to that subject.

VI.—LANGUAGE AS A SIGN-SYSTEM[1]

Relation as between Archetype and Type, with their respective Synonyms and Modification

When any two psychical real entities, any two ideas—whether perceptions, remembrances, or factitious mental images—have, either at the same instant, or at two contiguous or nearly contiguous instants, been present to the mind, each of them (such is the effect of this conjunction, however transient) acquires in the event of its reappearance a tendency to draw forth and introduce the other ; and the more frequently the conjunct appearance is repeated the more apt, *cæteris paribus*, is this tendency or probability to ripen into actuality.

This tendency is equal and mutual ; and, forasmuch as when considered in this most simple point of view, the two objects thus associated present not any points of difference by which either can be distinguished from the other, they are not, while considered in this point of view and no other, susceptible of different names.

When in respect of order of time, any difference between the two has place, in this difference may be found (it might be supposed) matter sufficient to serve as the ground for the formation of a difference in respect of name. But innumerable are the instances in which no difference·in point of *time* can be found to have place ; and even when a difference of this sort might perhaps be observable, to such a degree is it fugitive and questionable as to be altogether incapable of affording any permanent and sufficient practical ground for a permanent difference in respect of name.

At the same time, so it is that, for the two ideas in a

---

[1] [*Works*, Vol. VIII, pp. 331–2.]

pair of ideas thus associated, two different names, and those employed throughout a large portion of the field of thought, have been provided.

To the possibility of putting to any kind of use this difference in respect of name, some difference in respect of nature was an indispensable requisite. Of this necessary difference, a source was found in the order of *importance*. For designating the object regarded as superior in the scale of importance the word *archetype*, or thing signified, was employed ; for the other, the words *sign* and *type*.

In so far as any importance is considered as belonging to both, and if to both, in so far as any difference is considered as having place in their respective degrees of relative importance, that to which the highest degree is ascribed will be considered and spoken of as the archetype, or thing signified ; that to which no more than an inferior degree of importance, or what is, perhaps, more common, no importance at all is regarded as belonging, will be spoken of as the type or sign.

If, while importance is considered as belonging to both, no difference of level is considered as having place between their respective situations in the scale of importance, either may be considered as possessing the character of archetype, or thing signified in relation to the other, which in that case will be considered as operating in the character of type—performing the function of type or sign.

In so far as no degree of importance is regarded as belonging to either of them, no source of denomination can in that case be found for either of them ; neither of them presenting any pretension to the character of archetype, neither of them is capable of being designated by any such denominations as that of *type*.

The condition requisite to the establishment of this conjunction being so extremely simple, and such as in the nature of things cannot but be of continually repeated occurrence, design, human design, cannot but have been necessary to the exemplification of it.

But if, even without design, *i.e.* an exertion of the will applying itself to that purpose, it be capable of taking place, much more is it with and by design.

Of the production of this effect by design, language, in all its various forms, is the most extensive exemplification ; within the field of its operation, almost all other exemplifications are included.

In the case of language taken in the aggregate—the aggregate, composed of ideas or other psychical entities, capable of being expressed by language, being considered as constituting the aggregate archetype or thing signified ; the aggregate of the sounds employed for that purpose, constitute, with reference to it, the aggregate type or sign ; this aggregate type or sign being considered as the archetype, the aggregate of the images which, under the name of *letters*, are employed for the designation of those sounds, constitutes with reference to the aggregate of those same sounds, the aggregate type or sign.

Symbol, index, indication, token, badge—the ideas attached respectively to these words, are so many modifications of the idea attached to the word sign.

Though in the nature of the case, as above, no object of perception be incapable of being, in the character of type or sign, made to serve for bringing to the mind's view any other, yet, by reason of their natural permanence, or capacity for permanence, the signs most naturally and frequently applied to this purpose are of the *visible class*.

So extensive and, considered in its totality, so adequate to the purpose of designation is the collection of signs of which language is composed that any other sign or lesser aggregate of signs, to which on any occasion it happens to be applied to any part of the same purpose, is considered in no other light than that of a substitute to that supremely useful instrument.

Part II
SPECIAL PROBLEMS

I.—MOTION, REST, AND RELATIVITY.[1]

ALL bodies we are acquainted with, it is universally agreed, are compounds, as it were, of solid matter and empty space. All bodies, viz. the ultimate particles of solid matter which enter into their composition, are separated by intervals of space, in which no matter at all, at any rate none that we have any acquaintance with, is contained. To the different distances at which, in different states of its existence, the component particles of the same body are placed, are owing, in some degree, the different textures of which it is susceptible, and which, under different circumstances, it exhibits to our senses.

Take, for example, any mass of matter whatsoever : suppose an apple—the apple let it be from which Newton derived the first hint of the attraction of gravitation ; . . . the particles of solid matter of which this apple is constituted are each of them at a certain distance from each of the several others. How happens it that they are not more distant. What is the cause of such their propinquity ? The necessary fiction above spoken of provides an answer and says : The *attraction of cohesion* is the cause by the operation of which they are thus kept together. How happens it that they are as distant as they are ? What is the cause of such their distance ? Here again steps in the same useful respondent, and answers : It is by mutual *repulsion* that they are thus kept asunder.

It is to distinguish it from the attraction of *gravity*,

---

[1] [*Works*, Vol. VIII, pp. 129–30.]

of which presently, that the attraction, termed the attraction of cohesion, has acquired that name. Of this species of attraction, repulsion, it has been seen, is the constant companion and antagonist ; each of the opposite and mutually balancing effects have equal need of a fictitious cause. *Repulsion* is the generic name applicable to other cases. *Attraction of cohesion* is a specific one. To match with this its antagonist, the particular species of repulsion here in question requires its specific name. Repulsion corresponding to the attraction of cohesion, let this be that specific name ; or rather, an appellation thus multitudinously worded being too cumbersome for use, say, the *repulsion of cohesion* : and though taken by itself, and without explanation, the appellative would, upon the face of it, be self-contradictory, yet by this explanation, to which by its texture it would naturally point, it may perhaps be found not altogether unfit for use. Instead of this appellation, or for variety along with it, if for attraction of cohesion the appellation *internal attraction*, or *intestine attraction*, be employed ; for repulsion of cohesion, the term *internal repulsion*, or *intestine repulsion, may be employed.*

In the *Attraction of Gravity* may be seen one of the fictitious entities to the operation of which, in the character of causes or sources, the birth of motion, howsoever modified, may, as far as we are acquainted with it, be referred. To the repulsion of cohesion, to this one simple cause, will, it is believed, be found referable, with equal propriety, the death of all these several motions ; which, at the conclusion of the conflict maintained by the various species of attraction, endowed with their several unequal degrees of force, remains—constituting the only force by which matter is retained in that state of composition above mentioned, which seems essential to its existence ; and by which the whole multitude of its particles are prevented from being crowded together into one mass.

To account for the difference of bodies in point of distance, a sort of nominal entity is feigned, to represent the cause of it, and *Motion* is the name by which this imaginary cause is designated. Motion is thereupon considered (for such are the shifts that language is reduced to) as a sort of receptacle in which bodies are lodged ; they are accordingly said to be *in* motion, as a man is said to be *in* a house.

By laying out of consideration everything that concerns the particular nature of these bodies respectively ; everything, in a word, concerning them, but the difference between the distance or interval between them at the one time and the distance or interval between them at the other, we obtain the abstract idea, for the designation of which the word *motion* is employed. In speaking of it, we speak of it as if it were itself a substance : a hollow mass into which the body, the really and independently existing body, whatever it be and how vast soever it be, is capable of being put, and which is capable of being communicated to that body : and so in regard to bodies in any number.

A philosopher, says the old Greek story, denying the existence of Motion, another, to refute him, got up and walked. Good for a practical joke, not so for a serious refutation. Of the existence of the faculty of locomotion the denier of the existence of motion was not less perfectly aware before the experiment than after it. What he denied was—not the universally exemplified, and universally known, and acknowledged matter of fact that the same body is at one time in one place, at another time in another, and in that sense the existence of motion—but the existence of any real entity corresponding to the appellation motion ; any entity real and distinct from the body or bodies in which the motion is said to have place. . . .

Rest is the absence, non-existence, or negation of this imaginary receptacle. When, after observation taken of the two bodies in question, at two different points of time, no such difference of distance is found, they are said to have been during that length of time each of them at rest. Rest is thus a sort of imaginary pillar—or anchor, to which, in the English language, they are considered, or at least spoken of, as being fastened.

Enclosed in that receptacle, or fastened to this pillar or anchor—one or other is at every point of time the condition of every object to which the name of *body* has been attached.

The truth is that, absolutely and properly speaking, in as far as observation and inference have extended, motion is the state or condition in which, at every point, every body is, and so for ever is likely to continue. Rest is not the state of our own sun, about which the planet that we inhabit moves. If a state of rest were predicable of anything, it would be of the ideal point in the expanse of space, the *centre of gravity*, as it is called, about which the sun on the one part and the planets on the other are observed or supposed to turn. The observations and inferences thus applied, in the first instance, to our sun, have been extended to those other bodies to which, to distinguish them from those companions to our earth called planets, we give the name of fixed stars ; but which, determined as they have been by these observations and these inferences, it has seemed good to our astronomers not to tie to the above-mentioned pillar but to put all together into the above-mentioned receptacle.

So it is then, that, for the purposes of discourse, as well as of thought and action, the pillar is not less necessary to us than the receptacle. For this purpose, rest requires to be distinguished into *absolute* and *relative*. Absolutely speaking, as above, no one body is at rest ; but on this our little planet, the theatre of all our little doings and sufferings, bodies in abundance are to be found, which, as between any two given points of time, having been at the same distance from each other, have, during these two points of time, together with the whole interval, if any, that has been between them, been at rest. Upon the whole, then, absolute rest is not exemplified anywhere ; but, on the surface of our planet, exemplifications of relative rest may be found everywhere. These things considered, henceforward as often as *rest* is spoken of as having place, relative rest, and that alone, will be intended.

II.—SUBSTANTIVE AND ADJECTIVE[1]

Of the import of all the several sorts of conjugates actually existing and imaginable, the basis is the import of the noun-substantive.

A noun-substantive is the name of some entity, real or fictitious.

By a real entity, understand a substance—an object, the existence of which is made known to us by one or more of our five senses. A real entity is either a person or a thing, a substance rational, or a substance not rational.

By a fictitious entity, understand an object, the existence of which is feigned by the imagination—feigned for the purpose of discourse—and which, when so formed, is spoken of as a real one.

These sorts of fictitious entities may be classed in different ranks or orders, distinguished by their respective degrees of vicinity to the real one.

First comes motion—fictitious entity of the first order. To speak of a motion, we are obliged to speak of it as if it were a substance. We say, he or it is 'in motion'; thus speaking, we speak of a motion as if it were a place, a portion of space, and the person or thing situated in that place.

The absence or negation of motion is rest; we say that person or thing is *at rest*; speaking thus, we speak of rest as being a sort of substance—suppose a tree or a stone—and the person or the thing as being in a state of contiguity or relation to it.

Considered with reference to our senses, every particle of matter, perceived or perceptible at the *time* at which, or with reference to which it is considered, is either in a state of *motion* or in a state of *rest*.

---

[1] [*Works*, Vol. VIII, pp. 325–6.]

The state of rest is the negation of the state of motion. With reference to the same object, no particle of matter can therefore be in motion and at rest at the same time. To say that it is or can be, would be a self-contradictory proposition, resolvable into a pair of mutually contradictory propositions.

But take any body composed of a number of particles of matter, then so it is that, of and in that same body, while part, *i.e.* some of those particles, are in a state of motion, other parts may at the same time be in a state of rest.

When of any body it is said : " That body has been in motion ", what is meant is that, at or in different portions of the field of time, that body has occupied different portions or positions in the field of space.

As atoms or minimum portions may be conceived as having place in the field of space, so may atoms or minimum portions in the field of time.

If speaking of any body—suppose the play-thing called a peg-top—I say : " This body is now in motion " ; then, if by *now* I mean no more than a single atom or minimum portion of time, what I thus say cannot be exactly true, since, as above, for motion to have had place, or to have place, two atoms of time at the least are necessary.

But if, speaking as above, what I mean by *now* is a portion of the field of time, containing any number of atoms greater than one, then the proposition delivered by me in those same words may be true.

In general, the word *now*, when applied to motion, is understood as applicable with propriety. Why ? Because, in the utterance of the proposition to that effect, atoms in great number are employed.[1]

Here, then, we have a division of the states of which things, *i.e.* portions of matter, are susceptible, and that division an exhaustive one ; of states of things, and

[1] In the above distinction in regard to *existence*, and thence *thought*, may be seen the necessary basis of the distinction of qualities into active and passive, and of verbs into transitive and intransitive.

thence and therefore of the objects of thought, in so far as they come within that same denomination, viz., portions of matter.

States of things, when at rest, are their positions with reference to one another in the field of space.

States of things, when in motion, are motions.

Considered abstractedly from volition, a *motion* is termed an event ; a simple motion, a simple event ; a complex motion, a complex event.

Considered as the result of volition, a motion is termed *an act, an action*, an operation.

In the word *position*, we see already the name of one fictitious entity, and thereby, in so far as it can be said to be visible, one fictitious entity. In the word *motion* we see another.

Taking into consideration any body which we have been considering as having been in a state of motion, we thence take occasion to ascribe to it a *quality*, viz. *mobility* ; the quality which consists in the capacity of being, or aptitude to be, put *into*, and thence to be *in* a state of motion. Antecedent to our idea of this quality, mobility must have been our idea of the correspondent *state*, viz. a *state* of motion.

To substance we ascribe qualities ; to motion also we ascribe qualities. It is by this circumstance that of motion the import is placed, as it were, nearer to that of substance than that of qualities. Substances have their qualities ; they are large, small, long, short, thick, thin, and so forth : motions have their qualities ; they are quick, slow, rising, falling, continued, discontinued, regular, irregular, and so on.

If, then, *motion* be termed a fictitious entity of the *first* order—viz. that which is nearest to reality—mobility, and so any other quality, may with reference to it be termed a fictitious entity of the *second* order.

Here, then, we have an additional class of fictitious entities, of fictitious substances. We have largeness, smallness, length, shortness, thickness, thinness ; we have, moreover, quickness, slowness. We might have as well as rising, *risingness* ; as well as falling, *fallingness* ; as well as continued, *continuedness* ; as well as discontinued, *discontinuedness* ; we have as well as regular, *regularity* ; as well as irregular, *irregularity* ; attributes as well of substances as of motions.

Already has been brought to view, though as yet without special notice, a different sort of conjugate, the noun-adjective—*large, small, long, short, thick, thin,* and so forth.

This sort of conjugate, in what consists its difference from that which is the name of a quality ? In this : when we speak of *largeness,* there is largeness ; we speak of the fictitious substance so denominated, without reference made to any other object. On the contrary, when we say *large,* we present the idea of that same quality, but accompanied with the intimation of some other substance which is endued with that quality—some other object in which that quality has existence and is to be found. We put the mind upon the look-out for that other object, without which it is satisfied that the expression is incomplete ; that the idea presented by it is but, as it were, the fragment of an idea—a fragment, to the completion of which the idea of some object in which the quality is to be found is necessary.

In a word, the *substantival name* of a quality presents the idea in the character of a complete idea, conceivable of itself ; the *adjectival denomination* of that same quality presents the idea in the character of an incomplete idea, requiring for the completion of it the idea of some object in which it may be seen to *inhere.*

In the order of invention, proper names come before common names. Common names are the result of generalization ; every common name is the name of a general idea.

III.—THE FICTION OF RIGHT[1]

Otherwise than from the idea of obligation, no clear idea can be attached to the word *right*.

The efficient causes of right are two :—

1. Absence of correspondent obligation. You have a *right* to perform whatever you are not under obligation to abstain from the performance of. Such is the right which every human being has in a state of nature.

2. The second efficient cause of right is—presence of correspondent obligation. This obligation is the obligation imposed upon other persons at large to abstain from disturbing you in the exercise of the first-mentioned sort of right. The first-mentioned right may be termed a naked kind of right ; this second-mentioned right, a vested or established right.

The word *right* is the name of a fictitious entity ; one of those objects the existence of which is feigned for the purpose of discourse—by a fiction so necessary that without it human discourse could not be carried on.[2]

A man is said to have it, to hold it, to possess it, to acquire it, to lose it. It is thus spoken of as if it were a portion of matter such as a man may take into his hand, keep it for a time and let it go again. According to a phrase more common in law language than in ordinary language, a man is even spoken of as being *invested* with it. Vestment is clothing : invested with it makes it an article of clothing, and is as much as to say 'is clothed with it.'

To the substantive word are frequently prefixed, as

---

[1] [*Works*, Vol. III, pp. 217–19.]

[2] Though fictitious, the language cannot be termed *deceptious*—in intention at least, whatsoever in some cases may without intention be the result.

adjuncts and attributives, not only the word *political*, but the word *natural* and the word *moral* : and thus rights are distinguished into natural, moral, and political.

From this mode of speech, much confusion of ideas has been the result.

The only one of the three cases in which the word *right* has any determinate and intelligible meaning is that in which it has the adjunct political attached to it : in this case, when a man is said to have a right (mentioning it), the existence of a certain matter of fact is asserted ; namely, of a disposition, on the part of those by whom the powers of government are exercised, to cause him to possess, and so far as depends upon them to have the faculty of enjoying, the benefit to which he has a right. If, then, the fact thus asserted be true, the case is, that amongst them they are prepared on occasion to render him this service : and to this service on the part of the subordinate functionaries to whose province the matter belongs, he has, if so it be, a right : the supreme functionaries being always prepared to do what depends upon them to cause this same service to be rendered by those same subordinate functionaries.

Now, in the case of alleged natural rights, no such matter of fact has place—nor any matter of fact other than what would have place supposing no such natural right to have place. In this case, no functionaries have place ; or if they have, no such disposition on their part, as above, has place : for if it have, it is the case of a political right, and not of a merely natural right. A man is never the better for having such natural right ; admit that he has it, his condition is not in any respect different from what it would be if he had it not.

If I say a man has a right to this coat or this piece of land, meaning a right in the political sense of the word, what I assert is a matter of fact ; namely, the existence of the disposition in question as above.

If I say a man has a natural right to the coat or the land—all that it can mean, if it mean any thing and mean true, is that I am of opinion he ought to have a political right to it ; that, by the appropriate services rendered upon occasion to him by the appropriate functionaries of government, he ought to be protected and secured in the use of it : he ought to be so—that is to say, the idea of his being so is pleasing to me, the idea of the opposite result displeasing.

In the English language, an imperfection, perhaps peculiar to that language, contributes to the keeping up of this confusion.   In English, in speaking of a certain man and a certain coat, or a certain piece of land, I may say it is right he should have this coat or this piece of land.   But in this case, beyond doubt, nothing more do I express than my satisfaction at the idea of his having this same coat or land.

This imperfection does not extend itself to other languages.   Take the French, for instance.   A Frenchman will not say, *Il est droit que cet homme ait cet habit :* what he will say is, *Il est juste que cet homme ait cet habit.   Cet appartient de droit à cet homme.*

If the coat I have on is mine, I have a *right* by law to knock down, if I can, any man who by force should attempt to take it from me ; and this right is what in any case it can scarcely be but that a man looks to when he says, *I have a right* to a constitution, to such or such an effect—or a right to have the powers of government arranged in such manner as to place me in such or such a condition in respect of actual right, actually established rights, political rights.

To engage others to join with him in applying force, for the purpose of putting things into a state in which he would actually be in possession of the right of which he thus pretends to be in possession, is at bottom the real object and purpose of the confusion thus endeavoured to be introduced into men's ideas, by employing a word in a sense different from what it had been wont to be employed, and from thus causing men to accede in words to positions from which they dissent in judgment.

This confusion has for its source the heat of argument. In the case of a political right, when the existence of it is admitted on all sides, all dispute ceases. But when so it is that a man has been contending for a political right which he either never has possessed, or having in his possession, is fearful of losing, he will not quietly be beaten out of his claim ; but in default of the political right, or as a support to the political right, he asserts he has a natural right. This imaginary natural right is a sort of thread he clings by : in the case in question, his having any efficient political right is a supposed matter of fact, the existence of the contrary of which is but too notorious ; and being so, is but too capable of being proved. Beaten out of this ground, he says he has a natural right—a right given him by that kind goddess and governess Nature, whose legitimacy who shall dispute ? And if he can manage so as to get you to admit the existence of this natural right, he has, under favour of this confusion, the hope of getting you to acknowledge the existence of the correspondent political right, and your assistance in enabling him to possess it.

It may, however, be said, to deny the existence of these rights which you call imaginary, is to give a *carte blanche* to the most outrageous tyranny. The rights of a man anterior to all government, and superior as to their authority to every act of government—these are the rampart, and the only rampart, against the tyrannical enterprises of government. Not at all—the shadow of a rampart is not a rampart ; a fiction proves nothing ; from that which is false you can only go on to that which is false. When the governed have no right, the government has no more. The rights of the governed and the rights of the government spring up together ;—the same cause which creates the one creates the other.

H

IV.—THE FICTION OF AN ORIGINAL CONTRACT[1]

With respect to this, and other fictions, there was once a time, perhaps, when they had their use. With instruments of this temper, I will not deny but that some political work may have been done, and that useful work, which, under the then circumstances of things, could hardly have been done with any other. But the season of *Fiction* is now over : insomuch that what formerly might have been tolerated and countenanced under the name, would, if now attempted to be set on foot, be censured and stigmatized under the harsher appellations of *encroachment* or *imposture*. To attempt to introduce any *new* one, would be *now* a crime ; for which reason there is much danger, without any use, in vaunting and propagating such as have been introduced already. In point of political discernment, the universal spread of learning has raised mankind in a manner to a level with each other, in comparison of what they have been in any former time ; nor is any man now so far elevated above his fellows, as that he should be indulged in the dangerous licence of cheating them for their good.

As to the fiction now before us, in the character of an *argumentum ad hominem*, coming when it did, and managed as it was, it succeeded to admiration.

That compacts, by whomsoever entered into, *ought* to be kept ; that men are *bound* by compacts ; are propositions which men, without knowing or inquiring why, were disposed universally to accede to. The observance of promises they had been accustomed to see pretty constantly enforced. They had been accustomed to see Kings, as well as others, behave themselves as if bound by them. This proposition, then, " that men are bound

---

by *compacts* ", and this other, " that, if one part performs not his part, the other is released from his ", being propositions which no man disputed, were propositions which no man had any call to prove. In theory they were assumed for axioms : and in practice they were observed as rules.[1] If, on any occasion, it was thought proper to make a show of proving them, it was rather for form's sake than for any thing else ; and that, rather in the way of memento or instruction to acquiescing auditors than in the way of proof against opponents. On such an occasion the commonplace retinue of phrases was at hand ; *Justice*, *Right Reason* required it, the *Law of Nature* commanded it, and so forth : all which are but so many ways of intimating that a man is firmly persuaded of the truth of this or that moral proposition, though he either thinks he *need not*, or finds he *can't*, tell *why*. Men were too obviously and too generally interested in the observance of these rules to entertain doubts concerning the force of any arguments they saw employed in their support. It is an old observation, how Interest smooths the road to Faith.

A compact, then, it was said, was made by the King and People ; the terms of it were to this effect :—The People, on their part, promised to the King a *general obedience* : the King, on his part, promised to *govern* the People in such a *particular* manner, always, as should be *subservient* to their happiness. I insist not on the words, I undertake only for the sense—as far as an imaginary engagement, so loosely and so variously worded by those who have imagined it, is capable of any decided signification. Assuming, then, as a general rule, that promises, when made, ought to be observed ; and, as a point of fact, that a promise to this effect in particular had been made by the party in question, men were more ready to deem themselves qualified to judge when it was such a promise was *broken*, than to decide directly and avowedly

---

[1] A *compact* or *contract* (for the two words, on this occasion at least, are used in the same sense) may, I think, be defined a pair of promises, by two persons reciprocally given, the one promise in consideration of the other.

on the delicate question, when it was that a King acted so far in *opposition* to the happiness of his People, that it were better no longer to obey him.

It is manifest, on a very little consideration, that nothing was gained by this manœuvre after all : no difficulty removed by it. It was still necessary, and that as much as ever, that the question men studied to avoid should be determined, in order to determine the question they thought to substitute in its room. It was still necessary to determine, whether the King in question had, or had not, acted so far in *opposition* to the happiness of his people, that it were better no longer to obey him, in order to determine whether the promise he was supposed to have made had or had not been broken. For what was the supposed purport of this promise ? It was no other than what has just been mentioned.

Let it be said that part at least of this promise was to govern in *subservience to Law* : that hereby a more precise rule was laid down for his conduct, by means of this supposal of a promise, than that other loose and general rule to govern in subservience to the *happiness of his people* : and that, by this means, it is the letter of the *Law* that forms the tenor of the rule.

Now true it is, that the governing in opposition to Law is *one* way of governing in opposition to the happiness of the people : the natural effect of such a contempt of the Law being, if not actually to destroy, at least to threaten with destruction, all those rights and privileges that are founded on it ; rights and privileges on the enjoyment of which that happiness depends. But still it is not this that can be safely taken for the entire purport of the promise here in question ; and that for several reasons. *First*—because the most mischievous, and under certain constitutions the most feasible, method of governing in opposition to the happiness of the people, is by setting the Law itself in opposition to their happiness. *Second*—because it is a case very conceivable that a King may, to a great degree, impair the happiness of his people without violating the letter of any single Law. *Third*—because extraordinary occasions may now and then occur, in which the happiness of the people may be better promoted by acting, for the moment, in *opposition* to the Law, than in *subservience* to it. *Fourth*—because it is not any single violation of the Law, as such, that can properly be taken for a breach of his part of the contract, so as to be understood to have released the people from the obligation of performing theirs. For, to quit the fiction, and resume the language of the plain truth, it is scarce ever any single violation of the Law that, by being *submitted to*, can produce so much mischief as shall surpass the probable mischief of *resisting* it. If every single instance whatever of such a violation were to be deemed an entire dissolution of the contract, a man who reflects at all would scarce find anywhere, I believe, under the sun, that Government which he could allow to subsist for twenty years together. It is plain, therefore, that to pass any sound decision upon the question which the inventors of this fiction substituted instead of the true one, the latter was still necessary to be decided. All they gained by their contrivance was the convenience of deciding it obliquely, as it were, and by a side wind; that is, in a crude and hasty way, without any direct and steady examination.

V.—ANALYSIS, PHYSICAL AND LINGUISTIC [1]

Of every *logical analysis*—of every system of logical divisions—the subject is a *logical whole*. But, any such logical analysis, nowhere could it ever have had a subject, but for that system of *primeval* logical analysis, which has had for its subjects *physical wholes*, and for its *results* those ideas which, at the very moment of their conception, were respectively accompanied and fixed by so many *names* or *denominations* :—signs, by means of which, in so far as those signs were the sort of names called *common* names, those ideas were, as it were, tied up into bundles, called *sorts, kinds, species, genera, classes*, and the like : the connexion being effected by another sort of logical instrument, which, as will be seen, is not *analysis*, but its converse, *synthesis*.

Of this double course—a course of *analysis* conjoined with a correspondent course of *synthesis*—the commencement must have had place in the very infancy of society ; and neither to the continuance nor to the extension of it can any conceivable bounds be assigned, other than those which apply to the extension and continuance of society itself.

1. Difference between a *physical whole* and a *logical whole* ; 2. difference between *physical analysis* and *logical analysis*, when both have for their subject a *physical whole* ; 3. difference between logical *analysis* and logical *synthesis* ; 4. operation and instrument by which *logical synthesis* is performed ; 5. necessity of an antecedent logical *analysis*, performed upon a physical whole, to the previous *formation*, and thence to the subsequent *analysis* of a *logical* whole ; 6. necessity of an act of logical *synthesis* to the formation of such logical whole : such are the

points, on all which, as soon as the definitions of the two species of *wholes* have been given, a conjunct illustration will be attempted.

By a *physical whole*, understand any *corporeal real entity*, considered as being in one mass, and without any regard paid at the instant to any parts that might be observable in it : for instance, this or that individual *plant*.

By a *logical whole*, understand that sort of fictitious *aggregate*, or *collection* of objects, for the designation of which any one of those names which, in contradistinction to *proper* names, are termed *common* names, are employed ; for example, the aggregate designated by that same word *plant*. The common name *plant* is applicable to every individual plant that grows ; and not only to those, but moreover to all those which ever grew in time past and to all those which will grow in time future ; and in saying, of any one of them individually taken—viz. of those that are now growing—" this plant exists ", there is no fiction. But the *aggregate*, conceived as composed of all plants, present, past, and future put together, is manifestly the work of the *imagination*—a pure fiction. The *logical whole*, designated by the word *plant*, is therefore a *fictitious* entity.

For the illustration of these several points, follow now a short history, which though at no time perhaps realized in every minute particular, must many millions of times have been exemplified in every circumstance which to the purpose of the present explanation is a *material* one.

Walking one day over his grounds, a certain husbandman observed a plant which was not of the number of those which he was employed in cultivating. Overhanging some of them, it seemed to him to impede their growth. Taking out his knife, he cut the plant off just above the root ; and a fire, in which he was burning weeds for the ashes, being near at hand, he threw it into the fire. In so doing, he had thus in two different modes performed, upon this physical *whole*, the physical *analysis*. By being cut as it was, it became divided into two parts, viz. the *root*, and that which was above the root : and this in the *mechanical* mode was the physical analysis performed upon it. By its being thrown into the fire and there consumed, of the portion so cut off as above, part was made to fly off in the state of *gas*, the rest stayed behind in the state of *ashes* : and thus in the *chemical* mode was the physical analysis performed upon it.

Not long after, came a daughter of his that same way, and a plant of the same kind which her father had thus cut down being left standing, her *attention* was caught by the beauty of it. It was a sweet-brier rose, of which one flower had just expanded itself. All parts of the plant were not alike beautiful. By one part her attention was more forcibly engaged than by the rest. It was the flower. To examine it more closely, she plucked it off and brought it near her eye. During its approach, the scent of it became perceptible ; and thus another sense received its gratification. To prolong it, she tried to stick the flower in a part of her dress that covered her bosom. Meeting with some resistance, the stalk to which, with a few leaves on it, the flower was attached, was somewhat bruised ; and now she perceived and distinguished another odour, which though not less agreeable, was somewhat different from the first.

All this while she had been performing upon this physical whole the logical operation termed *logical analysis*: performing it not the less, though, as in Molière's *Bourgeois Gentilhomme* Monsieur Jourdan [*sic*] when talking *prose*, without knowing it. The *instrument*, by which this mental *operation* was performed by her, was the fictitious entity *attention*. By the attention which she bestowed upon the flower, while no equal degree of attention was bestowed upon any other part of the plant, she analysed it—she mentally *resolved* or divided it—into *two* parts, viz., the *flower*, and all that was not the flower : and thus she distinguished part from part.

Again. By applying her attention, first to the *beauty* of the flower, composed as it was of the beauty of its *form* and the beauty of its *colour*, she performed in this same original subject *another* analysis, which though still a *logical* analysis, was productive of results somewhat different from those produced by the former ; for thus, in the same *part* she distinguished two *properties* or *qualities* ; viz. that of presenting to the sense of *sight* a peculiarly agreeable *appearance*, and that of presenting to the sense of *smell* a peculiarly agreeable odour. The *parts* were both of them *real* entities : the *qualities* were, both of them, *fictitious* entities.

Eager to communicate the discovery to a little brother of hers, she took him to the spot : she showed him the *plant* from which the flower had been plucked. The flower had already become a subject of conversation to them ; that part had already received the name of *flower* ; not having equally engaged her attention, the other part, like a sheep in a flock, or a pig in a litter, remained without any distinctive name.

Ere long her sweet-brier rose put forth two other blossoms ; being so little different from the first, each of these became *flower* likewise. From a *proper* name, flower thus became a *common* name.

In the course of another social ramble, a *mallow* plant, with a flower on it, met her eye. At a distance the flower was not yet distinguished from that of the *sweet-brier rose* —" Ah," (cried she) " here is *flower* again." The *sweet-brier*, on acount of its scent, which continued after the flower was gone, had been preserved : the *mallow*, having nothing but colour to recommend it, was neglected.

These rambles had not continued long, before other sweet-briers and other mallows met her eye. The former being regarded with interest, the other with comparative indifference, the occasion for distinguishing them in conversation was not unfrequently recurring. The *rose flower* became a *rose flower*, the *mallow flower* a *mallow flower*.

When the flower first observed was named *flower*, as

yet nothing but *analysis—logical* analysis—had been performed ; no operation of the nature of logical *synthesis* : of one individual object it was and no other that the word *flower* had been made the name. But, no sooner was the *second* flower observed, and the same name *flower*, which had been applied to the first, applied to this other, than an act of logical synthesis was performed. The *proper* name was thus turned into a *common* one ; and the fictitious entity, called a *sort*, a *kind*, a *species*, or a *genus* (call it which you please) was created.[1]

The *fictitious* entity being nothing at all, and the two *real* entities being each of them something, the *fictitious* entity itself did not contain within itself the two real entities, or either of them. But the name, which, after having occasionally been applied to each of the two *real* entities, became, by degrees, designative of the *fictitious* entity deduced from them, as above, by abstraction, continued to be employed for the designation of *either* of them and occasionally for the designation of *both* of them together : and thus, in a sense, which, although not strictly proper, has the advantage of conciseness, the one *fictitious* entity, the *species*, may be said to have contained, and to contain, the two individual *real* ones : to *contain*, viz. though not in a physical, in a logical sense.[2]

[1] *Genus* and *species* are words which cannot, either of them, be employed without impliedly asserting the existence of the other. Both are aggregates or names of aggregates ; *genus* is the whole, of which *species* is a part. Suppose but *one* aggregate, either of these names may as well be applied to it as the other ; or rather, and for the above reason, neither can with propriety be applied to it.

[2] Thus it is, that, considered as distinct from the individuals contained in them, these aggregates, as above, are but *fictitious entities*— the *names*, employed in the designation of them, so many names of *fictitious entities*. But, when compared with names of fictitious entities at large, these may be seen to have something peculiar in them, which, if he would avoid confusion and disputation, it seems necessary a man should have in mind. In this case, the same word which is employed to signify the fictitious entity, viz., the *fictitious aggregate*, is also employed to designate anyone of the individual real entities of which that aggregate is regarded as being composed : an homonymy, which may be seen not to have place in the instance of any other sort of fictitious entity, such as a *quality*, a *property*, a *relation*, and the like. Nor let it be said that because it contains real entities the aggregate called a *species*, a *genus*, a *class*, is itself a real entity. For by the word *plant*—taking *plant*, for example, for the aggregate—are designated

The analysis thus unconsciously performed by the maiden on the first-observed sweet-brier rose, viz. by not only all plants existing at the time of the speaking or the writing of that word, but also all plants that ever have existed and all plants that ever shall exist in future—and even all plants that, without existing, shall be but conceived to exist : and to these last, at any rate, the term *real entity* will hardly be regarded as properly applicable. But though, in addition to the several individual objects, to which the word *plant* is applicable, no real entity corresponding to it has *place* out of the human mind, yet, *within* that receptacle, by the same *name* of a *fictitious* entity, a *real entity*, a *general idea*—an entity which, though not corporeal, is not less *real* than that which is produced in it by the sight or touch of an individual plant—is produced. To convince himself of this, the reader need but ask himself whether after, and by thus reading the word *plant*, his mind is not put in a state more or less different from that which it was in before this word was read by him. If this be not enough, then let him say, whether by the proposition, *plants have a property which minerals have not*, three distinguishable mental sensations at least—not to speak of any others —have not been produced in his mind : three perfectly distinct *ideas*, each of which is of that sort which is termed a *general* or *abstract* one. Yet, to some philosophers, it has, somehow or other, been matter of supposed discovery, that there are no such things as general or abstract ideas : not considering that, if this position of theirs were true, nothing that they say in proof of it would have so much as the least chance of being productive of the effect they aim at ; or, to speak still more generally, scarcely would anything they say be productive of any more effect than would be produced by so much nonsense. Yes : by the word *plant*, or the word *plants*, when read, an effect, a sort of *feeling*, or *mental image*, is as really produced, as by the sight of any individual plant—and it is a clearly different one. In the one case it is an *abstract idea* ; in the other case, an *impression* : but in the one there is just as much reality as in the other. Of the evidence of the existence of the general idea, the probative force is even nearer, and more promptly and surely satisfactory, than that of the existence of any individual *plant*, from which, by abstraction, that general idea was deduced. In the former case, the evidence is *perception* ; in the other case, it is but *inference*—ratiocination, and *that* such ratiocination as many an acute mind (Bishop Berkeley's for instance) has not been satisfied with.

In speaking of *genera* and *species*, two sources of indistinctness and confusion, and (if observed) of perplexity, are continually presenting themselves. One is the difficulty which, on the appearance of a generic or specific name, is found, in determining whether it is the fictitious entity, the aggregate *itself*, or only the *name* employed for the designation of it—that, in the character of the subject of the proposition, the word is intended to bring to view. The other is the penury and imperfection under which language—the best constructed not excepted— still labours : viz. in respect of its furnishing no more than these two names, for the designation of the results of any number of ramifications, which, in a system of logical division, there may have been occasion to bring to view. Hence it is that the same word which, with reference to this or that other is a *generic* term, is *specific* with reference to a third. Hence again the continually recurring question—is this a *generic* or a *specific* name ? and the dispute with [which] that question is pregnant is altogether an interminable one.

applying her attention to one part, while it was not applied to the other, had for its object the *real* entity, the physical whole. It may be termed the *primeval* or *primordial* analysis : for by no other sort of logical analysis will it be found capable of having been preceded. The analysis by which the rose-flower became *rose-flower*, and the mallow-flower, *mallow-flower*, had for its subject no other than the fictitious entity, the logical whole, viz. the *whole* designated, fixed, and, as it were, created, by the denomination *flower*, so soon as, after having been employed merely as a *proper* name, it had come to be employed as a *common*, and thence a *specific* name. It may be termed the *secondary* analysis, or *analysis of the second order.* In her young mind, and in this its simple form, this secondary mode of analysis had nothing in it of science, nothing of system. But, in it may be seen the germ of all those systems of division, which, being framed by scientific hands, have spread so much useful light over every portion of the field of art and science.

The maiden had for her sweetheart a young man, who, though not a member of the Company of Apothecaries (for the company had not yet received its charter) had, on his part, been engaged in a little train of observations, to an improved and extended series of which, together with the experiments which they suggested, some thousands of years afterwards that most useful and respectable community became indebted for its establishment.

He had observed his dog, after a full meal, betake itself to a grass-plat and gnaw the grass : a sort of article which, when hungry, it had never been seen to meddle with. To this sagacious swain the maiden was not backward in reporting her above-mentioned discoveries. It might, perhaps, have been not altogether impossible to obtain a communication of some of these observations and discoveries of his, for the purpose of adding them to hers. But, for the explanation of what has here been endeavoured to be explained, what has already been reported of the damsel's will, it is hoped, be found to suffice, without any further trial of the reader's patience.[1]

Some thousands of years after appeared Linnæus. In

[1] In their present shape the conceptions above brought to view would not have been formed, nor consequently would this section have been penned, but for a very recent glance cast on the *Logic* of Condillac. More than once, at different times, had that little work been glanced over or at least glanced at ; never without its presenting itself in the character of a mass of confusion from which little or no information was to be reaped. *Analysis* is the name there given to the instrument by which everything is there supposed to be done : everything by that *one* instrument ; in every case that one instrument the same. Language-making was *analysing* : and " *analysis* itself was but *a well-made language* " (pp. 88 ff., 121 ff.). On looking at the work once more, observation was made of such passages in which—always under this one name, *analysis*—an explanation is given of the mode for the distinguishing of which the epithet primeval has herein-above been just employed. Now for the first time presented itself to view matter which seemed capable of being put to use. A resolution was accordingly taken, to endeavour to derive such instruction as might be found derivable from it. Its claim to *attention* being now recognized, thus it was that, by a closer application of that faculty, those distinctions which have above been seen were brought to view. *Logical analysis* of the *physical whole, logical synthesis* performed upon the qualities—upon the *parts* which had been produced by that *logical analysis*—these, together with the logical analysis of those aggregates which were the products of that *logical* synthesis, were in the logic of Condillac seen, all of them, designated by and confounded together under the one undiscriminating term *analysis*. For the subject of the *primeval* analysis, Condillac, before he came to the *plant*, had employed a magnificently furnished château ; for the present occasion, a couple of plants seemed quite sufficient, without any such encumbrance as the château. Moreover, of the sort of work here in question abundance must have been done before there were any such things as châteaux.

Yes (says somebody), and so there was before husbandmen's daughters amused themselves with gathering flowers. The ancestors of husbandmen were shepherds ; the ancestors of shepherds, hunters. In certifying this genealogy Geography joins with History.

Assuredly (it may be answered), man had need to provide food before maidens had need to gather flowers. But, to provide food, man must somehow or other have been in being, and able to provide it. Here then the explanation would have been entangled in the mysteries of Cosmogony—a subject which, besides its inexplicability, is altogether foreign to the present purpose. No doubt that for *attention*, and thence for *analysis*—to be performed, as above, upon these *physical wholes*—and thence for *synthesis*, and thence for *logical analysis*, to be performed upon the *logical wholes*—results of these *logical syntheses*, demands much more urgent as well as much more early, must have been produced by eatable *fruits* and *roots* than ever can have been produced by *flowers*. But, by any such illustration, we should have been sent to the Garden of Eden : and of that garden no map being to be had sufficiently particular for the present purpose, there we should have lost ourselves.

Pluming himself as it should seem upon the discovery, and bringing the course of that interval, not only in the language in which he wrote, but in every lettered language at least, not indeed with perfect steadiness, but still without much dispute or variation, a name corresponding to the word

it to view as such thrice in two small 12mo. pages, Condillac (pp. 114, 115) will have it that languages are but so many *analytic methods—méthodes analytiques* ; meaning, as far as he can be said to mean anything, the results of so many analytic—purely analytic—processes. He sees not that so far from being an analytic process, the process by which the principal and fundamental materials of all languages—viz. *common* names—are framed, is of a nature exactly opposite to that of analysis ; viz. *synthesis.* True it is that this *synthetic* is necessarily preceded by an *analytic* process ; viz. by the one above explained under the denomination of the *primeval* or *inerudite* analysis : a *logical* analysis performed upon *physical wholes.* True it also is that, to the *wholes* which are the results of this synthetic process—with the exception of those *minimums* which are in immediate contact with individuals—another analytic process may to any extent be applied, viz. the scientific or *logical* analysis performed upon these logical wholes. But how promptly soever they may succeed to each other, *disaggregation* and *aggregation*—putting asunder and putting together —never can be one and the same operation, never can be other than opposite operations ; and but for and by means of the aggregative process, not a single word—not a single instrument—would the philosopher have had wherewith to put together this his not sufficiently considered account of the formation of language.

One of these days—the sooner the better—by a still closer application of the faculty of *attention,* a more discerning eye will perhaps discover and bring to light similar imperfections in the account given of the matter in these pages ; and thus it is that by still closer and closer application of that same faculty additional *correctness, distinctness,* and *comprehensiveness* is given to man's conceptions, in relation to each and every portion of the field of art and science.

Of the aggregations thus formed, some have been better made, others worse. Those which he regards as having been better made were (he assures us) the work of *Nature ;* those which were worse made, the work of learned men—meaning such whose labours in this line he saw reason to disapprove of. Nature being a sort of goddess, and that a favourite one—by ascribing to this goddess whatsoever was regarded by him as good, he seems to have satisfied himself that he had proved the goodness of it : and by so concise an expedient—an expedient, in the employment of which he has found but too many successors as well as contemporaries and predecessors—he has saved himself no small quantity of trouble.

Nature is a sort of fictitious personage, without whose occasional assistance it is scarce possible (it must be confessed) either to write or speak. But, when brought upon the carpet, she should be brought on in her proper *costume*—nakedness : not bedizened with *attributes*— not clothed in *eulogistic* any more than in *dyslogistic* moral qualities. Making minerals, vegetables, and animals—this is her proper work— and it is quite enough for her ; whenever you are bid to see her doing **man's** work, be sure it is not *Nature* that is doing it but the **author,** or somebody or other whom he patronizes and whom he has dressed up for the purpose in the goddess's robes. . . .

plant had been in use to be employed in the designation of any one of those physical objects, to which, when individually taken, that same denomination continues to be applied.

For the same length of time accordingly, a *logical whole,* possessing this vast extent—a *logical whole,* formed by the logical process called *synthesis*—had been in possession of the sort of existence which the nature of an object of this sort admits of.

For the purpose of distributing, according to such of these properties as were at the same time most easily observable, most steady in their union, and most interesting to man, whether in the way of use or harm, such individual plants as from time to time should come under observation—and *this* to the end that such names might be given to them, whereby, for the purpose of putting to use their useful properties, or excluding the operation of their pernicious properties, they might, when seen, be recognized—various sources of division had occurred to various scientific observers. By none of them had this useful object been completely accomplished. To Linnæus it appeared, that it was in the *flower* that the most apt source of division was to be found : inasmuch as, for the determination of the principal and most comprehensive divisions of a vast logical whole, certain differences, in respect of the form in which that part manifests itself, might be made to serve with as yet unknown advantage. Why ? Because, with those differences in respect of the flower, other differences in respect of some of the properties most interesting to man—differences pervading the entire mass of each individual plant—had been observed to be conjoined. Thence, by seeing what sort of a thing the plant in question is, in respect of the flower, a guess may be formed, better than can be formed by any other means, what sort of a thing the plant is in other respects.

From this view a conception may be formed of the disadvantage under which every system of logical division comes to be framed. In this way no two things can be put asunder, but what have first been put together. To no other objects can this mode of analysis be applied other than to *logical wholes*—objects which are altogether the product of so many antecedent logical *syntheses*. But, in the first place, the primeval logical analysis, performed upon individual objects—this process, notwithstanding this its scientific name, having taken its commencement at the very earliest stage of society, cannot but have had for its operators the most unexperienced, the most uninformed, and unskilful hands. In the next place, the *synthetic process*, by which the results of that analysis, fragments detached by abstraction from these physical wholes, were placed as it were under so many different common names, and by those names bound together by so many logical ties—this likewise was a work, which, though not yet concluded, nor in a way to be soon concluded, must in its commencement have been coeval even with that of the primeval process, to which it has been indebted for all the materials on which it has had to operate : coeval with the very first crude effusions, or the results of which the matter of spoken, and thence of written language, came, by continual additions, to be composed.

Thus stands the matter, in regard to those names of aggregates in the signification of which are comprised such individual objects as are purely corporeal. How then stands it (says somebody) in regard to objects of the *pneumatic* cast, *real* and *fictitious* ? The answer is—to apply to this division of the objects of thought the triple process, just above described, would require a full and detailed explanation of the nature of those *fictitious* entities, which, by reason of the similarity of the aspect of their names to that of the names of corporeal objects, all which names are *real* entities, are so continually confounded with real ones. But to suggest the question is almost all that can be done here. To attempt anything like a complete answer would be to transgress beyond endurance the proper limits of this work.

VI.—SUMMARY[1]

Entities are either *real* or *fictitious* : real, either *perceptible* or *inferential* ; perceptible, either *impressions* or *ideas* ; inferential, either *material, i.e. corporeal* or *immaterial, i.e. spiritual.* Material are those of which the principal divisions are exhibited in the *Ramean* tree : of such inferential real entities as are immaterial, examples may be seen in the Almighty Being, and in the human soul, considered in a state of separation from the body.

By *fictitious entities* are here meant, not any of those which will be presented by the name of *fabulous, i.e.* imaginary *persons,* such as *Heathen Gods, Genii,* and *Fairies,* but such as *quality—property* (in the sense in which it is nearly synonymous to *quality) relation, power, obligation, duty, right,* and so forth. Incorrect as it would be if the entities in question were considered as being, in point of reality, upon a footing with *real* entities as above distinguished, the supposition of a sort of *verbal* reality, so to speak, as belonging to these fictitious entities is a supposition without which the matter of language could never have been formed, nor between man and man any converse carried on other than such as hath place between brute and brute.

Fictitious as they are, entities of this description could not be spoken of at all if they were not spoken of as *real* ones. Thus a *quality* is spoken of as being *in* a thing or a person : *i.e.* the thing or the person is spoken of as being a *receptacle* and the *quality* as being something that is contained *in* it.

As in the case of all words which have an immaterial as well as a material import, the root of the *immaterial* will be found in the *material* ; so, to explain the nature

[1] [*Works*, Vol. VIII, pp. 126–7.]

I

and origin of the idea attached to the name of a *fictitious* entity, it will be necessary to point out the *relation* which the import of that word bears to the import of one or more names of *real* entities : *i.e.* to show the *genealogy*, or (to borrow an expression from the mathematicians) the *genesis* of the fictitious entity.

From the observation by which, for example, the words *duties* and *rights* are here spoken of as names of fictitious entities, let it not for a moment so much as be supposed that, in either instance, the reality of the object is meant to be denied in any sense in which in ordinary language the reality of it is assumed. One question, however, may be ventured to be proposed for consideration, viz. whether, supposing no such sensations as *pleasure* or *pain*, *duties* would not be altogether without force, and *rights* altogether without value ?

On this occasion, in the case of the name of a fictitious entity, a distinction requires to be made between the *root* of the *idea* and the *root* of the *word* by which it is designated. Thus, in the case of *obligation*, if the above conception be correct, the root of the *idea* is in the ideas of pain and pleasure. But the root of the *word*, employed as a sign for the designation of that idea, is altogether different. It lies in a material image, employed as an *archetype* or *emblem* : viz. the image of a *cord*, or any other *tie* or *band* (from the Latin *ligo*, to bind) by which the object in question is *bound* or fastened to any other, the person in question bound to a certain course of practice.

Thus, for the explanation of a fictitious entity, or rather of the name of a fictitious entity, two perfectly distinct species of operations—call them *paraphrasis* and *archetypation*—will, in every case, require to be performed ; and the corresponding sorts of propositions, which are their respective results, formed ; viz. the *paraphrasis*, performing the function of a *definition*, but in its *form* not coinciding with any proposition to which that name is commonly attached.

The *paraphrasis* consists in taking the word that requires to be expounded—viz. the name of a *fictitious* entity—and, after making it up into a *phrase*, applying to it another phrase, which, being of the same import, shall have for its principal and characteristic word the name of the corresponding *real* entity. In a *definition*, a phrase is employed for the exposition of a single word : in a *paraphrasis*, a phrase is employed for the exposition of an entire phrase, of which the word, proposed to be expounded, is made to constitute the principal or characteristic word.

Archetypation (a word employed, for shortness, rather than *archetypophantia*, *i.e.* indication of the archetype or pattern) consists in indicating the *material image* of which the word, taken in its primeval sense, contains the expression.

Thus, without being drawn out into form (an operation for which a multitude of distinctions and discussions would be found requisite) in the case of the word *obligation*, both the *paraphrasis* and the *archetypation* may be deduced from what is indicated above.

Rhizophantia, indication of the *root*, might serve as a common or generic term applicable to both.

To return to *analysis*. It is by an operation of the nature of *analysis*, *primeval* analysis, that the ideas designated by the several names of *fictitious entities* have been formed. Unfortunately, in the case of these *fictitious* objects, the description of the way in which the analysis must, or may, have been performed, will be matter of much more difficulty than in the case of the above-mentioned *real* ones.

Not to leave the field of fictitious entities, and with it the corresponding part of the field of *logical analysis*, in the state of an utterly *dark spot*, thus much has here been hazarded ; and here it is high time that what has been said on the subject of *analysis* should be brought to a close.

Unfortunately, here are not only *new words*, but these in a multitude greater by the whole number than would have been employed, could the ideas intended have at any cheaper rate been conveyed. But he who, in any branch of art and science, *ethics* itself not excepted, is resolved not to have anything to do with new words, resolves by that very resolution to confine himself to the existing stock of ideas and opinions, how great soever the degree of incorrectness, imperfection, error, and mischievousness which may in those ideas and opinions happen to be involved. . . .

APPENDIX A

LEGAL FICTIONS [1]

What you have been doing by the fiction—could you, or could you not, have done it without the fiction ? If not, your fiction is a wicked lie : if yes, a foolish one.

Such is the dilemma. Lawyer ! escape from it if you can.

But no : the distinction is but in appearance ; folly none in either case, except in so far as all wickedness is folly : mischievous in every case the *effect;* in every case wicked, if it had any, the *purpose.*

Fiction of use to justice ? Exactly as swindling is to trade.

The fictions with which the substantive branch of the law has been fouled belong not to the design of the present work.

The fictions by which, in so much greater abundance the adjective branch is polluted, may be distinguished in the first instance into two great classes : the falsehoods which the judges are in the habit of uttering, by themselves, or by the officers under their direction ; and the falsehoods which they cause to be uttered by the suitors.

1. Take for the first case, as one of the most striking ones, that of common recoveries ; [2] though it belongs to the substantive branch with as much propriety at least as to the adjective.

The judges formed a plan for making business, by enabling the proprietors of entailed estates to cheat their heirs. The king, as is said, through policy, or perhaps through negligence, gave them their own way. A sham action was brought against the proprietor : the proprietor, by direction of the judges, named a creature of theirs, the crier of their court, a man worth nothing, as the man of whom he had bought the land, and who stood bound to prove the title to it a good one, or, on failure, to give him another estate of equal value. The father lost the land ; that is, got the power of doing with it what he pleased ; but no injury was done to the children, because the father, and through him, they, his children got

---

[1] [*Works*, Vol. VII, pp. 283–7.]
[2] [2 Blackstone, 357. Fines and recoveries were abolished by 3 & 4 Will. IV. c. 74.]

the crier's land instead of it.   This the judges, receiving their
fees, never failed to testify ;   it is entered upon the record.
A record is the very tabernacle of truth ; let it say what it
will, no man is permitted to dispute the truth of it, or of any
part of it.

Sham equivalent as above to heirs ; sham security to
defendants ; sham security to plaintiffs ; sham notices to
both, and more especially to defendants ; sham pretences to
one another for cheating one another of business.   To give
the list and the explanation of all those shams, with the
consequences drawn from them, would be to heap volume
upon volume.   It is of such matter that the system of procedure,
as displayed in the books of practice, is composed.

Such is the matter of a record : everything is sham that
finds its way into that receptacle, as everything is foul that
finds its way out of Fleet-ditch into the Thames.

The spice or two of truth, buried here and there amidst
those heaps of falsehood, serve but to make the compost the
richer, and the better adapted to the purposes of misconception
and deception ; in a word, to the service of the ends of
judicature.   They serve to favour the operation of the *double-
fountain* principle.[1]

2. Take next the case of sham bail, and sham pledges of
prosecution.

In the infancy of the technical system of English procedure,
the performance on the part of the plaintiff of an operation
called by the name of *finding security* was established in the
character of a condition precedent to the subjecting a man,
in the character of defendant, to make answer in any way to
a judicial demand.   The security was real, but eventual only,
and not deposititious : a pair of friends binding themselves
(though by promise only, and not, as in case of pawning
goods, by actual deposit) to pay a sum of money, preliquidated
or not preliquidated, certain or uncertain, in case the plaintiff
should lose his cause.   *Pledges of prosecution* was the name
given to these friends.[2]

No such pledges are in any case found : a certificate of
their being found is in every case given ; and the certificate
is among the countless host of lies, notorious lies, without
which English judges know not how to administer what in
their language goes by the name of justice.

So in the case of sham bail, on part of the defendant.   The
defendant pays an attorney, who pays an officer of the court

---

[1] [*Works*, Vol. V, pp. 14, 512, and Vol. VII, pp. 308–9, 339.]
[2] Blackstone, III, Append. xiii.

for making in one of the books of the court an entry, importing that on such a day two persons bound themselves to stand as sureties for the defendant ; undertaking, in the event of his losing his cause, and being ordered to comply with the plaintiff's pecuniary demand, either to pay the money for the defendant or to render his body up to prison. No such engagement has been taken by anybody.—The persons spoken of as having taken it, are not real persons but imaginary persons ; a pair of names always the same, John Doe and Richard Roe.[1]

The impossibility that this vile lie should be of use to anybody but the inventors and utterers of it, and their confederates, is too manifest to be rendered more so by anything than can be said of it.

In the original institution of this security, the " pledges of prosecution ", as little regard was paid to the ends of justice as in the subsequent evasion of it.

Had any regard been paid to the ends of justice, the judge, were it only for the purpose of ascertaining what security the nature of the case required and what it was in the plaintiff's power to give, would have examined him *viva voce* ; not to speak of the many other indispensable purposes to which the same operation would have been subservient. Instead of that, this part of the duty was turned over to a subordinate officer, of which there was but one for a whole county, the sheriff. This officer, either he was personally responsible for the

---

[1] This operation English lawyers, heaping fiction upon fiction, call *appearance* : a word which in their vocabulary has at least half a score different meanings ; but that which it has in the language of common sense is not of the number. Whatever be the number of them, they all agree in this, viz. that they signify some operation which, in every instance, is completely useless to the purposes of justice, oppressive to suitors, useful to none but the fraternity of lawyers.

A written order is delivered to a man, commanding him to appear on a certain day in a certain court of justice, under a certain penalty. On the day mentioned, he appears in the court mentioned and stays there the whole time of its sittings ; this does not save him from the penalty. An English judge (such is the force of usage in hardening men in iniquity) scruples not to sanction this instrument of deception by his signature.

Think you to make an English lawyer comprehend how it should be possible that appearance, when the scene of it is in an English court of justice, should mean appearance ? The adjunct *personal* will be apt to present itself as capable of conveying the intimation. Appearance simply—appearance of the defendant in court—means indeed, it may be said, appearance of somebody else in another place ; but personal appearance—personal appearance of the defendant in court—cannot surely be understood as meaning anything else but the appearance of that person in that place. Vain expectation !—personal is added, and the meaning of the word appearance is still, in the conception of the man of law, exactly what it was before.

eventual justifiability and solvency of those pledges, or he was not. Responsible for them, for twice as many persons as there were actions brought in a year within a whole county, he would have been continually exposed to almost certain ruin. Not responsible for them, two secure instruments of injustice were lodged in his hands ; for the acts of this sub-ordinate officer were not, like those of his superiors, the judges, exposed to the scrutiny of the public eye. One was, to consult his own ease and safety by reporting the im-possibility of finding two such pledges. The other was, to make the like report for the benefit of his friends ; including all such persons as, for the convenience of getting rid of troublesome demands of all sorts, might find their account in purchasing that distinction at his own price.

Not such, however, were the considerations which dictated the evasion which ensued. Of the due application of this security (had it been susceptible of any useful application in such hands) the effect would have been the depriving the justice-shop, the *officina justitiæ*,[1] of a number of good cus-tomers. For, to a man's being a good customer to the lawyers of all sorts, so long as the suit lasted (which was as long as they could contrive to make it last) it was not necessary that the demand should have any merits to support it, or the demandant the value of a farthing left in his purse, to pay in the name of satisfaction to an injured defendant at the end of it. On the part of the judge, any such inquiry (it may be said) would have been impracticable. Nothing more easy to say ; nor anything more true : because, from the first of their opening, it had been the care of those great shops to put down all the little ones. Without hearing all suitors in the first instance, justice, it is true, could not be done to any of them ; and true indeed it was, that for three or four sets of judges, sitting in Westminster Hall, to hear as many persons in the character of suitors as all England could supply has from first to last been physically impossible. But what was possible, and not only possible but easy, was from the whole of that extent of country (and from ten times that extent, had there been as much) to receive fees ; giving, in return for those fees, scraps of written lawyers's slang in due form of law.

The plea of impossibility offers itself at every step, in justification of injustice in all its forms. The plea is as true as so many other pleas are false ; but the impossibility is in each instance the work, not of nature, but of the judge.

[1] Blackstone's *Commentaries.*

No man (says the man of law, in one of his maxims) ought
to take advantage of his own wrong. What !—no man ?
No lawyer, no judge, take advantage of his own wrong, when,
under the system of procedure which has had the judges for
its authors, it is thus out of their own wrong, and nothing
else, that an apology, or anything in the form of apology, is,
or can ever be cooked up ? What !—no man ? Yes ; no
man : subject of course to the exception, which, when anything wrong is forbidden by us, is constantly to be understood ; viz. an exception in favour of ourselves, and such
other persons to whom it is our pleasure to impart our licence.

True it is that under this system of yours it is impossible,
without exception impossible, ever to do justice. Nothing
was ever more true. But the impossibility, whence comes it ?
From yourselves. First you make the impossibility, and then
you plead it. And wherefore was it made, but that it might
be pleaded ?

3. Business-stealing, or jurisdiction-stealing, falsehoods.

King's Bench stole business from Common Pleas ; Common
Pleas stole it back again from King's Bench. Falsehood,
avowed falsehood, was their common instrument. B. R. let
off one lie ; C. B. answered it by another.[1] The battle is in
all the books.[2]

Quoth client to attorney, " Such a one has forged a bond
upon me." Quoth attorney to client, " Don't dispute it ;
forge a release." *Vero o ben trovato ;* this advice is also in the
books. If true, it shows that it was not for nothing that so
good a scholar had been to the great school, the school kept
by the king himself at Westminster. *Regis ad exemplum ;*
such was the pattern followed by him. *Ingenuas didicisse
fideliter artes, Emollit mores. . . .*

Vide the case of the story-telling club in Joe Miller. Per
Archer, cabbage as big as St. Paul's ; per *Merryman,* boiler

---

[1] [This was caused by the 13 Car. II. st. 2, c. 2, which required that
the true cause of action should be stated in the body of the writ, before
a defendant could be arrested, upon affidavit that the cause of action
amounted to £10 or upwards. As the bill of Middlesex was only framed
for actions of trespass, upon which a defendant could not be arrested
for a breach of civil contract, the King's Bench was ousted of its
jurisdiction. In order to get out of this difficulty, the judges invented
the *ac etiam* clause, by which the defendant was to be brought in to
answer the plaintiff of a plea of trespass *and also* to a bill of debt.
A few years after, Lord Chief-Justice North, in order to get some of
his business into the Common Pleas, also added an *ac etiam* clause
to the writ of *capias,* in order to give his court jurisdiction.—Note by
J. S. Mill.]

[2] Blackstone's *Commentaries* ; Sellon's *Crompton* ; North's *Life of
Lord-Keeper Guildford,* etc., etc.

as big as St. Paul's church-yard. *President*—Cui bono ?
Merryman—to boil brother Archer's cabbage.

Thief to catch thief, fraud to combat fraud, lie to answer
lie. Every criminal uses the weapon he is most practised in
the use of ; the bull uses his horns, the tiger his claws, the
rattle-snake his fangs, the technical lawyer his lies.   Un-
licensed thieves use pick-lock keys ; licensed thieves use
fictions.

Unwilling to be left behind, Exchequer stole with both
hands at once, stole from both its neighbours.   In design,
they were all three much upon a par ; but as to success,
whatever may have been the cause, the thefts of the Exchequer
have been little more than gleaning.

Among the falsehoods which judges caused to be uttered
by the suitors, a division may again be made into those
which they contented themselves with encouraging and those
which they compelled the suitors to utter.   In the one case,
the powers of reward alone were employed in the generation
of the lie ; in the other case, the irresistible force of punishment
is called in to secure it.

A sample of the simply permitted lies has been already
seen, in the instance of the written pleadings in general—
and more especially of special pleading at common law—and
the initiative pleadings called bills in equity.   The habitual
utterance of these falsehoods is exactly commensurate and
co-extensive with the range of the *mendacity-licence* above
mentioned.

These exercises of professional genius and morality, if they
do not in common parlance come under the head of *fictions*,
come not the less under the head of falsehoods ; falsehoods
hatched in the same heads, and in pursuit of the same ends,
the ends of judicature.

Of the falsehoods which are forced into the lips of the
suitors, or rather (since in that way little would be to be got)
into the paws of their professional assistants, a specimen may
be seen in those falsehoods [1] the utterance of which is rendered
necessary on pretence of *certainty*.   The specimen is a rich
one : falsehood upon falsehood ; for the reason (as we have
seen) is as rich in hypocrisy, as the practice itself is in
falsehood.

When a thing happened in one or other of two ways, and
you cannot tell in which, you must not say so ; that would
be *uncertain* : your indictment or your declaration would be

---

[1] See *Works*, Vol. VII, pp. 275 ff. (*Rationale of Judicial Evidence*,
Chap. XVI, " Written Pleadings ", § 4.)

void for uncertainty. You must say it happened in both. On these terms, and on these only, you are right in law ; not the less so when the fact is impossible. And so if there be half a dozen or a dozen such alternatives—which there are, and more, in every day's practice.

The practice is, to tell as many different stories, as there are ways in one or other of which it is supposed the fact may have happened : it is spoken of as having happened in each of those ways ; each story is called a count. Thus, if there are two such counts, there is one of them perhaps true, one certainly false ; if half a dozen counts, one perhaps true, five false.

A man was murdered, by being knocked on the head and thrown overboard ; whether dead or not when thrown overboard is uncertain. Two counts : one, that the man was knocked on the head, and died of the blow ; the other, that the man, the same man, was, at the same time and place, thrown overboard, and died of drowning. Here was the same man killed twice over ; and this for the better information of the supposed murderer, that he might the more clearly understand the charges he had to defend himself against. Had the fact been truly stated, the murderer would have been acquitted. This case occurred not much more than twenty years ago. The indictment stood the scrutiny of twelve judges.[1]

So again *in non-criminali*. To take the sort of case of all others the most commonly exemplified. A man owes you £20 and no more ; you are or are not certain as to the precise description of the debt or the evidence by which you shall be able to prove it. Your attorney, with his special pleader under the bar, with or without the advice of a barrister to boot, gets a declaration drawn with half a dozen counts in it, less or more ; say half a dozen. Here, then, you are made to demand six separate sums of £20 each, stating them as different, and saying of each that it is due to you ; total £120.

What shall we think of that man, but above all of that judge, who seeing this, or not seeing it, proclaims the necessity of certainty ; and is indefatigable in his eulogiums on the law, for the rigour with which it exacts the presence of that best ornament in all legal instruments ?

Uses of these forced falsehoods :—

1. Half a dozen or a dozen or a score of stories told instead of one ; so much the more made business.

2. Chance of mis-statement, real or supposed : whence

---

[1] [Leach's *Crown Cases*, p. 569, case of Hindmarsh, 1792.]

application for nullification ; certainty of a motion and an argument ; even chance of a fresh suit ; at any rate, more made business.

3. Verdict taken in a court alleged not to be the proper one ; application in consequence : more made business as before.

4. The business having thus been rendered incomprehensible to a jury, what is given as their verdict is none of theirs, but settled somehow or other among the men of law ; neither is the judge himself responsible for it. On one or other of all these counts, the plaintiff takes the verdict at his peril ; that is, the plaintiff's lawyers take it, at the peril of their client : if they take it wrong, so much the worse for the client, but so much the better for the lawyers. The lawyers make the verdict, the jury stare. Jury trial for ever !—sacred palladium of English liberty !

5. Confirmation of arbitrary power in the hands of the judge ; the jury serving as a stalking horse. Incapable of judging for themselves, conscious of their own incapacity, juries become helpless and do as they are bid. How should they do otherwise ? They know not what is done ; they know not how to help themselves. If the court likes the verdict, it stands ; if not, it is got rid of. The verdict, if an unjust one, cannot, on the score of its injustice, be got rid of without reasons. But in this way, just or unjust (reasons being out of the question) it may be got rid of with equal ease.

6. The state of the law rendered more and more incognoscible.

By wrapping up the real dispositions of the law in a covering of nonsense, the knowledge of it is rendered impossible to the bulk of the people—to the bulk of those whose fate depends upon it. What meets their eyes is gross and palpable nonsense : a man dead and alive at the same time ; a dead man and a live man the same person ; thirty or forty days making altogether but one day ; a man constantly present in a place where he never set his foot ; the same man judge and party, and justice all the better for it. In jargon such as this, no man in whose brain the natural provision of common sense has not been eaten out by false science can avoid beholding so much vile and scandalous nonsense ; but if, by the help of that portion of common sense which each man's fortune has imparted to him, it were possible to him to divine what disastrous sense may be at the bottom of this nonsense, the nonsense would miss its mark.

7. Legislator and people confirmed in the habit of bowing

down to falsehood and absurdity, and recognizing them as being, what lawyers are continually proclaiming them to be, necessary instruments in the hands of justice. If without them justice never *is* administered, what conclusion more natural than that it never *can be*?

8. Corrupting the morals of the people. Wheresoever the use of fiction prevails, and in proportion as it prevails, every law-book is an institute of vice; every court of judicature is a school of vice.

Put into the hands of your son the *Commentaries* of Blackstone? Send him to attend the courts at Westminster? For learning jurisprudence, yes; but for cherishing in his bosom the principles of veracity, of sincerity, of true honour? Stay till you have made your daughter get by heart the words of Piron and Lord Rochester.

9. Corrupting the intellectual faculties of the people. To what a state of debility and depravation must the understanding of that man have been brought down, who can really persuade himself that a lawyer's fiction is anything better than a lie of the very worst sort—that the whole mass taken together, or any one particle of it, was ever of any the smallest use to justice!

Fiction may be applied to a good purpose, as well as to a bad one; in giving support to a useful rule or institution, as well as to a pernicious one. The virtues of an useful institution will not be destroyed by any lie or lies that may have accompanied the establishment of it; but can they receive any increase? The virtues of a useful medicine will not be destroyed by pronouncing an incantation over it before it is taken; but will they be increased?

Behold here one of the artifices of lawyers. They refuse to administer justice to you unless you join with them in their fictions; and then their cry is, see how necessary fiction is to justice! Necessary indeed; but too necessary; but how came it so, and who made it so? [1]

[1] A man to whom you lent a horse—does he refuse to return it? Not the smallest chance will they give you for getting the animal back again, unless you say he *found* it. This is what you are forced to do when you bring an action of *trover*; by which, by the bye, you will not get your horse after all, if the defendant chooses to keep it, paying the price which the jury have happened to set upon it.

A man to whom you let your house for a year—does he at the expiration of the time refuse to quit it? Not a chance will they g for obtaining possession again of your house, unless you trun foolish story about two persons, real or imaginary, one of whom the other out of it. This is what you are forced to do, in brir action of ejectment.

On the other side of the Tweed, where no such lies are told

As well might the father of a family make it a rule never to let his children have their breakfast till they had uttered, each of them, a certain number of lies, curses, and profane oaths ; and then exclaim, " You see, my dear children, how necessary lying, cursing, and swearing are to human sustenance ! "

they contrive somehow or other to put a man in possession of his horse, or of his house ? An English court of conscience, would it do its business any better than it does were it to refuse to make a man repay the thirty shillings he had borrowed of you, unless you would declare that, instead of your lending him the money, he had found it.

APPENDIX B

THE CLASSIFICATION OF FICTIONS
By GEORGE BENTHAM

[In addition to Bentham's own MSS. and posthumous papers, material for the study of his theory of Fictions is to be found in the " Outlines of Logic " which his nephew George published in 1827. The uncle financed this work after its rejection by a commercial firm, but it was eventually sold for waste paper, owing to the bankruptcy of the publishers, when only sixty copies had been sold.

It will be observed that at certain points the treatment is less cautious than that of the original, which the nephew first translated into French in order to attain stylistic freedom—at the same time borrowing freely from the logical jargon of the day.

Nearly half a century later when George Bentham was at the height of his fame as President of the Linnean Society, Jevons corresponded with him about his discovery of the ' Quantification of the Predicate ', previously attributed to Sir William Hamilton (who reviewed the book in 1833 without mentioning this item). In the " Contemporary Review " for May, 1873, will be found an article by Jevons, for whom the very much more important section on Fictions seems to have had no interest.[1]

In the following pages certain footnotes have been incorporated in the main text, the cumbrous system of italicization has not been strictly adhered to, and an occasional abbreviation is indicated by square brackets].

The word *Entity* is that most extensive and all-comprehensive term which is used to designate every subject matter of perception, thought, or discourse, every *being*, every *thing*, every *operation*, every *property*, whether real, abstract, or fictitious, whether reckoned as certain, contingent, or impossible, by any mind, at any time, in any place. Every noun-substantive, every substantive expression, in any language, is the name of an *Entity* [and the term *Entity* cannot be defined *per genus et differentiam*].

Entities in general may be referred to the following classes,

---

[1] See the writer's *Jeremy Bentham, 1832–2032*, pp. 34–5.

or in other words, the summum genus *Entity* may be divided as follows.

I. A *real* Entity is one which has a physical existence ; that is, one which is perceptible by means of any of our *senses*, as a *rock*, a *star*, a *man*, etc. A real entity must therefore be an *individual*, or a *collection* of individuals *definite* in number, as a *landscape*, an *army*, a *man on horseback*, etc. But, if by these expressions a *class* be meant, they are no longer names of real, but of *collective* entities, of which mention will presently be made.

II. An *inferential* Entity is one which we believe to have real existence, but which is imperceptible to any of our senses ; such is, in relation to every man, the Divinity he worships ; such is our *mind*, or the *thinking part* of our frame.

III. A *fabulous* Entity is one which has been believed in by others, but to the existence of which we attach no belief. Such are, with relation to us, the Heathen Gods, which were inferential entities with relation to those who believed in them. Between real or inferential and fabulous entities there is no distinct line of separation, even with relation to one individual mind, as belief admits of every degree from *positive* to *negative* certainty.

IV. A *collective* Entity is the result of the operations of abstraction and generalization. Certain properties possessed by one entity, or by several entities in common, are abstracted from all other properties which those entities may happen to possess, and an indefinite number of individuals are imagined as being all endowed with those abstracted properties ; these individuals form a *class*, and are designated collectively by a *common name*. Every *common name* is therefore the name of a *collective entity*, of an indefinite number of individual entities considered with respect of certain properties common to all the entities so *contained* in the class. Where those entities are *real*, the class which contains them is a *physical* collective entity ; where they are *fictitious*, the corresponding collective entities are also *fictitious*.

V. A *fictitious* Entity is one which neither has, nor is supposed to have, any real existence, but which is grammatically spoken of as real. We say : colour is a property, benevolence is a quality ; and yet we do not suppose that *colour, property, benevolence,* or *quality* are really existing objects. These four words are therefore names of fictitious entities.

Fictitious entities as well as real are referable to classes, which classes may be termed collective fictitious entities.

Fictitious entities are individualized by referring them to real objects ; as, for example, *the colour of that object, that man's benevolence.*

As to a subdivision of these several heads, it is only in regard to real and to fictitious entities that it appears to be necessary on the present occasion.

In the case of real entities, the summum genus is commonly designated by the word matter, which may be divided into *bodies* and *substances*, according to whether the individuals referred to are or are not, for the particular purpose in view, supposed to be limited in configuration. Thus *man, tree, house*, etc., are names of classes of bodies, *metal, bone, flesh*, etc., are names of classes of substances.

These two genera, bodies and substances, are susceptible of regular and distinctly-characterized divisions and subdivisions, which may always be rendered all-comprehensive, that is, such as that, when taken together, they shall comprehend every conceivable real entity. Such an operation, however, is foreign to the present purpose, being the subject matter of physical science.

But fictitious entities can by no means be so easily reduced to order. The vague and indefinite nature of the operation of *fiction* renders the classification of its results a very arduous task. In the following sketch I have endeavoured to refer them to a few general heads ; but, such is the difficulty of bringing them under all comprehensive genera and species, that, in some instances, it will be found that the lowest species here mentioned, must, for the purpose of exposition or ulterior division, be considered as summa genera. Such are, for example, some of the jurisprudential fictitious entities, here classed under the head of Immediate Results of Political Operations.

I. Physical fictitious entities are such as relate to real individuals. A real individual may be considered as being either in *motion* or at *rest*. Thence the division of physical fictitious entities into *motions* and *states* of things. Physical *actions* and *operations* are species of motions more or less complicated.

States of things or *properties* may be divided into *absolute* and *relative*. The absolute properties of a body are such as have place independently of any other body, and consist in the effect which that body produces upon our mind. The relative properties of a body are such as result from its comparison with another body.

All the substantives given as examples under this head of *states of things or properties* are to be reckoned as names of

K

properties. Some of them are commonly used in other senses also, as for example, organization, which means either the operation of organizing or the property of being organized. It is in the latter sense that it is here to be understood. This is an imperfection in language much to be regretted, but which, I fear, cannot be easily remedied. There are, in fact, but few instances, comparatively speaking, where there is a substantive in use for the designation of properties, and, on many occasions, it might not even be desirable to make use of it, should it exist. Thus the adjective is a very common and a very useful abridged form, as, for example, when we say that an object is *red*, we mean that it is endowed with redness, a species of absolute properties. If we say that it is *large*, we refer to largeness, a species of relative properties. Sometimes properties are designated in the verbal form, as, for example, *he can move*. By this expression is understood, that he is endowed with that species of absolute properties which cannot be substantively expressed otherwise than by some such hard word as locomoveability. The words *before*, *behind*, *above*, *below*, are examples of relative properties expressed in the adverbial form. That language is the most convenient for use, in this respect, which enables the writer to choose, on each occasion, that form of expression which is best suited to his particular purpose.

The summum genus of absolute properties is *existence*. Its division may be founded on various principles or sources. Thus, for example, we may divide Existence :

1. According to the degree of *belief* attached to it, into certainty, contingency in its various degrees, impossibility, etc.

2. According to the degree of *perceptibility* by any one of our senses, into presence and absence (that is, the being within or without the reach of any of our senses), in respect either of place or of time, or of both. Absence in respect of place may be subdivided into attainability (the property of being susceptible of becoming within reach), unattainability, etc. A corresponding division of absence, in respect of time, is into past and future.

3. According to the particular *sense* by means of which the properties are perceived. Thus . . . 1. by the sense of sight, we perceive colour and its species, opacity, and transparence, etc. ; 2. by the sense of hearing we perceive sound and its species ; 3. by that sense of tasting, taste and its species ; 4. by that of smelling, smell and its species ; 5. by that of feeling, either alone or combined with sight, we perceive form and its species ; quantity, number, and size, and their species ;

consistence and its species, such as solidity, fluidity, gazeity, etc.

4. According to the *intrinsic nature of the properties*, into organization and inorganization, animation and inanimation, etc. Animation comprehends all the physical powers or faculties which are all absolute properties.

Relative properties or relations may be referred to the following heads : 1. Relations of contiguity and distance in place. Propinquity and remoteness are degrees of distance. These relations may also be subdivided into inherence, exclusion, the properties of being above, below, behind, before, etc. By inherence it is understood that one body is a part of another. Absolute identity in place cannot exist (in regard to real entities to which alone it must be remembered, these properties relate) without reference to succession in time, and therefore belongs to the head of relations of time and place combined. 2. Relations of simultaneity and succession in respect of time. Coexistence is simultaneity ; but generally implies duration, which also belongs to this head. To succession may be referred previousness and subsequentness, propinquity and remoteness in time. 3. Relations of time and place combined. Succession in time may be combined with identity, contiguity, or distance in place. Simultaneity can only be combined with contiguity and distance in place. 4. Relations independent of time or place, *i.e.* relations of identity and diversity. Similitude, dissimilitude, and opposition are degrees of diversity. These relations are susceptible of all or nearly all the several divisional operations which are above performed on absolute properties.

II. Tactical fictitious entities. Those entities belong to the class of relations and are commonly termed relations of subalternation. Such are the relations of genus and species, of subordination, superordination, co-ordination, etc.

III. Noological fictitious entities. They consist of such as relate to the intellect. To this head may be referred :

1. The absolute properties of the mind, *i.e.* its powers or faculties.

2. The relative properties of the mind, such as intensity of its faculties, sanity and insanity of the mind, etc. But whenever any expression of approbation or disapprobation is conveyed, it does not belong to this head, but to a species of ethical fictitious entities.

3. The several operations performable by means of these faculties.

4. The immediate results of these several operations, viz.

impressions and ideas, with their several species, simple or combined.

IV. Pathological fictitious entities, which relate to the sensitive mind. These are denominated sensations, and comprehend pleasures, pains and neutral *sensations.* Pleasures and pains have been subdivided into fourteen heads by Mr. Bentham in his *Table of the Springs of Action.*

V. Ethical fictitious entities, or such as relate to desire and will, that is to the desiring and volitional mind. These may be classed under the following heads :

1. Properties of the desiring mind, or *desire,* and its species. With relation to any event or object *desire* may be divided into *positive desire* or hope, and negative desire or fear ; and either of these may be subdivided according to its object. Thus, hunger, thirst, ambition, curiosity, are species of desire, distinguished by their respective objects, viz. *solid food, liquid food, social pre-eminence, acquirement of knowledge.*

2. *Motives* for ethical operations ; a species of entities, intimately connected with the preceding, but distinguished by the additional intimation of the relation they bear to operations.

3. Ethical *operations,* which are either *moral,* such as *approbation, vituperation, entreaty, refusal,* etc., or political, such as *command, empowerment, obligation, punishment,* etc.

4. Immediate *results* of ethical operations. Such are (*a*) with relation to moral operations, neutral, laudatory, and *vituperative* qualifications of fictitious entities, viz. *reputation, virtue,* and *vice,* with all their several species ; (*b*) with relation to *political* operations, *command, obligation, right, power,* etc.

5. Ethical *relations.* Such are society and conditions in life, *moral* or *political.* Moral conditions are those of *friendship, inimity,* etc. Political conditions are *trades, professions, situations, places, offices,* etc.

This last head comes very near to that of physical relations, but differs in this, that it is not by the perceptive, but by the conceptive faculty, that they are attached to the idea of the persons to which they relate. A barrister, for example, is not perceptibly different from a solicitor, like a tall man from a short one. *Barristership* and *solicitorship* are ethical fictitious entities [whereas *tallness* and *shortness* are physical fictitious entities].

INDEX

Printed in the USA/Agawam, MA
July 20, 2010

542860.035